African Art

ITS BACKGROUND AND TRADITIONS

AFRICAN ART

Its Background and Traditions

TEXT BY René S. Wassing

CURATOR AT THE MUSEUM VOOR LAND-EN VOLKENKUNDE, ROTTERDAM

PHOTOGRAPHS BY Hans Hinz

PORTLAND HOUSE · NEW YORK

Translated by Diana Imber

Library of Congress Catalog Card Number 68-28387

Copyright ©1968 in Switzerland by Office du Livre, Fribourg

English language rights reserved by William S. Konecky, Inc.

This 1988 edition published by Portland House,
a division of dilithium Press, Ltd.,
distributed by Crown Publishers, Inc.,
225 Park Avenue South, New York, New York 10003.

Printed and bound in Hong Kong

ISBN 0-517-66271-X

h g f e d c b a

CONTENTS

Abbreviations:

Pl. i to xxiv: Colour Plates
Pl. i to 120: Black-and-white illustrations in the text
Cat. i to 120: Black-and-white illustrations in the catalogue
★: An asterisk before a number refers to a textual reference in the outer
column of the page

LIST OF PLATES

COLOUR PLATES

BLACK-AND-WHITE-PLATES

FOREWORD

In this work, in an attempt to avoid the well-trodden paths, I have taken as a starting point the close relationship between the art of Black Africa and the culture from which it arose.

A survey of the whole cultural field renders it possible to understand the complex human conditions that together form a conscious community. Every community of this kind makes sure of its own continuity by numerous binding rules, which alone allow relations between members.

One of the factors which permits an individual to establish human contact through the rules and attain communication with his fellow men is the urge to express himself, to create something. This urge is manifested in different ways by many peoples: in poetry, song, music and dance, sculpture and painting. The man whose talent in these fields has produced exceptional creations which suit the valid criteria of his community, can be described as an artist, and his creations as works of art.

However, I must make it clear at once that the conception of 'artist' as we know it, is unknown in many non-Western communities, as in Africa for example. It follows therefore that certain individuals in every community are recognized as leaders in a particular field, and their works are preferred to those of their colleagues. But the *leitmotiv* is function, the purpose of an object, rather than a standard of criticism founded on purely aesthetic principles, though these may not be lacking altogether.

When the Western world first discovered African art it was enthusiastic about the objects produced by African culture. Because this art is so severely functional that without its collective cultural background it is scarcely to be understood, I have tried here to arrange the works in relation to their function as expressed in different cultural aspects.

Plastic art forms the richest vein in Africa, the greater part of this book is therefore devoted to it, and because this type of art flourished above all in West and central Africa it follows that I shall concentrate on these regions, leaving East and South Africa slightly to one side because they offer—in the plastic arts at least—less material for discussion.

Finally I must emphasize that as a result of this approach, based principally on the function of art in African cultures, the cultural significance is much to the fore. It is essential that the objects should be really understood and not enumerated singly like a cultural inventory of individual African tribes.

Rotterdam, April 1968   R.S.W.

1

INTRODUCTION

Before we can embark on a discussion of the art of Black Africa we must clearly understand what is meant by the words 'Black Africa' and 'art'. First the country and the people. The designation 'Black Africa' is apparently simple: it is a collective term used to cover a large number of ideas and values, but it produces an impression of unity that is false and unsupported by the facts. The reality is much more complex and many-sided, and displays surprising differences in landscape, climatic conditions, races and cultures. All these factors must be considered where they impinge on art. However, it is possible to limit this broad concept of Black Africa straight away: first, the part of Africa we shall discuss lies south of the Sahara and secondly, the inhabitants of that region are black and physically members of the main black race, always described as Negro. The white and Arab elements of the north are here irrelevant, as are the white and Asiatic elements of East and South Africa. They have no bearing on Negro cultures.

The idea of art is charged with decidedly subjective overtones, hence the word is not easy to define. Fundamentally it is a Western idea developed in the mental climate of Western philosophy and applied to the expression of Western culture. In all periods people have measured it by their own standards, which were naturally not relevant. Many works of art that were once accepted have not stood the test of time, while others are still held in high esteem. A work of art is the creation of a man whose own personality is in some way reflected in material, form and content, whether it is sculptural, plastic, graphic, spatial or musical. The symbols he employs must also be comprehensible to others, for

only thus can his work rise above the individual and take on a wider role.

Another factor is the idea of beauty, which is always applied in a subjective way. There is no absolute standard of beauty, because criteria change continually. If this is true of the familiar art we have known since childhood, considerably more attention must be paid to these factors when dealing with non-Western, and especially African art. Whenever we non-Africans talk of African art we apply—however we may try to avoid it—the standards we are accustomed to use in our own culture. The same is true of all non-Western art. Even the names of foreign art-forms reveal their strangeness: primitive art, exotic art, *art sauvage* and so on. And here it is essential to comment, if not in detail, on the expression 'primitive art'. The phrase should really be understood in a cultural-historical sense, but it always has the slightly pejorative meaning 'naïve', or, in the true sense of the word, 'first', as if European art were unquestionably on a more sophisticated, later and higher cultural level. Many people, however, do not find this combination of discriminative attitudes with pure art-criticism to be a double-standard, and therefore inconsistent.

Since the tendency today, especially in America, is to describe all non-Western art as primitive art, with no distinction, for instance, between the art of the Australian aborigine and that of the refined Balinese (admittedly also without the double meaning of the word primitive discussed before), it seems to me better in the case of Africa to call it African, or Negro, art.

It is not entirely impossible that a study of African art will discover parallels between our artistic values and

* Pl. 1

those of Africans. But far more frequently the two cultures are completely opposed because different standards apply. In order, therefore, to be able to understand the canon it is essential to know something of the background to African art. For centuries Africa's creative urge has borne fruit and examples that have been preserved—rock-painting, objects in stone, clay, bronze, wood and other materials—still arouse our wonder. Such hereditary examples of African culture will be admired unhesitatingly as the finest artistic creations of the Black World. It must, however, be remembered that the artists did not consciously set out to create a work of art. They considered a piece a success if it fulfilled the task set, a task which was primarily functional. Whatever function a piece might have—economic, magical or religious—the aesthetic principle never became an end in itself, in the manner of 'art for art's sake'. Aesthetic appreciation and criticism of the material culture of Africa is a Western invention founded on a discovery made not long before, the development of which runs parallel with the developing concept of art in Western history.

Historians make no mention of appreciation of African art in the fifteenth and sixteenth centuries when the white and black men first met. Everything the white man saw seemed either strange or barbaric and was without exception judged idolatrous and therefore to be condemned. Time passed and the eighteenth and nineteenth centuries saw the era of great explorations, travellers and conquerors returning with trophies and the spoils of war, exhibiting them in their houses as testimony to their personal valour. After the colonisation of

Africa had become a regular institution in the nineteenth century and connections with Europe were well established, the stream of exotic and strange pieces from Africa became a flood. Such objects, collected at random on the spot by sailors, merchants, missionaries and officials, were regarded as curiosities useful for entertaining friends and acquaintances. Sometimes the pieces were bought by collectors and housed in '*cabinets de curiosités*' beside other fine specimens. Nor should we deride these collections of rarities for often we have only them to thank for the rescue and preservation of unique pieces.

Many of these private collections have ended up in museums, where, once their value was realized, they laid the foundations of ethnographical collections that are invaluable today, not only as art-objects but as material for research on African man and his culture.

European artists were the first to recognize the aesthetic value of these objects. Picasso, Braque, Matisse as well as other painters, derided by the public as *fauves* (wild beasts), working at the close of the *Belle Epoque* and forming the *avant garde* of the twentieth century in their search for new forms of expression, were the first to raise African sculpture from anonymity and to recognize it as art. They were attracted by the strangeness, the difference of the figures. A special charm attaches to these pieces, an aura, beyond the form itself, that was capable of describing a completely different world by means of expressions unknown in Europe. This was the answer to the search that would enable the artists to break through the heavy barriers of convention and to follow paths that would undoubtedly lead to the liberation of the individual. It is evident that African examples

undoubtedly influenced the discovery and development of new styles such as Cubism and Surrealism, though whether African art influenced the singularity of these styles is questionable; however, at some period of their career many artists have delved deeply and unhesitatingly into the rich vein of form presented by African sculpture, as for instance some of Lipchitz's sculpture, which derives from tomb-figures of the Kota tribe in Gabon.

African art—once discovered—quickly received its just acclaim. The ethnographical collections aroused curiosity and were the springboard for a new field of study—anthropology—which, during the nineteenth century, was widely preoccupied with non-European communities. Attempts were made, by studying known types of social structures, to construct genealogy, beginning with the problematical archetype—the most primitive form—from which more complex types had gradually developed. This theory of evolution established beyond doubt—so it was believed—that the West represented the highest and by far the most advanced form of civilization. Although this evolutionary theory has fortunately long been abandoned, the heavily tainted word 'primitive' has survived.

From the science of anthropology the discipline that we now call cultural anthropology evolved, that is the study of man and his culture in a worldwide sense. Obviously the modern anthropologist turns his attention to art because it forms a part of the whole culture. He also tries to explain art from the standpoint of its general cultural background.

However the Western art-collector, whose range covers the art of different peoples, sees it from a completely different point of view. He eagerly follows his personal taste. In his search for quality he is guided by aesthetic standards and intuition, while his main object is to raise the standard of his collection. Cultural background is usually of little interest to him, the principal thing being the beauty of a given piece. It is not mere chance that African and Oceanic art has so great an appeal. We have already seen that the early twentieth century experienced a tendency to simplify form. After the Second World War this tendency spread over the whole field of architecture, industrial design, literature, sculpture and painting. Everywhere there was a search for the substance of things and non-essentials were abandoned. These are exactly the characteristics presented by African art. Form and line are direct and strong, the choice of colour is harmonious. It is an art that exactly conforms to Western standards of beauty; this is at least true of bronze and wood sculpture, if rather less so of ivory and stone-carving, weaving and textiles.

Of the wood-carvings, figures and masks take first place. They can express far more to the art-collector than, for instance, a raffia basket or a shield. And this intentional choice made by the collector is responsible for the one-sided character of so many collections of African art. Such collections do not try to represent every aspect of African art; the collector is much more inclined to confine himself to aesthetically satisfactory objects. There is also the question of rarity; the rarer a piece, the greater value to the collection.

The anthropologist uses completely different methods

to form a well-founded aesthetic judgement. Of course he also needs a well-developed aesthetic sense; but principally he tries to establish the position held by a particular object within its own culture, and to assess the standards of criticism valid in the community in question, which may coincide with his own, but could well be totally opposed. An anthropologist may also be inclined to classify more human activities as art than would the collector. It is possible that everyday objects, made for an immediate need and afterwards perhaps discarded, could have an aesthetic value for him, where to a collector they seem negligible. This brings us to the frontier between art and craft. It is a very controversial and nebulous subject, though it is not of great significance here. Many African products that are, in the Western sense, purely the work of craftsmen, may nevertheless be counted as art. In this field too, the European, strongly individual, is free to decide for himself. Ideally the collector should also be an anthropologist, so as to combine the two methods which alone allow the complete understanding of the prophetic nature of a single work or of a whole art-collection. In this book we shall study the traditional art of Africa and also the tribal art which has developed very slowly within strict social customs. It reflects the image of Africa, undisturbed over many centuries, and this ethnological purity is in part responsible for its beauty.

This work is an attempt to see African art, on which a great deal has already been written, afresh from the standpoint of a collector-anthropologist and to give it a new dimension which will help to broaden our understanding by introducing the living element, which ex-plains the how and why. The philosophies and creeds which gave birth to this art will speak for themselves, so that an ancestor figure, a mask or any other object will not only be the splendour of a collection, but alive and expressive. Keita Fodeba expressed this idea most forcibly. At the time when he was Director of the Negro Ballet of Guinea he saw two masks in the Musée de l'Homme in Paris which enchanted him so strongly that he felt as if they were trying to rouse him in an imaginary discussion over the meaning of existence.

That is primarily also the intention of this book: to bring African works of art, so long collected in Europe and America, to life, as living testimony of their traditional significance for the splendid men and communities of Africa.

THE AFRICAN AND HIS ENVIRONMENT

As I have already said, a general picture of Africa is very complex as it is made up of many factors. The same is true of the black man, or Negro, the name of the peoples dwelling south of the Sahara. Ethnologically they belong to the chief indigenous black race. The African continent, however, is not peopled exclusively by Negroes, but by a number of related Negro, and several non-Negro, races. Together they form the people of Africa. A racial map will show a host of groups that are distinguished by definite marked physical and racial characteristics.

BUSHMEN

The Bushmen are acknowledged today to be the oldest African race, on the evidence of prehistoric archaeological sites. Originally their territory spread far into Pl. 1 central and North Africa, but in the course of time they were pressed further and further south until now they Pl. 2 are to be found in South-West and South Africa in the region of the Kalahari desert. The race known as Bushmen differs radically from the true Negro, but does display some similarity with the Hottentots. The most important characteristics are: small stature, wrinkled, yellowish-brown skin, small hands and feet, prominent cheekbones, broad flat nose, narrow eyes and eyelids with wiry hair wound in spiral curls. The women are steatopygous, that is inclined to fat around the hips and buttocks.

Bushmen, who scratch a living in one of the most thankless territories imaginable, have nevertheless adapted perfectly to their natural surroundings. While they are, technologically, the most primitive of African tribes, they succeed in finding food for a continuing community by hunting and the search for edible roots, plants and insects. In circumstances where the struggle for existence is a daily reality one would scarcely expect to find a great deal that could be classed as art. And yet, even the crudely scratched designs on the ostrich eggs used as water-vessels display an aesthetic sense. The women also work the ostrich egg into small discs bored with holes, and these are highly valued as trade barter with the Herero and neighbouring tribes. The Herero use them for ornament. The technique of making ostrich egg discs must be very old because they have been found at several different prehistoric sites, for instance in the Sahara.

NEGRITOS OR PYGMIES

The Negritos, or Pygmies, live today in the thick, primaeval, tropical forestland of central Africa. Their chief physical characteristics are: small stature (usually not more than four feet nine inches tall), skin colour varying between light and reddish brown (rarely black like the Negroes), fuzzy body hair, in tight curls on the males, and crinkly head hair. Head and rump are relatively big, but the legs are short. Three groups of Pygmies may be distinguished according to the territory—north-east Congo, the region of the Ubangi river, and Gabon. The best-known are the Mbuti Pygmies of the Ituri forest in the Congo. They withdrew into the impenetrable

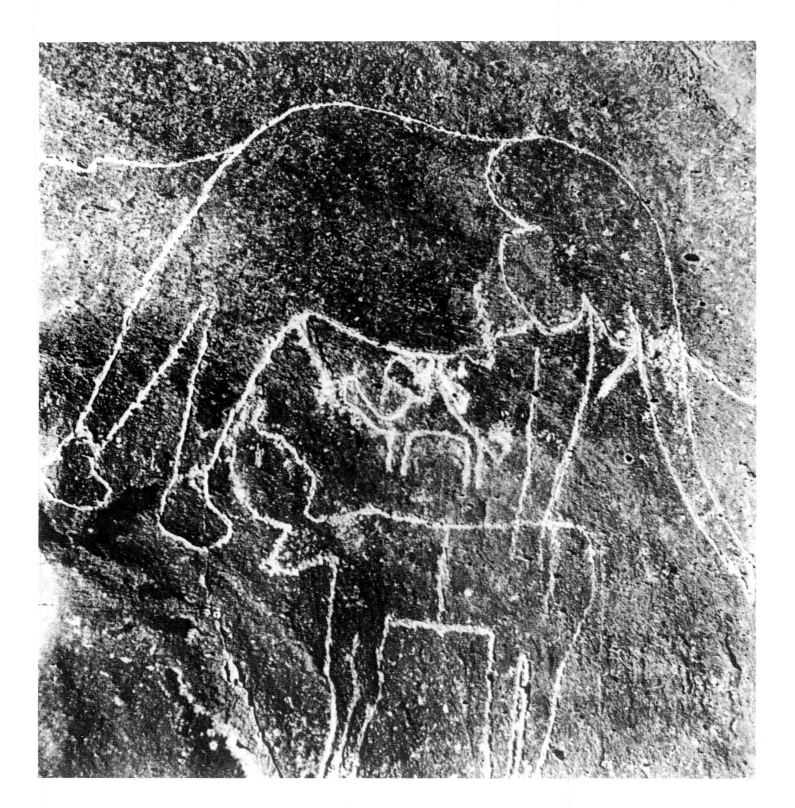

forest to avoid pressure from other peoples. The Pygmies like the Bushmen, lead the nomadic life of the hunter and food-gatherer and have also adapted themselves very well to their surroundings. Despite their isolation they retain some contact with Negro peoples who have penetrated their territory: they help the Negroes to clear the forest for plantations, receiving in exchange all kinds of desirable goods such as iron and weapons. This inter-relationship sometimes goes so far as to alter the social structure of the Pygmy community; the Pygmies even adopting the language of the Negroes. The Pygmies sing well and have a remarkable facility for yodelling.

NEGROES

Even the Negro himself is anything but homogeneous. They are culturally as rich and subtle as they are racially complex, their ancestry being inextricably mixed with other races. There are, nevertheless, several racial characteristics which justify the concept of Negro.

The Negro race spread widely over Africa, from West Africa, central and different parts of East Africa to Ethiopia, although it is in West Africa that we find the people who have best preserved the features of their race. They comprise a large part of the inhabitants of Senegal, the coast of Guinea, Nigeria, west Sudan (Mali and Upper Volta), Cameroun and part of the Congo. These 'true' Negroes, sometimes also called Sudan Negroes, are about five feet eight inches tall, have black skin, curly hair, longish faces with a broad flat nose and thick curved lips. They are divided into many peoples and groups and have, apart from racial characteristics, several linguistic features in common. The innumerable languages and dialects of West Africa all belong to the Sudanese group, centred on the Guinea tribes speaking Twi-Ewe, and the tribes of Nigeria speaking Kwa-Yoruba. The tribes here were often distinguished and named by the language they spoke, a phenomenon also encountered elsewhere in Africa.

To turn now to the best-known Negro peoples and tribes. The word tribe is loosely used today and it is justifiable historically even though its population may have so increased, sometimes to more than a million, as to warrant the description of a people.

The natural surroundings of the West African Negro can be divided into two very different types of landscape: the almost treeless grasslands, or savannah belt, that reaches from Senegal in the west to Ethiopia in the east, and the forest that extends southwards from the savannah belt and runs parallel with it along the west coast as far as Ghana, continuing on into eastern Nigeria and well into the eastern Congo. The two types of vegetation have in many ways been decisive factors in the appearance and development of special features in the different cultures of these territories.

The best-known representative of the Negroes indigenous to the savannah belt in Senegal is the Wolof tribe. Generally their skin is very dark. Nowadays they are mostly Muslims, although they have not entirely abandoned the original beliefs of their ancestors. Two other tribes live in the same territory: the Tukuleur and the Serer.

To the east of Senegal, in Mali and Upper Volta, there are several closely-related tribes who are described as Mande or Mandingo, accordingly to their language. They are tall and slim with fine features and a rather lighter skin than the surrounding tribes. The best-known are the Bambara whose wooden carvings display interesting abstract forms. The Kasonke, Soninke and Malinke also belong to this group. Also in Mali live the Bozo fishing people and in the south the tribe of Dogon, who still preserve much of their original culture. Their rich mythology figures in the many-faced masks that play a special role in the cult of the dead. The Kurumba, whom we meet south of the Dogon in northern Upper Volta seem to be artistically related to the Dogon.

Another group, linguistically linked, comprises the Songhai in south-east Mali and the Niger Republic, the people of the Mossi in Upper Volta and the Gurunsi of northern Ghana. The Songhai have interbred with the Tuareg and Fulani resulting in narrower noses and a lightening of the skin, although the racial features of the Negro remain dominant.

The Mossi, the most important tribe in Upper Volta, have retained their characteristics despite interbreeding with the Songhai and Fulani and still cling to their ancient, predominantly agricultural customs. Several tribes from northern Ghana must also be mentioned, because they were greatly influenced by the Mossi. They are the Dagomba and Mamprusi, the Konkomba (also living in the north of Togoland), the Tallensi, Dagari and Kasena who occupy the fringe of territory under Mossi influence. The Bobo, of west Upper Volta have managed to preserve their own culture despite pressure from Islam, and, like the Dogon, they have developed an impressive mask-cult.

The Lobi always lived in isolation and probably on that account have remained rather backward, a characteristic reflected in their art. Nevertheless their woodcarvings often have a very distinct character. The large Senufo tribe dwells south-west of the Lobi, on the Ivory Coast, extending outwards to Mali and Upper Volta. They make a living by agriculture and cattle-rearing too, but, apart from farmers, several other groups have developed who devote their time to wood-carving, iron-work and bronze-casting. These objects were made for various rites and very fine pieces come from the territory of Korhogo in Senufo country.

Further east, in northern Togo, north Dahomey, north Nigeria, north Cameroun and Chad live many peoples who are culturally very different though racially closely related. These people, each one the product of several sources, formerly led very isolated lives and even today have little contact with the outside world. In northern Togo, for instance, the agricultural people called Kabre are scarcely affected by other tribes, while in central Nigeria it is the so-called 'pagan' tribes known by the names Kadara, Birom, Zaranda and so on who have been gradually driven back by more highly-developed tribes (Nupe, Gwari, Jukun and so on) into the rough interior of central Nigeria, where today they pursue a primitive kind of agriculture.

In mountainous northern Cameroun live the Kirdi and the Mandara, and on Lake Chad, the Sara. In the same territory we find the Kanembu, Kanuri and Baghirmi, Muslim tribes closely intermingled with the Arabs. Formerly they founded powerful dynasties.

If we now turn to the Negro peoples in the forest south of the savannah belt, we also find many different cultures, each one stamped with distinctive features borrowed from close neighbours.

In Guinea the rice-cultivators called Baga are the best-known. They also advanced into the territory of the Susu, extending along the coast as far as Sierra Leone. In the borderland between Guinea and Sierra Leone live the Kissi, also rice-farmers. To the north lie the Toma. The dominant people in Sierra Leone are the Mende and the Temne, less important are the Kpelle and the Bulom.

In the borderlands of Guinea, Sierra Leone and Liberia

are many tribes who are closely related culturally, for instance the Dan, Kran (also called Gere) and the Kono.

In all these tribes the secret society forms part of the social structure. The best-known societies or guilds are the male *poro* guild and the female, *bundu* or *sande* guild. Different artistic styles are well displayed in the masks of these societies, the styles of the Mende, Dan and Gere being very remarkable.

Numerous intermediate styles have developed by exchange, though usually the marks of the original style

are not lost. The Kru are a good example of this because their masks often display features of the Gere style. The Kru whose territory extends across Liberia as far as the Ivory Coast, live for the most part on coastal strips where they have shown themselves to be bold sailors. They were called Kru from their language, which is spoken by many small tribes.

The Liberian Negro is the integrated African, descendant of American black slaves who returned after 1821 as free men.

The Baule and Guro, (Cat. 58) important tribes living in the west of the Ivory Coast, have produced a great variety of plastic art. The Baule, descendants of the Agni people, are not only fine and exceptionally sensitive wood-carvers, but also masters of the art of bronze and jewellery. Their style is clearly separated from the Guro but even here there is an exchange of influence, which may add greatly to the difficulties of exact attribution of many pieces.

In south-west Ghana we encounter people, who, like several of the tribes of southern Dahomey and Nigeria to be discussed later, present a typical overall picture that justifies description of them as an entity. These are people who are assembled in federated tribes, a type of organization often described as a state, and which, because the centre of the state is a capital city with a chief, called a king, have come to be known as city states. The kings, whose power was primarily founded on their sacred status, also had a sharply-defined profane power, which was extended by vassals far beyond the immediate environment of the capital city. The king surrounded himself with a splendid court, to which the finest craftsmen were attached and who made cult objects of all kinds in the service of the king. It is possible to speak of a court style that is distinct from the art of the common people. These royal courts still exist today although their power has been strictly limited since colonial times. In Ghana the people of the powerful Akan federation form influential states. To these belong the Ashanti, the Fanti, Ahanta, Nzima and the Ga. In Dahomey, on the other hand, there are the Fon, who are a branch of the large Ewe tribe, the Yoruba, with their centre in west Nigeria, and their eastern neighbours the Bini. Large tribes also live in east Nigeria, in the delta of the Niger and the mouth of the Cross river. Their culture, however, is very different from that of western Nigeria though they too are dominated by the secret society. These tribes are known by the names Ijo, Ibo, Ibibio, Anyang and Ekoi. The Hausa is an important tribe of northern Nigeria. They are Negroes speaking a Hamitic language and are largely Muslim. This tribe too formerly belonged to the founders of states, whose names live on in descriptions such as Kano, Katsina, Daura, Biram and so on.

Finally there are some tribes and groups in the northeast Congo who also belong to the true Negro race, the best known of which are the Zande, with several branches, and the Mangbetu and Lugbara of northwestern Buganda.

BANTU

Bantu is the name given to a race inhabiting large areas of East, central and South Africa. Originally it was a definite linguistic group called Bantu; but the name has been extended to cover all Bantu speakers. Nowadays it is used as a generic term for the Negroes.

The word Bantu consists of the particle *ntu*, meaning man, and the prefix *ba* forming the plural. Hence its meaning is 'the men', namely those belonging to one tribe. It follows that many of the Bantu tribes have names beginning with *ba*: Bakuba, Barundi, Bakota and so on. In other words, Kuba-men, Rundi-men,

Kota-men. Therefore in discussing the tribes I shall adhere to the literal translation, dropping the prefix *ba*.

Several groups are loosely termed Bantu who, although they speak related languages, have mingled more or less freely with other races; in consequence many differences have arisen. The Bantu intermarried primarily with Hamitic peoples who, arriving in successive waves, settled in the country. There was also miscegenation with the Bushmen and other groups, but on the whole the Bantu Negro's appearance is easily distinguishable from that of the Sudanese.

The Bantu are generally of powerful, muscular physique. The hair is curly, the face broad with high cheekbones, a large forehead and thick lips. The nose is broad, with a decided bridge, and often very narrow nostrils. The skin colour is mostly chocolate brown, but may vary from black to light brown.

The cultures of the Bantu are rarely entities. Some tribes are so wide-ranging that they should really be classed as a people, because they have a well-developed political system, while there are others which have never branched out beyond a simple tribal foundation.

The Bantu are divided according to territory:

1. The eastern Bantu in Buganda, Kenya, Tanzania, Zambia, Malawi and part of Mozambique.

2. The southern Bantu who dwell south of the Zambezi in Rhodesia and South Africa, in Swaziland, Botswana, Lesotho and South-West Africa.

3. The western Bantu live in the territory extending from Angola to southern Cameroun in the north, including the Congo and Zambia in the east as far as the Great Lakes of East Africa.

The Ganda, Nyoro, Ankole, Rundi, Rwanda, Kavirondo, Sukuma and Nyamwesi are tribes of the eastern Bantu, who live in the regions of Lakes Victoria, Albert, Tanganyika and Kivu, that is in Buganda, Kenya and Tanzania. These are the lake-dwelling Bantu. The tradition of these people is that they originally came from the north. One thing is certain, that the autochthonous people has become closely mixed with the Huma or Hima, a powerful Hamitic shepherd people who, in more recent times arrived in great numbers from the north and settled here, leaving their mark on the cultures of the indigenous populations.

Here, as in many parts of West Africa, kingdoms developed and that of Ganda played an important role even into recent decades. The extent to which the nomadic shepherds influenced these cultures can be deduced from more or less important additions to their culture. Many of the kings, who live in large palaces, retain huge herds of cattle, the significance of which far outweighs purely economic reasons and is deeply rooted in religion —a regular phenomenon of the Hamitic shepherd people. The same veneration is reserved for the sacred royal drums as for the king himself, who was—at least before colonial times—the incarnation of divine authority.

Among other tribes, the Nyoro for instance, in which the mixture between the two races and cultures was not so strong, a completely different situation holds sway. Two social classes developed: the Hamitic Hima becoming overlords of the Iru who were the original farmers of the district. In the Nyankole tribe the contrast between the two classes is even stronger.

In Kenya, east of the Lakes and to the north of Kilimanjaro, live the Kavirondo, Kamba and Kikuyu, while to the south of them in Tanzania we find the Chagga and, east of Lake Tanganyika, the Sukuma, Nyamwesi and Nyika. The Swahili, who originally came from the Lamu islands, are spread widely along the east coast. Below them to the south live the Ngonde and Nyakyusa. Here, too, the racial picture is very mixed and the cultural aspects are just as variable, due to immigrations from the north in earlier times.

The Bantu, though primarily an agricultural people, are also herdsmen, preponderantly of sheep and goats, which seem here to be held in the same esteem as cattle in the neighbouring shepherd tribes.

A typical social feature of the Bantu, especially noticeable in the Kamba and Kikuyu tribes, is the division of the males into clearly defined classes according to age.

The Swahili are one of the best-known tribes of East Africa. During the course of time they have absorbed many Asiatic elements from Arabia, Persia and later even from India; in fact, since they mingled relatively freely with all these people they can no longer really be counted as pure Bantu, even though their Negroid features remain dominant. Their language, despite many foreign loan words is, nevertheless, Bantu. It has gradually become the *lingua franca* of large parts of Africa and even spread as far as the Congo and Mozambique.

The southern Bantu, those living south of the Zambezi, have settled in Rhodesia, Mozambique, South and South-West Africa, but their southerly migration took place only in modern historical times, for in the seventeenth century when the Dutch first came to South Africa, they found scarcely any Bantu in the *hinterland*. In the course of their migration the Bantu have not only absorbed many foreign elements into their own culture, but have also partly mingled with indigenous peoples. Consequently the southern Bantu today form anything but a homogenous group, and comprise several subsidiary tribes spread all over the Union of South Africa.

In Rhodesia and Mozambique the Shona and Chopi tribes are important, also the Tsonga who inhabit the coastal regions. South of them live the Ngoni with their subsidiaries the Xhosa and Mpondo in the Union of South Africa. And in the east of the Union live the Swazi in Swaziland, the Ndebele and the Zulus of Natal and Zululand. The Zulus, a large people comprising many tribes, were at one time a powerful fighting force united by the much-feared Chaka, against the invading Boers. In the centre of the Union the most important tribes are the Venda, the Sotho in Lesotho, the Tswana in Botswana, incorporating also the Kwena, Ngwato, Tawana and Ngawaketse. In South West Africa the important tribes are the Herero and the Ovambo.

The country here is full of contrasts. Mountain ranges, chains of hills, fruitful valleys, grassland, arid plateaux and deserts are the natural environment of the Bantu. Strife over grazing grounds not unnaturally often led to bloody wars, because cattle were all-important to their lives. The Zulus especially were bold warriors, which may have been caused by the system of age-grouping, as it was the young who were the militant group. Even today cattle are the most important thing. In the centre of every Bantu village stands a kraal, a round, fenced enclosure that serves to hold the cattle at night. Men alone tend and watch over the beasts and different ceremonies and taboos concerning cattle appear to be related to similar Hamitic customs. This is a point I shall discuss later.

The western Bantu are centred in Congo-Kinshasa, and radiate outwards to Angola, Congo-Brazzaville, Gabon, the southern part of Cameroun and Zambia. These Bantu tribes played an historical role as the prototype of the idea of the Negro from the mysterious Dark Continent. Split into innumerable tribes and sub-tribes they managed to survive in the midst of the tropical jungle of central Africa. Tribal organization was well established here and developed sometimes into powerful social-political groups with a king as their chief. It was certainly not only the environment but also this social factor that principally favoured the birth of many kinds of art, such as wood-carving, and allowed them to achieve an exceptional standard of beauty and perfection.

If we separate the innumerable Congo tribes into four groups an overall picture emerges with opportunity for more detailed descriptions of individual tribes. And here it is noticeable that the great rivers often play a part in forming geographical boundaries.

In the west, in the valleys of the lower Congo and lower Kasai live the Congo, Vili, Mayombe and Bwende Pl. III tribes. It is known that, before the advent of the white man, the Congo controlled a powerful state at the mouth of the river, whose influence was felt over a large area. In the fifteenth century the Portuguese soon converted the whole kingdom to Christianity. From Pl. 5, 6; Cat. 53

that time on, periods of prosperity alternated with times of decline until, during the colonial period, very little remained of the former power of the Congo kings. On the other hand this region, subjected as it was to a constant influence from Europe, developed a very interesting process of acculturation with consequences which are often apparent today, as did the other tribes mentioned above as well as the Congo. This syncretism is only faintly discernible in mythology whereas the plastic arts reveal much more clearly how great was Christian influence. Sixteenth- and seventeenth-century crucifixes, figures of Saint Antony and other objects cast in brass, obviously Roman Catholic in origin, have been preserved. But there are foreign elements from still later periods such as figures of Europeans as priests, hunters and colonial officials. In general the artistic style of this territory is very realistic and themes from everyday life are preferred.

To the east of these tribes in the area of Stanley Pool live the Teke, Wumbu, Mfumungu, Yanzi and Sengele. In lands stretching between the Kwango and the lower Kasai live the Yaka people who show a preference for polychrome in their plastic art, especially in initiation masks. A characteristic and frequent feature of their figures is the triangular snub nose.

In the same area we find the Mbala, Bembe, Huana, Suku and Holo. The Kuba, living in the region between Kasai and Sangkuru include several tribes, whose nucleus is the Bushongo (the 'knife-throwing people'). The Bushongo founded the powerful Kuba empire whose highly developed social-political organization stood out as a remarkable exception among the Congo peoples. The Kuba still have a king called the *nyimi,* a symbol of ultimate power to his vassals. Court life in Musjenge is still run on traditional lines and the many courtiers, among them priests, artists, historians, musicians and dancers, are even today exponents of a living, indigenous culture which far outstrips that of other central African tribes. The Kuba federation can best be compared with the Negro states of the Yoruba or Akan in West Africa. It is scarcely necessary to say that art was greatly stimulated here too and its products are among Africa's finest works. Not the portrait figures of kings alone, but ceremonial objects, such as wooden goblets, tobacco pipes, boxes and bowls display an exceptionally sensitive aesthetic sense, inherent not only in the form of the objects, but also in the rich, geometrical ornamentation seen at its best on their embroidered raffia-work.

North of the Kuba dwell the Lele, the Songo Meno, Dengese, Ekonda and Nkuchu, relatives of the Mongo and Kundu. The southern group is represented by the Pende whose territory stretches as far as north Angola. The Pende masks, used principally for boys' initiation rites, display an extraordinary variety of expression. Nor should the small amulet masks carved in ivory be forgotten. Neighbours of the Pende are the Jokwe and the Lunda, whose territory also extends beyond the borders of Angola. The Jokwe, among whom the initiation of boys plays an important part, make impressive masks of bark which are used at the rite of circumcision. Finally chiefs' stools often have scenes from daily life carved on the stretchers.

The art of the Lunda displays a certain relationship with that of the Jokwe and both have influenced other

tribes more or less strongly, the Bena Kanioka and the Kete for example.

The Bena Lulua, Salampasu and Songe should also be mentioned. Wooden figures of the Bena Lulua usually have a long neck and tall, slim body, covered all over with a complicated tattoo design. The peculiar style of the Songe is seen in the fetish figures decorated with feathers, animal teeth and snakeskin, that give a very uncanny impression with their open mouths, sharp chins and fierce eyes made of cowrie shells.

In south-eastern Congo, in Katanga especially, though also to some extent in Kasai, we find another important people, the Luba. The old Luba kingdom with its sacred kingship and efficient organization of

state power extending over a number of neighbouring tribes, has now completely lost its former political might. But the heritage of earlier days is still seen in a variety of sub-styles, so intermingled, however, that it is often difficult to fix an exact origin to an object from Luba territory. The wooden carved figures are generally finely rounded in form with a round face in which the large half-closed eyes seem to gaze into another world. A particular characteristic of many of these figures is a cross motif set behind the head to form part of the hair-style. In Luba art the human figure often forms part of a larger piece. For instance there are chiefs' stools, neck supports, bowls, three-pronged spear-holders and so forth that are supported by one or two caryatids.

★ Pl. 7

Pl. 8; Cat. 107

Cat. 48

Among the sub-styles of the Luba, that of Buli on the Lualaba is justly famous for its definite clarity of form, while the powerful abstract style of the *kifwebe* (Pl. IV; Cat. 16) masks of the Luba-Songe is also remarkable.

The Eastern group comprises, among others, the Bembe, Rega or Lega, Buye, and Mbole. These tribes —especially the Rega—are in the western sense not very advanced. They still live in closed tribal communities in which social-political life is ruled almost completely by secret societies, for whose functions almost all art is created. Apart from wooden figures and masks, the small ivory masks of the Rega (Cat. 14) are well-known. The northern group between the Congo and Ubangi rivers as far as the Stanley Falls, also includes several tribes:

Ngala, Bwaka, Ngombe, Poto and Ngata. In the valley of the Welle live the Ngbandi and the Ababua. The styles of this region contrast sharply with those of the rest of the Congo. The forms of the wooden figures have a brutal appearance and incorporate only essentials. The objects are made principally for magic rites conducted by the secret societies.

Turning once more to the west coast of Angola, we find in the north the Congo and the Jokwe again, and, on the coastal belt of Loanda, the Ngola and Mbaka. Portuguese influence has been felt here for a long time. In the south live the Ovimbundu, in the central part the Mbangala and Ngangela with the Rotse in Zambia.

In Congo-Brazzaville the most important tribes are the Teke, Bembe and Sundi. The fetish figures of the Teke testify to a distinct style, using cylindrical or cubist forms. The Kuyu live to the north of the Teke and their ancestral mythological dance personifies the primaeval snake. This is achieved with the assistance of a *Kebe-Kebe* mask constructed from an impressive arrangement of woven fibre and feathers crowned by a small polychrome wooden head. Cat. 17, 42

Far to the north live the Kwele, represented by the heart-shaped, strongly stylized masks that are peculiar to this people. Cat. 18

Gabon tribes have much in common with the world of ideas of the Congo tribes. One explanation could be that many tribal wanderings have taken place here, resulting in deeply ingrained cultural memories. Whatever the reason it is astonishing what a rich vein this homogenous background proved for the art of the different tribes. First and foremost come the Pangwe

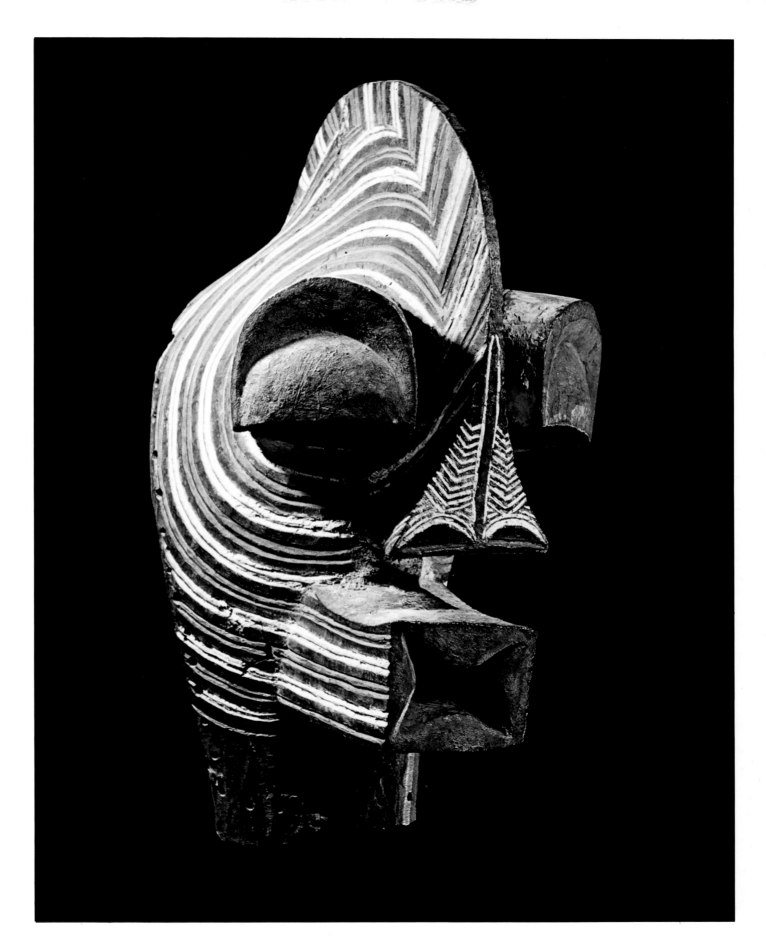

people, composed of several tribes mostly living in north Gabon. The southern Pangwe include the Fang, whose art, in contrast to the northern group, is strongly stylized. Many figures from this territory are figures of the dead made to be placed on the top of important   Cat. 28
funerary urns as protective spirits.

Tribes living on the Ogowe river have the same customs towards the dead and here too we find reliquaries, although the style of the figures is absolutely different. In the Kota tribe these tomb figures, or *mbulu-ngulu,* are   Cat. 29, 30
so stylized that nothing remains but a large, flat face   Pl. 9
covered with brass or sheet iron. In the south of Gabon live the Mpongwe, known also as the Lumbo, who use ritual death masks as incarnations of dead women. The white painted faces and half-closed slit eyes of these magnificent masks call forth the world of the dead in dramatic fashion.   Pl. V

Cameroun is in many ways a transit territory. Here we encounter, besides pure Bantu, Sudanese Negroes, while the mixture of languages and people is especially strong. Of the Bantu there are the Bafo, Duala, Bakwiri and Baza who live in the southern, primaeval forest. Where the forest falls away before grassland and savannah we find again quite different cultures: here kingdoms developed and palaces and courts became centres whence different styles spread out over the land. The Tikar, Barmum, Bali, Bamessing, Babungo, Bekom and Bamileke are the most important groups.
The style of the grasslands of Cameroun is easily recognizable: like the masks, faces on the figures have wide,   Pl. 10
staring eyes and round cheeks. Imposing wooden   Cat. 9, 103, 104
figures decorate porches and doorways in the palace.

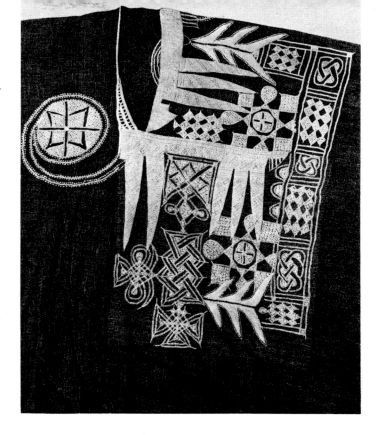

Cat. 94, 95, 101, 102

Pl. 11 *Hausa (northern Nigeria). Man's embroidered robe. Detail. Cotton. Koninklijk Instituut voor de Tropen, Amsterdam. (Cat. 71)*

Pl. 12 *Mandingo (Mali/Guinea). Sword in a leather sheath. Top of handle and end of sheath made of brass, l. 84 cm. Deutsches Leder-museum, Offenbach (Main).*

But great artistic skill is displayed in clay, bronze or mother-of-pearl in pipes, masks and chiefs' stools.

HAMITIC PEOPLES

The Hamitic people bring a completely new element into the racial pattern of the African races. In the light of present knowledge it is thought that they must originally have come from Asia Minor. Their homeland should be sought in south Arabia whence they travelled through Somaliland and Ethiopia to Africa. The Hamites, with the Semites, are considered to be a Mediterranean race, and a minor branch of the Caucasian or white race. Over

the centuries the Hamitic people penetrated in successive migratory waves into Black Africa and thereby forced the indigenous people in their path further southward. This process, which continued more or less unbroken over a long period, was the cause of racial interbreeding and cultural similarities, as one may see in the language relationships in East Africa.

The date of the first migration of the Hamitic peoples is not precisely known, but it was probably about the fourth century B.C. At that time classical Egyptian civilization was in flower on the Nile. The expression Hamitic, like Bantu, describes chiefly a language grouping. From the racial-historical point of view it comprises a number of racially different peoples, the outcome of various mixtures between Negro and Hamite. To the northern Hamites belong the North African Berbers, the Tuareg of the Sahara and the Fulani in West Africa. The eastern Hamites comprise the modern Egyptians, the Galla, Danakil and the Somali in Ethiopia.

Racially the northern Hamites are the purest. We must, however, ignore them here, as they are representatives of the white race and their culture has nothing in common with those men dwelling south of the Sahara. An exception must, however, be made for the Fulbe, also called Fulani or Peul, a large, nomadic shepherd people whose origin has never been properly established. After many migrations they found a home for a time in Senegal, but in the thirteenth century they set off eastwards, gradually spreading over the whole savannah belt of West Africa. During this migration they broke up into several groups, some of

whom remained faithful to the nomadic life, for instance the Peul in Mali, the Bororo in Niger and the Fulbe in Nigeria. Other groups, converted to Islam, founded an enormously powerful religious and political warrior state, which in the eighteenth and nineteenth centuries fought a 'holy war' against the Hausa kingdoms of Nigeria. From this clash of powers there resulted the Fulani emirates of northern Nigeria. The best-known of the thirty seven emirates existing today are: Sokoto, Kano, Nupe, Katsina and Bornu.

Of course the anti-figurative influence of Islam prohibited the production of genuine plastic art-forms, but there is a good deal of applied art. The Fulani, and other Mohammedan peoples of West Africa circumvented the decree forbidding representation of animals and humans, and the creative urge found an outlet in their love of decoration. Embroidery on the Sultan's robes Pl. 11, Cat. 71 and finely worked leather ornament on weapons, Pl. 12 purses and horse-trappings gives an excellent picture of Islamic-African art.

NILO-HAMITES AND NILOTES

These two races are to be found in North-East and East Africa. The Nilo-Hamites live in Kenya, northern Buganda and north Tanzania. They display the Hamitic racial characteristics in a much more marked degree than the Bantu and the Nilotes. They are tall, slim men of an average height of five feet eight inches. They have other Negroid features beside their curly hair, but their noses are remarkably narrow. Their languages be-

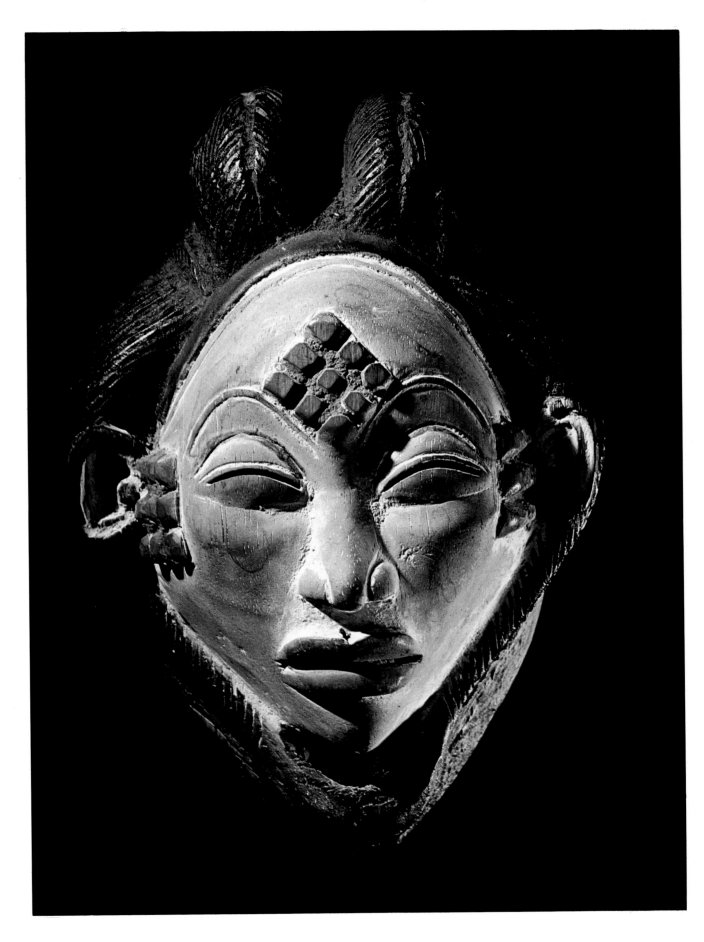

Pl. VI Masai (Kenya). Woman wearing rich ornament.

long to the Nilotic group, but nevertheless show Hamitic characteristics. The Nilo-Hamites live entirely of their large herds and their manner of life is dictated by them. The same is true of those of them who have given up the semi-nomadic life in favour of a settled existence, for although they may now be tillers of the soil their cattle are still very important. This race is represented in Kenya by the Masai, Nandi, Suk and Kipsigi and in the far north of Kenya west of Lake Rudolph live the Turkana and Karamojong.

The Masai, who have spread as far as Tanzania provide a classic example of the division into age-groups already mentioned in connection with the Bantu. This age-division is strictly enforced by the Masai and the male community is subject to numerous responsibilities and taboos.

The Nilotes are centred on the White Nile in the southern Sudan. They are the Nuer, Dinka, Shilluk and Latuko and farther south the Acholi in Buganda.

The foregoing general survey of the African peoples has produced several ideas and phenomena that must now be discussed in greater detail, because they form important cornerstones in this essay. First and foremost the word and the idea of 'culture' must be clarified. The word, as it is used here, has nothing to do with the narrow, popular conception of culture: theatre, concerts, ballet, exhibitions of painting and so on. It is the essential quality that divides man from animals. By culture we understand all the acquired characteristics that a community of men possesses. Or, in the concise phrase of the American anthropologist, Herskovits, "Culture is the man-made part of the environment." Every community, however small and however simple its structure, is bound by many restrictive standards and rules of conduct necessary for communication. Theoretically endless different possibilities could be realized in a culture, but in reality we find that man always chooses a few only and uses them as a foundation for his system. It is a process that is never fulfilled and therefore static, but is in a continuous state of development. Changes may come about through inventions and discoveries from within, or they may be provoked from outside. Then they are the result of cultural contact and are known as acculturation. Their effect is to influence small sections or single elements and, as the process develops, a culture may change completely or only in a minor way.

An accompanying factor in the development of specific cultural elements is the geographical situation of a human community, though environment is not always decisive in the development of a type of culture. It creates certain possibilities while imposing definite limitations, but no more than that. In the light of these assertions it is possible to divide peoples into groups, according to the kind of culture they have developed. For this, the most important point is the method a people develops to exploit the natural assets of their environment, which leads to the division between food-gatherers, fishermen, hunters, farmers, cattle-breeders and industrialized peoples. Of course reality does not always fit so neatly into this artificial and standard pattern, and there are many combinations and transitional stages, leading to a very high degree of variety within a single culture.

In Africa the Bushmen are gatherers and hunters. For centuries they lived in almost complete isolation, hence their culture still displays a simple structure. The community is separated into small self-sufficient groups formed of a few small families. Every adult member is solely occupied with the pressing daily task—the search for food. Possibilities for variation in this existence are few, resulting in specialization, and leaving little room for activities that might have inspired a kind of art.

The position with the central African Pygmy is very similar. They have adapted their hunting technique to the deep forest and some have become fishermen. The Pygmies are not so isolated as the Bushmen and their contact with the Bantu has brought foreign elements into their original culture with some acculturation.

Agriculture is absolutely different. Farming communities are bound to the soil and have a settled existence. Conditions for the establishment of larger communities are met and villages can be built. Dwellings which will serve as permanent homes are constructed with greater care. The population increases and there is consequently time to spare for different kinds of work, which is applied of course principally to the tilling of the soil and to the primary needs of the community. But also it can be used for secondary, less immediate ends, producing a wider variety of activities. Handicrafts develop: weaving, pottery, metal-work, wood-carving etc. Only the needs of the individual group are served at first, but as soon as production oversteps this mark trade begins and trading centres which have to be protected by a political organization arise. Thus the foundation of a state can be the result of this kind of development.

We saw that the Sudanese Negroes of West Africa were primarily farmers. Their cultures are essentially based on soil husbandry. Many eastern and south-eastern Bantu people are also farmers, who have developed a terraced system of agriculture in the highlands.

A different form of farming is practised by the Droe Negro in the forest lands of the West African coast, and also by the western Bantu. It could be called agri- or even horticulture, as it is practised in small plots of land reclaimed from the rain-forest, where plants are cultivated that for the most part are not dependent on the seasons, but can be harvested all the year round.

The true cattle-breeder in Africa is the Hamite, and the Bantu of East Africa, who is strongly influenced by him. If we examine these cattle-rearing cultures there is no doubt that their structure is determined by the overwhelming significance of their herds. Pasture land, the territory within the borders of which the cattle are grazed, is all important. There is no permanent dwelling-place. All work is connected with cattle and the shepherd's life does not offer great outlets for other activities.

Besides these simple examples of agriculture and cattle-rearing there are intermediate forms in Africa. They are most frequently found in East and South Africa where the cultural assimilations among the agricultural Bantu and the Hamitic shepherd people have gradually been fully developed. The communities are settled. They tend their cattle in the neighbourhood of their village, or they lend the cattle in exchange for agricultural produce. Fixed dwellings and division of work have created secondary needs which make the cultural picture much more complex.

MATERIAL ASPECTS OF ART

We have seen that cultures of Africa display fundamental differences and those based on permanent agricultural holdings have the greatest potential for variety. In them a larger number of potential workers allows freedom to develop skills on work of secondary importance. This is one of the causes of the birth of African art.

However, there are two more important causes which are also fundamental to the African communities. The first is the outcome of the highly developed system of kinship. Several different branches of a central family form a clan. Several clans form a tribe and tribes may be extended to peoples.

A clan is a unilateral exogamous kinship group, whose members are all traditionally related, either patrilinearly or matrilinearly. Members of a clan trace their ancestry to a common clan ancestor, a mythological ancestor figure, who may be male or female, human or animal.

The second and related cause is the ancestor cult. The ancestors are intermediaries between the living and a distant, vaguely conceived supreme Being. The institution of divine kingship and the formation of powerful states derives from this.

When we consider the art of Black Africa and define the provenance of objects it is noticeable that West and central Africa have always produced the most and the best pieces. East and South Africa are not nearly so well represented. Hence it is the Sudan Negro and the Bantu who have made the greatest contribution to what we call African or Negro art. The three conditions mentioned above are especially applicable to these two groups.

The Hamitic people, basically shepherds and hence not in a position to develop a material culture, have produced relatively little art. The same is true of the somewhat similar cultures of the Bushmen and the Pygmies. It follows that we shall be concerned here primarily with the first two groups, though the others will not be completely ignored.

The deep-seated differences evident between the Negro peoples are exemplified by the divisions of different artistic styles. Every tribe has a style deviating from that of its neighbours; but sub-styles—regional or even absolutely local—sometimes arise within the same tribe. As a general rule it is no longer possible to trace the origin of a particular style as the material for comparison is nearly always lacking. Despite this, many researchers have tried to explain the origin and development of a particular style on a hypothetical basis. One example is the art of the Akan people of Ghana: it is believed by Eva Meyerowitz to have originated in ancient Egypt. The styles of the ancient Ife and Benin have also been linked with the Mediterranean and Egypt (Frobenius). These hypotheses are, however, not yet proven. The techniques of these highly developed West African cultures especially that of bronze-casting, as well as their style, reached such a sophisticated level that one can scarcely credit an autochthonous African origin, a supposition which is reinforced by the complete absence of similar techniques elsewhere.

Specific characteristics in style can, however, be traced to recognized phenomena, that formerly penetrated a culture from without and were subsequently absorbed. The portraits of Portuguese warriors in ancient

Benin art are a good example. The first Portuguese who reached Benin in 1458 must have made a profound impression on the court artists, for many figures were produced. Another instance is offered by Congo representations of mother and child: Fraser sees here an imitation of Christian Madonna figures. Other examples of Christian influence spread by the Portuguese in the Congo have already been mentioned.

Very few discoveries reveal that the origins of a style can date back to prehistoric Africa. The finds made by Bernard Fagg in northern central Nigeria near the village of Nok are relevant here. The first stone and clay heads found by him there were complemented in the '50's and '60's by the horde, possible ten times greater, and found in the same district, of fragments of figures and other objects that clearly point to a developed civilization flourishing in this region about the 800-700 B.C. Beautiful objects, found recently in Ife and its environs, probably offer a link between the Nok and the Yoruba culture of Ife.

In other cases, however, questions as to the origin of a given style remain unanswered. The crouching figures made of steatite—called *pomdo* by the Kissi in Sierra Leone—were mysterious pieces found in the earth and subsequently assimilated into the ancestor cult. The Dogon in Mali have the archaic Tellem figures, the origin of which remains unclear. The Dogon themselves attribute them to the Tellem tribe, traditionally supposed to have lived in Dogon territory. Anthropologists, on the other hand, assume that the Tellem figures represent an earlier stage in the development of Dogon art.

Surprising discoveries are constantly being made all over Africa. In the last few years clay figures and funerary urns have come to light in the Nigerian estuary, ⋆ Pl. 13 the origins of which are unknown. And in the territory of the Sao, south of Lake Chad, clay figures and remnants of decorative objects in bronze have been found. For the time being, however, all these finds are far too fragmentary to form the basis for conclusions.

The different styles of African art have now become almost completely determined. It is the community that gives birth to a style which carries the distinguishing marks of its imaginative world. Every clan—every ⋆ Pl. 14 tribe even—has tried to represent in art its mythological ideas, its ancestral beliefs or faith in a Supreme Being, and consequently has provided numerous objects, the production of which is subject to the same strict community laws as other things. Special people were always employed to make such exceptional objects, specialists chosen for their skill and versatility in this kind of work. The craft was handed down from father to son and sometimes they formed complete clans or guilds, which had the sole right—or duty—to practise their special craft in the service of the community. It is ⋆ Pl. 15 not, therefore, surprising that fine works of art were produced by their accumulated skills.

The conditions evident in the farming communities, ⋆ Pl. 16 where the craftsman worked for a whole village, are to be found in an even greater degree in professional people working for the court. The best of them can be called artists, even though we do not know their names, and many pieces have achieved fame as works of art. It does not follow, however, that everything of this kind

Pl. 14 Nok culture (Nigeria). Left : Head from Wamba. Fragment. Terracotta, h. 14 cm. Right : Figure. Terracotta, h. 16.5 cm. 5th to 1st century B.C. British Museum, London.

Pl. 15 *Sierra Leone.* Nomoli *crouching figure. Steatite, h. 19 cm. Koninklijk Instituut voor de Tropen, Amsterdam.*

Pl. 16 *Dogon (Mali).* Tellem *figure with raised arms. Wood with sacrificial crust, h. 117 cm. J. Boussard Collection, Paris.*

produced in Africa is necessarily first class. A general survey will be gained by walking through the galleries and the store of a museum: the public sees only the best pieces upstairs, while the less valuable are kept below, although among them there may be interesting and rare examples of regional styles. In the traditional world of Africa the concept of artist, as we understand it, is unknown. The man we call an artist is just one of the community like any other, only it happens that he is better at wood-carving than his friends, or that his weapons prove to be of more practical design than those of other smiths, or perhaps a woman's weaving is more attractive than that of her friends. Such people earn a reputation in their own and neighbouring villages and receive commissions when someone wants an especially fine and good piece. The 'artists', then, were originally known by name. But as is always the case with a people without writing their names were soon forgotten and they are remembered only by their work. This statement is as true for the plastic arts as for literature, music and the dance. In Africa the dance (Pl. 17) is highly developed, though unfortunately its aesthetic quality is not yet everywhere recognized.

Even though tradition kept unrelenting watch on the observance of unwritten laws, personal expression always found and took advantage of outlets, however small. This explains individual deviations on a theme within a particular style. Our knowledge of African art is not so far advanced that we can distill and group together individual styles. Probably the one and only example of this is the Luba style from Buli in the Congo,

Pl. 17 Nyamwesi (Nzega district, Tanzania). Dancer in full dress. Musée de l'Homme, Paris.

Pl. 18 Luba (Master of Buli, Congo-Kinshasa). Chief's stool with caryatids. Light-coloured wood, h. 53.3 cm. Koninklijk Museum voor Midden-Afrika, Tervuren. ★ Pl. 18

Pl. 19   From Douentza village (Mali). Cloth sewn together from narrow strips. Cotton with coloured designs. R. S. Wassing Collection, The Hague.

Pl. 20   Fon (Dahomey). Appliqué cloth. Reproduction of a lion-hunt. Cotton, brightly coloured. Museum voor Land- en Volkenkunde, Rotterdam.

mostly wood. Wood of many different qualities is available everywhere, even in the savannah. As a material it is a comparatively easy to work, which perhaps accounts for the preponderance of wood-carving in African art. But there are also many other vegetable raw materials: calabashes, fruit stones, raffia, fibrous barks, cotton, bamboos, rattan, reeds, resins and so on.

Of the animal stuffs ivory is the most important, followed by all the different kinds of horn, skins, wool, feathers, shells and teeth all of which were used at one time or another.

where it can be accepted that all the figures in this style were done by the same artist.

Traditional rules were especially strict where ceremonial and ritual objects were concerned, their appearance being rigidly linked with stereotyped models. In more profane themes the artist was freer to follow his own ideas. However great the resulting differences, the stylistic features determined by tradition are always manifest. This attachment to tradition—even if often subconscious—is characteristic of the styles of Black Africa: the giant ritual masks in a certain style will display the same features as a detail on almost any everyday object of the same people.

The African artist has a wide variety of materials to choose from. Usually they are of vegetable origin,

Bronze, brass and iron are the most important metals; rather less frequently gold, silver and aluminium are used, but also other minerals such as stone, glass, clay and dyes.

African techniques developed to an astonishingly high level, which is very surprising considering the primitive tools. The wood-carver used a short-handled mattock-shaped axe with a flat leaf-shaped blade attached either by binding or splicing. The chisel and knife were only used for detailed work and finishing. However large the seats, house-pillars or reliefs, and however much careful work was to be applied to the details, the object was almost invariably hewn from a single piece of wood. Drums, dug-out canoes and so on were hollowed out with fire, and poker-work is found everywhere.

Weaving was done with many different kinds of loom. The best developed form is the horizontal pedal loom. This type is specially widespread in West Africa. The narrow bands of material produced on these looms are usually sewn up later into clothes and covers (Pl. 19). The tribes of the Kasai and Kwilu territories in the central Congo have developed a special technique: here the women weave a kind of plush-like raffia on diagonal looms. The pattern is knotted in broad bands during the weaving process and these are shorn afterwards. Insertion of a pattern can be done in many different ways. It can be woven in with coloured thread. All the black and white and coloured wool or cotton cloths woven by the men in West Africa are produced in this way. Appliqué work on cloth is often found among the Fon of Dahomey. Their gay patterns include figures of men and beasts

*Pl. 20 *Pl. 21 Benin (Nigeria). Bronze plaque with three chiefs in ceremonial dress. Court style. H. 37.2 cm. 17th century. British Museum, London.*

Pl. 22   Bamum or Tikar (Cameroun grasslands). Royal pipe with an ele-phant's head. Brass, h. 16.5 cm. Museum Rietberg, Zurich.

Pl. VII   Baule (Ivory Coast). Raffia-work with plangi *and* tritik *decora-tive technique. Fragment. Museum voor Land- en Volkenkunde, Rotterdam.*

and historical episodes from the lives of their rulers. An example of template technique is seen in the so-called *adinkra* cloths of the Ashanti in Ghana. Here small patterns cut from a plate are stuck with a resinous paste on to the material. The tie and dye technique *(plangi)* is found in west Sudan, on the Ivory Coast and in the Congo. In this method of designing small pieces of the material are gathered and tied together. When the piece is dyed they remain untouched and appear afterwards as light ornament on a dark background. Another reserve technique practised in Africa by the Bambara of Mali and in the Cameroun, is batik. The patterns are drawn with an alkaline soap and the material dipped into a mudbath. When the soap is removed the parts

Pl. VII

★ Cat. 72

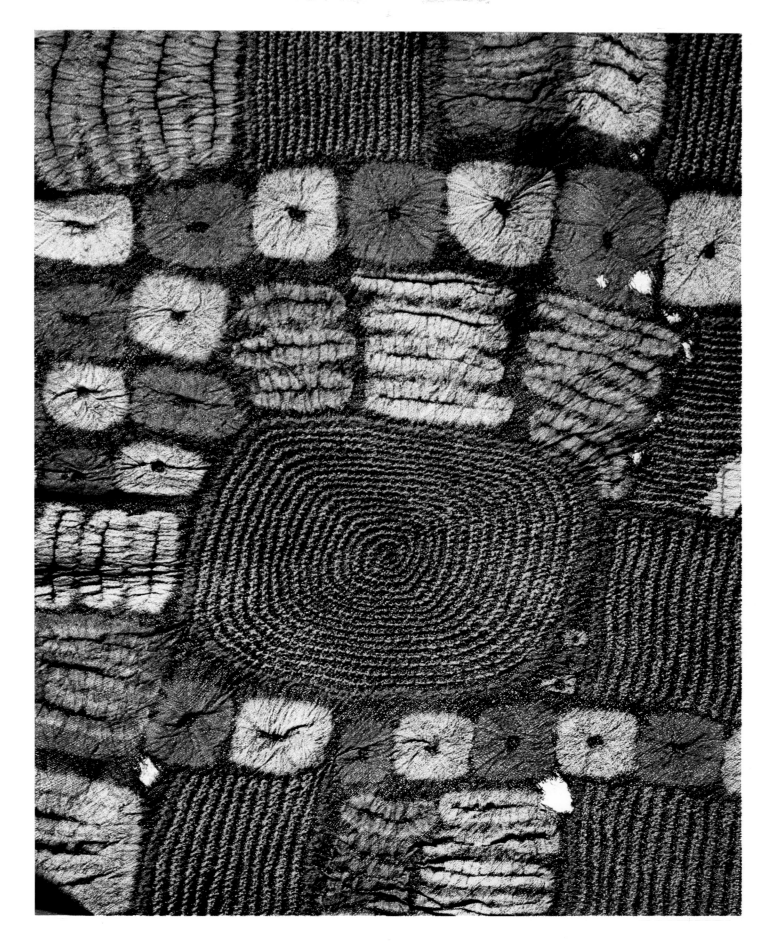

Pl. 23 Afo (northern Nigeria). Potter decorating a clay vessel.

Pl. 24 Bamum (Cameroun grasslands). Pipe-head belonging to a chief. Detail. Clay, overall height 110 cm. Ethnographisch Museum, Antwerp. (Cat. 95)

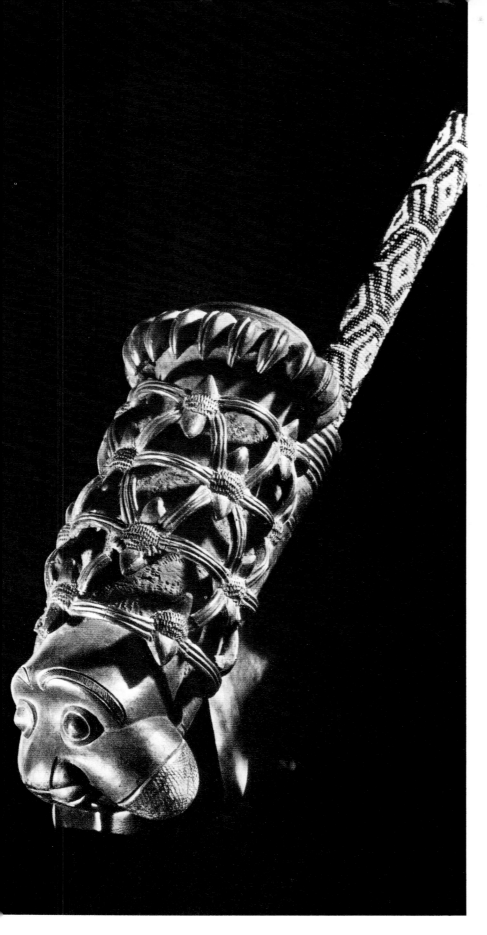

covered by it emerge as reserve or undyed patterns. Instead of mud the people of Cameroun use indigo as a dye.

Plait-work is found all over Africa, in fact there are too many different techniques to discuss each one individually and it must therefore suffice to mention only the mats, used either on the floor or walls, everyday objects which are often finely hand-woven in complicated, geometric or naturalistic patterns of some artistry.

There are examples of every different kind of plait-work, displaying an artistic sense for form and decoration; one need only mention the flat bowls and the baskets from Rwanda, whose conical lids have dark tips and a harmonious zig-zag ornamentation.

All objects cast in bronze or brass were made by the *cire perdue* method, a technique that flourished in the old kingdoms of Ife and Benin.[2] Traditionally it is said to have been discovered in Ife and to have been introduced to the Benin court later. It was always closely connected with the court and the artists made portraits of their rulers in bronze—kings, queens, princes and princesses—while ritual pieces and flat plaques (Pl. 21) for the palace walls depicted courtly scenes. This art was never surpassed anywhere in Africa. Brass-founding (Pl. 22) spread over large parts of West and central Africa where it was also maintained as a court art. In colonial times however it degenerated rapidly and the products of today are generally worthless.

The lost wax method *(cire perdue)* is as follows: a clay form is made and covered all over with beeswax. The details are often applied with wax thread or little drops of wax. A layer of clay is then placed over the wax model and as soon as it has hardened the wax is melted away by applying heat to the model. Now metal is poured through one or several pouring holes into the space where the wax formerly lay. When the metal has cooled the outer clay cover is broken off and the inner kernel removed. Countless objects were made in this way. The technique was also used for the production of gold ornaments. The Baule and Akan produce objects, paraphernalia of high rank and royalty, such as dignitaries' staves, insignia, dagger-handles, sandals and so on, that are often veneered with gold plate. The use of gold was very limited in early times and kings and their close relatives alone had the right to wear this symbol of divine power. When the Ashanti kings commanded their goldsmiths to make a gold piece the necessary quantity of gold dust was carefully weighed out. They used the small, so-called gold weights made of brass. These small weights are miniature works of art in themselves. There are two kinds: flat, rectangular, small blocks, the top surface of which is decorated in high relief, and very small weights sculpted in a form representing a proverb or a figure of speech, and displaying a rich imagination.

In wrought iron-work two kinds of bellows are used. The type with two quiver-shaped, carved wooden air-sacks was widespread throughout the tropical forest as far as East Africa, while the kind of bellows using clay chambers is more common in the savannah. Iron and steel are most commonly used for weapons. Smith's work has reached a high standard of perfection in many tribes and one can therefore justifiably speak of artist-smiths. In former times ceremonial as well as more utilitarian hunting weapons were made, and looked upon as signs of rank. Some masterpieces have become known, especially in the Congo, for instance the ceremonial axes of the Songe and neighbouring tribes, the handles of which are decorated with small heads.

The Dogon and Bambara of Mali have smiths who produce wrought iron ritual pieces besides agricultural tools and weapons. They usually represent human figures made from a single piece of iron and intended to be placed on graves or altars. The Senufo of the Ivory Coast are also famous for their wrought iron cult objects. Cat. 61

Silver is principally used as ornament and it is found wrought into armbands, anklets and spiral neckbands. It is also used for chasing, for knives and other weapons. This craft is especially developed among the Kuba of the Congo. Cat. 60

Pottery is almost exclusively the women's preserve in Africa, who employ several recognized techniques: round pots made without a wheel and hollowed out with a simple turning movement of the hands; or the clay coiled in concentric spirals and its surface afterwards rubbed smooth. Utilitarian pottery has attained such a state of perfection in many tribes that aesthetics play an important part. The finely worked pottery vessels of the Bali, Bamum, Bangungun, and other tribes of the Cameroun grasslands became splendid objects of art and this is equally true of the large clay pipe-heads with the appearance of ebony of the Bamessing and Babungo. The Mangbetu of the north-east Congo and also the Zande, whose ideas of beauty lead them to bind the heads of their babies to force the head Pl. 23

Pl. 24

Pl. 25   Zande (Congo-Kinshasa). Portrait vase. Clay, h. 21 cm. Koninklijk Instituut voor de Tropen, Amsterdam. (p. 54)

Pl. 26   Mangbetu (Congo-Kinshasa). Ceremonial spoon. Wood, h. 30 cm. Museum Rietberg, Zurich. (p.55)

into a long protuberance behind, have made wonderful
Pl. 25   portrait vases of the long-headed women.

Glass for the production of beads is smelted in Africa, but by far the larger proportion came into the country at the time of the slave trade. It is really extraordinary what can be made of this cheap material. The Zulus of South Africa were probably the greatest artists, using the minute beads to fashion all kinds of attractive ornaments. Very fine bead work was also done in East Africa, and the Tutsi tribe estimated beads highly enough to use them on the king's headdress.

Whatever art Africa has produced—and art criticism in its widest sense must surely concede that many
Pl. 26   of the handicrafts rank as art—the objects were always made for a definite purpose. Whether they are ancestor figures, magical cult objects, musical instruments, ornament or utilitarian pieces, functional design is all-important. Naturally there are some exceptions but as a rule objects were never made simply for the sake of their beauty. That they can however satisfy the highest artistic sensibility has been generally accepted for several decades.

What then was the real significance of these objects? And what effect did they have on the civilizations where they took root and to which they belong? Undoubtedly they all played an important part, were cherished and regarded with awe. The world of Africa gave them birth and touched them with life. Now, pulled up by the roots, they are dead. Polished and clean, they are precious works of art in foreign collections and today the mysterious secret of their glorious African past is only recognized by a few.

ART IN ITS RELATIONSHIP TO CULTURE

We must now proceed to a detailed analysis of the concept of culture which has already been mentioned several times in passing. If we are to understand how a particular culture functions and how its members succeed in welding a unified society it is necessary to analyse its component parts. Each one itself embraces numerous cultural and in some way interwoven, elements. If we now pursue these several elements and subject them to a detailed inquiry we can establish the reasons for the particular way a culture developed. In fact every culture is very complicated, processes are continuously evolving and in consequence many features overlap. Even single elements will not necessarily appear under one heading but are likely to be encountered in various contexts.

In this survey I propose to examine individual elements under whatever heading seems most appropriate. I have therefore grouped them into broad cultural divisions as follows:

1. SOCIAL LIFE

SOCIAL-FAMILIAR ASPECT

This includes all the different phenomena, which relate the individual to his human surroundings, *i.e.*, primarily, his relations with his family, and, over and above this, to the extended family or *lineage*, and to the clan. Important elements: birth, sex, age, initiation, relations, marriage, death.

SOCIAL-POLITICAL ASPECT

The institutions and phenomena which define the individual in his relationship to other members of the community. Important elements: age-groups, rank, secret societies, power, war and peace, law.

2. ECONOMICS

All activities connected with production, distribution and consumption: hunting, agriculture, cattle-rearing, division of labour, riches, barter and money.

3. RELIGION AND THE SUPERNATURAL

Under this heading are grouped all those phenomena that express either profane and worldly, or sacred and mythological orders: cults, priesthood, myths, rites and magic.

4. INTELLECTUAL COMMUNICATION

All the media of communication, language and writing.

5. TECHNOLOGY

The relationship between technology and its function in the art of different African cultures.

6. PLAY

This heading will embrace play of all kinds; relaxations, dancing, music, science and art.

SOCIAL LIFE: SOCIAL-FAMILIAR ASPECT

BIRTH AND YOUTH

The child begins to take part in social life as soon as it is born. It is already a member of a patri- or matrilinear social structure, although many years must pass before it is held to be a man, with rights and responsibilities; it is as yet a small creature needing only the care of its parents. A patrilinear society is one which traces its ancestry through the male side. The bond with the father and his brothers determines the clan name given to the child, and his education, heritage and succession. A matrilinear society is one which traces its ancestry back through the female side. Here the bond with the mother and her brothers, especially the elder brother, is decisive. The uncle, not the father, is responsible for the child's welfare.

Both these systems appear side by side in Africa and it is therefore impossible to draw a line between the areas occupied by patrilinear and matrilinear societies. In general, however, one can establish that the Sudan peoples of West Africa are patrilinear, whereas a large number of the Bantu tribes in central Africa are matrilinear. It should not, however, be forgotten, that there are many exceptions to this rule. Some communities display both patri- and matrilinear features in their structure; the clan names for instance may be matrilinear, while the succession is patrilinear.

★ Cat. 98, 99

Patrilinear peoples are: the Yoruba, Bini, Ibo, Dogon, Bambara, Senufo, Mandingo, Hausa, Fulani, Mende, Tallensi, Fang, Masai, Kikuyu, Ngoni, Zulu.

Matrilinear peoples are: the Congo, Vili, Mayombe, Mbala, Yaka, Pende, Jokwe, Ashanti.

Bilateral are the Mbuti, Pangwe, Lunda and Luba.

Small African girls often carry dolls about with them long before it is time for them to marry and have children. These dolls are very simply made out of hollow reed, a maize cob or a wooden cylinder and seem to have little relationship with the human figure. Other dolls are made of wood, glass beads and odd pieces of material, and these have definite, if stylized, arms and legs. Such African dolls are never ordinary playthings. There is always a profound sense of preparation, even the very young girl is being prepared for marriage and the fertility which it demands. The dolls are imbued with a special kind of magic and must be protected and cherished if they are to fulfil their purpose.

On the Ivory Coast the Dan carve their dolls out of raffia palm-wood and decorate them with poker-work in the form of lizards and snakes. The Mossi of Upper Volta make dolls of reeds, which sometimes have nothing human about them except their earrings and these dolls too are decorated with geometrical poker-work. The dolls of the Jokwe and Kimbunde in Angola are made of a centre—either a gourd, a maize cob or wood—wound round with cord. Hair is simulated by pieces of twine to which tiny reeds, beads or cowrie shells are attached, like the hair fashions of the women and girls. In South Africa dolls are cylindrical and completely bound with strings of small many-coloured beads. Only the face is roughly indicated.

Generally the woman carries the doll until a child is born.

Pregnant women of the Ashanti in Ghana who want a beautiful child always keep an *akuaba* doll in their carrying cloth. If they want a boy then the doll has a flat, moon-shaped disc for a face, carved with a delicate nose, close-set almond-shaped eyes and arched eyebrows. The thin neck leads into a cylindrical body with two small breasts and horizontal arms without hands. These dolls are normally black. If a girl is wanted the doll takes another form. The small head is flat, narrow and rectangular and in the lower part the face has round eyes and arching brows. On the top of the head strands of hair stick up, and the doll also has a cylindrical body but no arms. Such dolls are always brown.

The Yoruba women in Nigeria often carry twin dolls or *ibeji* about with them. Twins are greatly longed for as it is believed that they bring luck and wealth to the family. In view of the numerous *ibeji* figures made by the Yoruba one might well conclude that twin births are relatively frequent. If one of the twins dies, which often happens since child mortality is so high, then the twin doll belonging to the dead child is cared for as carefully as the living child. Every four days (corresponding to the market week of the Yoruba) the *ibeji* figure is cleaned, oiled, rubbed with red *tukula* powder and dressed in clothes and beads as though it were alive. This is intended to show that the dead child is not forgotten and that it will be welcome should it decide to return to earth in a different body. When the surviving twin is adult he takes over the care of the *ibeji* figure, because the soul of the dead twin is inseparable from his own. The soul lives on in the doll figures and the *ibeji* have a special place on the family altar. Many *ibeji* have been preserved, and because the families know, as often as not, the name and generation of the person incarnate

in them it is, in many cases, possible to date them approximately. The faces of old *ibeji* are quite often worn away with constant polishing.

Faces and hair-styles of the *ibeji* clearly reflect the Yoruba style. Typical are the broad nostrils, large protruding oval eyes with round pupils, the swelling lips, horizontal, scored tribal marks and the round, very high-set ears. Generally the hair is bound together in single strands and tied on, but sometimes it forms a protuberant kind of crest running from front to back.

When a woman's time draws near, numerous precautions have to be observed so that the birth goes well. The medicine man must make his magic incantations and ritual objects, herbs and roots must be prepared. This will be discussed in greater detail later, in the context of religion. Offerings are also made on the altars of the ancestors.

We encounter the ancestors again and again in the African world. They are responsible for the laws governing life and they also protect the living from sickness and bad luck. Their souls still stay alive even though their earthly existence is ended. Sometimes it is believed that certain ancestors have returned to earth and taken possession of the body of a new-born child. The ancestor cult has an essential significance in every part of African life, so that it crops up again and again when other aspects of culture are being discussed. Pl. 28

Here we must turn our attention to the mother-and-child figures that are so common, especially in Congo art. Without doubt these carved wooden figures are fertility symbols and directly connected with the desire to have large numbers of children. Fraser suggested that these figures were related to the Christian Madonna, who holds the Christ-child to her breast. It is possible that this image, introduced by the Portuguese in the fourteenth century was adopted by the Africans and assimilated into the local style, as happened with many other European elements. There are some grounds for this belief but it must not be forgotten that precisely here, where the tribes are matrilinear, this aspect of woman, namely as the founder of a *lineage* or clan, incorporates in a wider sense the idea of the ancestral mother, and hence the central figure in their view of life. Only because of this could the other, similar idea have been introduced at all.

The Mayombe depict the mother figure seated with crossed legs on a small stand. The relatively large face, pointed breasts and general position give a very realistic and plastic effect, itself one of the most apparent characteristics of Mayombe art. The fine, slanting eyes, often inlaid with white glass set with black pupils, gaze out over the head of the child. The open mouth revealing the upper teeth, shows that the two front teeth have been removed and the rest filed to points. The hair often takes the form of a flat mitre. The shoulders and upper part of the breast are covered with tattoo marks. The child lies across the mother's lap, who supports it at the head and feet.

The neighbouring Sundi paint the figures white on a reddish brown background. Eyes and features are drawn in black lines and on the head is a broad, black Pl. 32; Cat. 51 cap. The mother-and-child figures of the Mbala are in a completely different style, expressive and powerfully composed, and the carvers of the Mbala prove

themselves to be careful observers in the many different kinds of figures they produce. The standing mother figures carry the child—almost as large—by their side. Both stare straight ahead. Some figures show the woman seated on a stool with knees drawn up and the child at her breast. The faces of these figures are broad with round foreheads. The eyes are long, oval, with hollowed-out, round pupils. The hair is short, shorn in two curved bands across the forehead with a comb running over the head to the back. Hands and feet are usually rather crudely carved and the fingers and toes are only summarily indicated. These Mbala figures are often rubbed all over with reddish-brown *tukula* powder, though this does not always have to be the case. The mother-and-child figures of the Bena Lulua, also in the Congo, have the characteristics typical of their style: elongated necks and bodies, muscular arms and powerful legs. The navel is very pronounced, protruding like a shining button. But most striking are the scarifications that cover the figure almost completely from head to thighs giving it an unearthly, almost uncanny radiance. This impression is strengthened by the appearance of the child, a wretched misshapen little bundle lying in its mother's arms. The unnatural proportions and almost surrealistic presentation of the human figure give these small black figures an immense power. They undoubtedly rank among Africa's finest works of art. There are similar female figures which are also connected with the fertility cult in which the child is absent.

The mother-and-child is found in other tribes than the Congo. In West Africa and in the Bantu tribes of South Africa we find the same theme although there

was no Portuguese or other Christian influence there. The motif is used in every conceivable different way to fit in with the style of the tribe. It is also remarkable that the mother-and-child groups are not always produced as an independent piece, but are often part of a utilitarian object with a completely different function. However, it is evident that, even in these cases, the idea of fruitfulness is always present.

Not only the female but also the male fertility symbol appears in African art, although to a lesser degree. This

Cat. 113

Pl. 33   type of object is rather rare in Western collections, possibly on aesthetic or moral grounds. Certainly these pieces were undoubtedly created out of a sensibility completely foreign to the western moralistic view, be-

Cat. 45   cause the male figures, whose exaggerated genitalia are a significant detail also play a part in the fertility cult. Phallic symbols are very numerous and may be used as striking ornament on almost any object. And the act of procreation, which we must also regard as an aspect of the fertility cult, is often used as a decorative detail on a larger piece. For example there are the famous chiefs'

Pl. 34, 35   stools of the Jokwe or the *ifa* oracle boards of the Yoruba. All these things have a functional meaning, and spring from the fundamental idea that there is a close connection between ancestors and heirs. This link must be kept strong by definite rites and ceremonial to ensure the community's future. The ancestors in this sense are those with close ties to a family or extended family, but they can only be counted seven or eight generations back. Later on we shall encounter ancestors who have a much wider significance, the venerated founders of a whole people. In many African tribes family ancestors are portrayed and there are countless variations on this theme. We no longer know the true provenance of many pieces that are described in collections as ancestor figures. Their local significance within the culture of a family was lost and their history forgotten when they were removed from the structure of the extended family to which they belonged. Ancestor figures were kept and cherished on the house altars with other cult objects.

The great value of these figures lies in the fact that they, better than almost anything else, represent most

Pl. 30 *Luba (Congo-Kinshasa). Mother-and-child* **figure. Black wood,** **h.** *56 cm. Museum Rietberg, Zurich.*

Pl. 31 *Kuyu (Congo-Brazzaville). Mother-and-child figure. Used in the* kebe-kebe *cult. Wood, h. 51.5 cm. Ethnographisch Museum, Antwerp.*

strongly the traditional style of a tribe or clan. Good examples are the ancestor figures of the Baule and Senufo on the Ivory Coast. The Baule picture their ancestors standing or seated on a stool or a chair. The proportions are never related to natural sizes, yet they achieve a remarkably convincing eloquence and dignity. The strongly moulded head, long neck, small pointed breasts and powerful legs give these figures a dimensional quality which is intense from every angle. Every face is endowed, by the incredibly finely-worked detail, with an individual expression, increased in the complicated hair-style of the Baule, who have thick curls and one or two plaits hanging down the neck. The male figures often have a long woven beard sometimes made of fibre. All these figures are tattooed in fine detail with the customary patterns on the temples, cheeks, neck, rump and arms. On old figures the effect of all these details is strengthened considerably by patination.

Pl. 36, a + b

Cat. 37

Pl. 37; Cat. 38 Ancestor figures of the Senufo, either seated or standing, display a more stylized conception of the male figure. In seated figures the footstool seems to be a continuation of the long body because its front feet coincide with the legs of the seated man. The powerful neck carries a protruding face that ends, in some sub-styles, in a sharply-pointed chin. The hair style is peculiarly complicated: it consists generally of a high narrow comb and stylized curls in the form of a beak combed forward over the front, back and both sides of the head.

The infant does not count as an independent member of the community. It is still completely dependent on the care of its parents and other members of the family. Nor is the behaviour of children strictly controlled,

Pl. 33 Kuba (Congo-Kinshasa). Vessel in the form of a crouching man. Dark-coloured wood, h. 23.5 cm. Museum Rietberg, Zurich.

Pl. 34 Pende (Gungu region, Congo-Kinshasa). Chief's chair, influenced by European design. Wood and leather, h. 97 cm. Museum Rietberg, Zurich.

although naturally they have to conform to the rhythms of life. They will be present at ceremonial events, such as dance festivals, which are the most important times in the life-cycle, and they soon learn the countless taboos connected with certain ceremonies and ritual places, because they are kept away lest they are harmed by emanations dangerous for a child. Most games are directed towards the part which boy or girl will soon be called upon to play, thus they learn through childhood games. Division of work according to sex begins while the children are growing up. Boys take over the job of guarding the cattle or practise making bows and arrows, shooting all kinds of small birds and animals. The girls on the other hand learn their domestic duties by helping their mother.

At this period the child's life knows no great disturbance, but with the onset of puberty many African children face a momentous change. Childhood is over and the new period of life is introduced by a *rite de passage*, a traditional ritual, that marks the step from one stage in life to the other. This is called initiation.

Boys' and girls' initiation ceremonies are on the whole the best documented of African rites, although some tribes do not practise it. Africa has innumerable rites and customs connected with initiation. But they all have the same basic intention: the end of childhood and the entry of the individual into the adult world, bringing new status and with it binding rights and responsibilities. It is impossible to generalize on the subject. The age of the novice, the length of the initiation period and the lapse of time between two initiation feasts may all vary from tribe to tribe.

Pl. 35   Detail of Pl. 34. Copulation scene.

Pl. 36 a + b   Baule (Ivory Coast). Ceremonial spoon with female ancestor
figure. Wood, h. 36 cm. Dr. M. Kofler Collection, Riehen/Basle. (p. 68)

Pl. 37   Senufo-Kiembara (Ivory Coast). Female ancestor figure. Detail.
Wood, overall height : 103.2 cm. Ethnographisch Museum, Antwerp.
(Cat. 38). (p. 69)

Some tribes only have male initiation rites, or only
female. Others have both. Initiation may be collective,
usually the case with boys—or it can, and this is usual
for girls, have a more individual character. It is not
absolutely essential that boys should be initiated as soon
as they are sexually mature, whereas the onset of men-
struation sets the time for a girl's official transition into
her new life. Many African tribes practise circumcision
at the initiation. It is believed that only this treatment
can prepare a novice for marriage and marriage is the
rite de passage that follows initiation in many African
cultures.

What is then the real significance of initiation? We
have seen that the individual achieves thereby a new

status in the community. But before the novice attains this goal he has to pass through a rigorous apprenticeship, which may last a few weeks, months or even longer. He is forced to stay during this time far from his family and village in the bush or in a rocky desert region, for in these often cruelly hard weeks he must experience at first hand all the knowledge that has been acquired by his clan. Boys are taught all the cult secrets, they learn the history of their mythical ancestors and the sacred dances and songs as well as their future rights and duties. The basic idea is that the novice dies a symbolic spiritual death. The symbolism is expressed sometimes in a terrifying monster that swallows up the boys. After this 'death' the boys, led by their mentors, pass through the supernatural world of mythology. They experience this perilous journey through privation, humiliation, pain and fear. It is supposed to harden them, and the more courageous their bearing the more useful they will afterwards be to the community. Once he emerges from these tests the novice is symbolically reborn as another being: he is a man, circumcised and now tattooed with traditional clan markings as a sign of his new status.

This element of the African cultures has probably inspired a greater production of art than any other. Most important of all are the masks. These masks endow the wearers with a completely different personality. Concealed by a mask and wrapped in a thick raffia cloak the initiand is unrecognizable to the novice. He is changed into one of those culture heroes of long ago who brought desirable and essential gifts to mankind: fire, crops, social order, and specific dances and rites.

During the initiation the masks become the ancestors themselves or become spirits and demons embodying the powers of nature. The words they utter are mysterious and the atmosphere is charged and tense. The masks are dangerous because supernatural powers live in them, therefore they are kept away from women and children for whom they spell death. When they are made, great care is exercised lest the ancestors whom they represent should be angered. *Cat. 1*

This association of ideas has produced an extraordinary variety in the sculptural development of African masks. The shape of the masks reveals in a most interesting way the type of supernatural creature and spirit imagined by the people. They may take the form of the human face, or that of an animal, or fantastic and fabulous creature. They may be horrific in their appearance, but can also be friendly or mysterious. Many are so abstract and surrealist that they merit the word unearthly. Often we know nothing about a mask and its function in the initiation rites, and the object itself is all that we have. There is, however, no doubt that the masks, wrapped in their thick cloaks and animated by the dance, represent incarnations of culture heroes and spirits. They depict events of primeval times repeated once more in the sacred drama.

At the initiation rites of the Jokwe in Congo-Kinshasa ★ Pl. 38, 39 and in Angola, when the boys are circumcised, huge masks made of fibrous bark, resin and woven material painted red and white are worn. These *kalelwa*-masks carry a large crescent-shaped band on the forehead, the ★ Cat. 5, 6 eyes are slits outlined in white and a semicircular plaque is fixed below the large square mouth. A variant of the

kalelwa (Pl. VIII) is the *chikusa* mask, ending in a tall point made of bark. This mask represents the spirit of madness and is one of the oldest types of initiation masks made by the Jokwe.

The wooden masks (Pl. 40) of the neighbouring Pende represent a dead man: with half-shut eyes under heavy lids, a sometimes rather crooked mouth and painting in white or brownish-red. These two colours are used, not by the Pende alone but by several African tribes as a symbol of death. There are also masks of this type with a wooden ruffled beard to which a raffia collar is attached. A host of other masks appear in the dance dramas of the Pende, all of which represent supernatural powers. These masks, called *minanji* either consist of a flat piece of bark, or they are woven of fibre and pulled over the head. The face is indicated only by large, cylindrical eyes, outlined broadly in white. The head is completed by a thick raffia collar fixed on to the mask itself.

The Yaka, (Pl. IX) Suku and Nkanu, who all live in the same district, practise initiation and circumcision. The rites, ceremonies and dances connected with it take place round the *mukanda* or 'initiation school'. The last stage of the initiation feast sees the newly-circumcised returning to the village as adults, where they dance in large helmet masks adorned with a thick raffia ruff. These masks also have painted white faces intended to resemble the face of the dead. The Yaka masks are crowned with decorative arrangements that vary a little in each one; they can be birds, squatting figures, rams' heads, or birth scenes, all of which recall specific mythological figures, or events connected with them. Very well known is the *kakunga* mask of the Yaka from Kwango;

Pl. 39   Baga (Guinea). Helmet mask in the form of a female torso, with a snake. Wood, painted in bright colours, h. 51 cm. Museum voor Land-en Volkenkunde, Rotterdam.

Pl. 40   Pende (Congo-Kinshasa). Mbuya initiation mask. Wood, painted reddish-brown, with a fibre cap, h. 34 cm. C. P. Meulendijk Collection, Rotterdam.

it represents the master of the circumcision rites. It is a large oval wooden mask with rounded forehead, cheeks and chin. The eyes are close-set and shut giving the mask a gloomy expression. Pointed teeth are visible in the small mouth. The whole face is surrounded by a raffia collar. Yaka masks often display the characteristic features of the Yaka style: snub nose and protruding ears.

Cat. 16   The *kifwebe* masks are especially fine and are widespread among the Luba and the Songe in the Congo. Opinions vary as to the function of these masks, but undoubtedly they were used for initiation rites as well as on many other occasions. These strongly abstract human faces are of two kinds: one, found among the Luba, is almost round. The other displays stylistic features of the Songe and has a round forehead narrowing downwards to a rectangular chin. The face is covered with parallel, curved and scored lines in white ridges forming a sharp contrast to the black surface of the mask and enhancing the abstract effect of the facial features. Within this frame details such as eyes, nose, and mouth are incised, varying from tribe to tribe. The large oval eyes with arched eyelids are nearly closed, and the nose is mostly triangular. The lips are formed in a horizontal figure of eight, though they may also protrude like a cube from the face. Apart from these white furrowed *kifwebe* masks there are some examples with a smooth surface.

Quite different in their way are the *mashamboy* masks of the Kuba of Kasai in the Congo. These imposing helmet masks are made from raffia and woven material. The almost square face is made of panther skin. Eyes and

Pl. IX Yaka (Congo-Kinshasa). Initiation mask. The headdress crowned with two fish made of wood, raffia-weave, fibres and bright-coloured painting, h. 71.5 cm. Ethnographisch Museum, Antwerp.

brows are sewn in as glass beads and shells. Above the wooden nose and mouth there runs a broad band of coloured glass beads arranged in zig-zag pattern. The face is surrounded by a row of cowrie shells; below the mouth several more rows of shells form a broad band like a collar. There is a similar band at the back of the head. Above the mask there is often a caplike tall peak, bent towards the front and decorated with glass beads and shells. One variant of this mask has a huge fan-shaped headdress made of birds' feathers and red material. The *mashamboy* masks belong to the chiefs and represent clan heroes. The *shene-malula* masks also come from Kuba territory. They depict a carved wooden human face with closed, slit eyes. The forehead and the part above the mouth are covered with small triangular notches, and curved stripes run down the cheeks. Nose and mouth have a band of coloured glass beads stretched across them, and the upper part is made of black raffia-work decorated with cowrie shells.

For their circumcision rites the Bembe from the Kivu territory in the eastern Congo use a very abstract mask representing the wood spirit, *kalunga*. It is a cylindrical helmet mask with two faces, so stylized that only two large oval discs with two round, small eyes on either side remain. Each eye forms the central point of a pointed lozenge. The top of the mask carries a large bunch of mixed feathers.

The Makonde in Tanzania use masks for the ceremonial initiation of girls also. During the ritual of the *midimu* dance the watching girls learn the sexual conventions. They use very thin carved, helmet masks, naturalistically imitating the human face and often decorated with real hair, tattooing and lip discs. The Makonde in Mozambique possess wooden masks with faces decorated in four spirals of small white beads on forehead, cheeks and chin. The long hair, beard and eyelashes are also made of human hair in this tribe.

Several examples of the use of masks for initiation have been cited and it is noticeable that masks used for this function nearly all have human features, whether they are naturalistic or stylized. But there is no definite rule. Both conceptions may appear in the same region. Sometimes the influence of a strong adjacent style inspires certain variations and it is also possible that specific ancestors are presented in human form, because they are thought of as human, whereas spirits connected with nature retain their fantastic appearance. Pl. 42, 43

For many African peoples the initiation just discussed is only the beginning of a series of different initiation ceremonies, which take place throughout the life of an adult man or woman. There are numerous secret societies, each one fulfilling a particular function in the community and requiring certain necessary skills for membership. This type of ceremony also uses masks, which will be discussed under the social-political heading. There are also innumerable animal masks, connected with agriculture and hunting. * Pl. 41 Pl. 44; Cat. 20, 21

However the subject of initiation is not exhausted because many other things besides masks appear at the ceremonies, for instance all the attributes of the dance, rattles, drums, trumpets and other objects directly connected with the mythological drama. Dance-rattles serve not only to intensify the rhythm of the dance, but sometimes also have a symbolic meaning. The Mayombe Pl. 45

Pl. 41 Bembe (Congo-Kinshasa). Stylized mask with double face. Wood, painted white and red, h. 48 cm. J. Boussard Collection, Paris.

Pl. 42 Fang (Gabon). Stylized mask . Wood painted white with kaolin, fibres, h. 32 cm. Formerly in the collection of Georges Braque, Paris.

on the lower Congo use a rattle for the *bakhimba* boys' initiation, known as *thafu malunga*. This rattle has two seated figures as ornament, incarnations of the rainbow snake *mbumba luangu*. The portrait of this snake is also found on other cult objects. It is often represented in

Pl. 43 *Salampasu (Congo-Kinshasa). Initiation mask. Wood, painted red and white, decorated with rattan and feathers, h. 77 cm. L. van Bussel Collection, The Hague.*

Pl. 44 *Dogon (Mali). Ape mask. Dark-coloured wood, h. 32 cm. E. Dodeigne Collection, France.*

duplicate, depicting the double rainbow as a symbol of supernatural, life-consuming forces. The ceremonial Pl. 46 drums of the Mayombe are full of symbolic images. They are constructed with animal and human figures flanked by two snakes and the scene is carved out of a

single block of wood and highly painted. The object is crowned by a diminutive, cylindrical skin drum.

The girls of the Venda in South Africa represent a snake in the python dance of their initiation; it is of course a fertility symbol. For this dance the rhythm is

beaten on a particular round, flat drum decorated with snake ornament.

Nor should the small masks of carved ivory that are Cat. 67, 68 produced everywhere in Africa be forgotten. They are often imitations of the large dance masks and can serve as an amulet or a sign of the wearer's initiation. Miniature masks of this kind are also made of wood or metal.

Quite different, but nevertheless playing a part in the initiation theme are the large wooden spoons of the Pl. 47; Cat. 73 Dan and Kran in West Africa. Two types are known: one has a handle like a broad man's face, frequently with two small horns on the head. The other type is carved like a human figure, the head forming the spoon, and neck and legs the handle. These spoons, called *po*, belong to the clan chieftains' wives. They are used at the end of the initiation period when the boys come home, during the dance and at the great rice festival. If the initiation, particularly the circumcision, takes place in a closed room, the special hut is often filled with objects, the purpose of which is difficult to discern. They are secret objects, comprehensible only to initiates. In the Yaka and neighbouring Congo tribes Pl. x the walls of the circumcision huts are hung with painted boards of thick bark, to each of which is attached a carved wooden animal. These animals (birds, tortoises, etc.) may be clan totems. The Dogon in Mali bring their boys to a cave for circumcision, the walls of which are painted with esoteric signs.

Once the initiation is over the individual takes his place as a full member of the community and he is often given another name along with his new status. Now he holds a specific place in the social structure and begins a

new life. The next *rite de passage*—marriage—follows soon afterwards. Marriage and wedlock are social events shared not only by the two candidates but by both sides of the extended family. The rules governing relationships severely limit the choice of a possible girl and usually the family chooses one from those available. This is, in fact, a transaction, an exchange. Formerly it was thought by observers that it was a purely commercial matter in which the woman was only a chattel with no rights of her own. However, marriage is by no means as simple as that. It is generally agreed that the prefered woman is henceforward lost to her clan, even her children will belong to another group and this loss requires compensation. The woman has some rights, for instance the man can never pass her on to another. The more valuable the bride-price, the prouder the bride. The bride's family gives her a dowry when she leaves and thus the whole transaction takes on the character of an exchange of presents between the two extended families, with a pledge from either side in the form of the bridal pair. This exchange serves to confirm the marriage. Obviously purely economic factors play a part, and especially nowadays under the influence of Western ideas. Hence in the Luba and Cameroun tribes, to mention only two examples, the price becomes abnormally high; apart from the usual presents, Western products, weapons and other foreign prestige objects, as well as large sums of money are also demanded. In traditional Africa the presents were at least partly of economic value, but in general they were ceremonial pieces. The bridal presents among the shepherd peoples of East and South Africa (the Nilotes,

Tutsi, Masai among others) were mostly cattle, while the Swazi of South Africa give the mother-in-law a cow at the wedding 'to dry her tears'.

The ceremonial presents given as the bride-price are not usually of a kind to excite the attention of the art collector. They are often wrought iron-work, weapon-like objects, comparable with lance-or spearheads except that they are bigger and heavier. This 'spear money' forms the bride-price in many parts of the Congo and there are other metal objects too, such as the cruciform bronzes called Katanga crosses. A large amount of personal ornament must also be reckoned in the bride-price, for instance the heavy bracelets and anklets of brass and the silver or brass spirals that are wound round both arms and legs. There are also conical metal leg-splints, which, once attached, can never be removed, and which effectively hinder the woman's gait. Whatever form the ideal of beauty takes, the value of the metal itself is the most important aspect. The wealth of the bride also sometimes includes old necklaces of coral, glass beads and cowrie shells.

MATURITY

Marriage reflects everyday life. The African home contains many decorative things, (Pl. 48) useful tools (Pl. IX), made solely for practical purposes but endowed with such a fine sculptural sense that they undoubtedly rank as art. First we come to the objects given to the newly-married pair. The Lemba of the lower Congo decorate the head of the bridal bed with carvings. Scenes

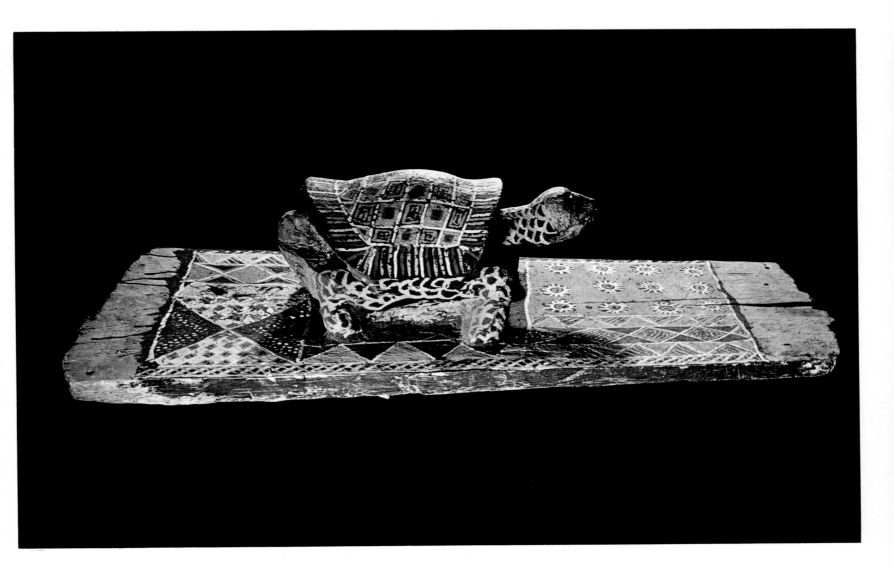

Pl. X Yaka (Congo-Kinshasa). Board with a tortoise, from a circumcision and initiation hut. Wood, painted, l. 85 cm. C. P. Meulendijk Collection. Rotterdam.

depicted therein show the young wife's uncle as the central figure, defining the importance of the uncle in the marriage negotiations. The Kuba exchange presents called *mboong a tul* at their weddings. These are models of everyday things made by the women by kneading the reddish-brown *tukula* powder, and they are attached to the cosmetic boxes. This *tukula* powder preserved in the boxes is supposed to have magic powers, and it is therefore freely used for painting the face and body at ritual dances, while ancestor figures and other cult objects are also rubbed with it. The plaited bridal baskets from Ethiopia, decorated with bead embroidery on the outside, the cover and the crossed handles, may also be mentioned in this context.

The simplest domestic things are those made of gourds and these offer many fine examples of applied art. Huge gourds are grown over the whole savannah territory of West Africa, which are much in demand in the markets. Cut in half, their hard outer shells lend themselves particularly well for use as bowls and vessels for food and water. In northern Nigeria these bowls are decorated with striped patterns of poker-work. Elsewhere, in Ghana for instance, the patterns are incised and stand out clearly against the yellowish-orange background. Animal- and circular patterns are common.

Gourd-bottles are used to carry water, palm-wine or beer. Sometimes they have handles or rings made of woven fibre. They are only natural products, yet they often display a beautiful flowing line equal to any modelling by an artist. Sometimes they are decorated with minutely-drawn mythological scenes, as for ins-

tance, the water-gourds of the Dogon shepherd boys.

Wooden vessels must be mentioned with the gourds. Extremely simple in shape, and therefore even more attractive are the flat bowls and tall gourd -shaped milk jugs and butter tubs of the Zulu and Sotho. In these a certain tension is attained by the contrast between the light body and the black handles and feet. Exceptionally fine too are the wooden covered bowls of the Rotse in

Pl. 49

Pl. 50

Cat. 89, 90
★ Cat. 88

★ Cat. 86, 87

Zambia and of the Subiya and Totela tribes who come under their influence. These oval bowls are sometimes similar to those of the Zulu, with animal figures as decoration on the flat cover. These beasts, elephants, buffalo, ducks and so on, are naturalistically and powerfully drawn. The same is true of other household goods of the south and east Bantu: spoons, head-rests, pipes, combs and so forth, all decorated with animals and human figures. Even when there are no figures and the object has only incised geometric patterns—for instance the bamboo milk containers of the Makonde, the head-rests of the Shona in Rhodesia and the covered bowls woven of root fibre of the Rotse—the graphic quality is apparent. This very definite style is ignored in many descriptions of African art in deference to the styles of West Africa, which in my opinion is unjust.

Let us now return to the north and consider the household utensils of the Congo peoples. Undoubtedly the difference is great: the pieces display the love of detail I have mentioned before, which is found on many everyday things.

First an example that is not unique of its kind, but which explains the social importance of things that we collect as works of art, but which originally had a completely different function. These are the so-called proverb covers from Cabinda and Loango on the Congo coast. Gerbrands has written a monograph on the function of these covers. In the Mayombe and other tribes of the region every woman has in her possession a number of wooden covers, on which well-known proverbs are modelled in the round. To understand them we must realize that the proverb was a powerful source

of magic against all injustice, not only in central Africa, but also among many people in West Africa. The village judge delivers judgment in the form of a proverb and the individual will use this formula to announce that he has been the victim of a crime, so as to gain the support of the community.

The proverb covers, however, do not concern social-political wrongs to be settled by a judge, but marital differences. When they become too great the extended family must be called in to settle the matter. The part played by the proverb covers is as follows: the scene, carved on the lid at the woman's request, represents the injustice of her husband's actions. As she serves him at table, she passes him the bowl with the relevant lid, when his misdeeds are immediately clear to everyone and the problem is at once laid before the community for judgment. Communal opinion, which is decisive, generally prevents a separation. Formerly a woman would have several of these proverb lids at her disposal, a comprehensive record of her married life. Occasionally in exceptional circumstances men could make use of the covers. And here too the purpose was to make a difficult situation public. The man usually saw to it that the wife was passed the lid by her uncle, so that her family, too, knew what was wrong and could therefore help to settle the quarrel.

The number of proverbs was enormous, they were known and used by everyone and recorded on the covers in symbols. For instance: the iron double bell *(ngonge)*, the ceremonial knife *(kiphaba)* and the ivory tusk are symbols of power. Half of a hard shell-fruit *(chiala mioko—caryopsis)* is a common symbol, because

* Cat. 78

* Pl. 51

* Pl. 52

when the fruit is ripe and picked from the tree it opens like the gesture of two hands making an offering. The fruit then is the symbol of hospitality. A coiled centipede signifies defencelessness. Three stones are necessary to balance the cooking pot, so all good things come in threes. Many of the other innumerable symbols are no longer intelligible to us and may well have had

several meanings which are only apparent in their proper context.

Pl. 53   The neck-supports or head-rests which were already mentioned in connection with the plastic art of the south Bantu, are found everywhere in Africa and especially in those places where the male and female headdress plays an important part in the costume. The neck-

support allows a person to sleep without spoiling the hair. As always with everyday things, many different forms are found, from the simplest wooden support to a richly decorated work of art.

The Nilotes, like the Shilluk and Karamojong in northern Kenya, and also the Masai, spend an enormous amount of time on their male headdresses. The Karamo-

jong build a kind of cap of clay on the head and this is finely decorated with incised lines and colours and completed by ostrich-plumes. Sometimes this fragile coiffure, baked hard in the sun, can last as long as a year. Only when the hair has grown so long that the clay cap breaks away is a new style modelled. Neck-supports are made of tough forked branches fixed in position with leather bands. Just as simple, but carved from wood, are the neck-supports that have inspired the countless variations encountered all over East Africa. This kind of support is smooth and bent upwards into a crescent shape with a cylindrical foot. The type spread all over the Congo and even appears among the Yanzi and Teke. A further stage of this type shows a very abstract human figure, whose arms and legs are set at such angles that the piece looks like a cross of Lorraine.

In the tribes of the central Congo (Kete, Kuba, Bena Kanioka etc.) the cylindrical foot often has a human face, or it is carved altogether into a man's torso without legs. The neck-supports also developed two cylindrical pillars which are either vertical or have an outward kink. An exceptional case is the double neck-rest of the Kuba; carved from one piece, its surface is incised with geometrical decoration.

In West Africa the neck-rest is comparatively rare. They exist in Dogon territory, but these people never use them themselves and attribute them to the legendary Tellem. Nevertheless excavations in a cliff not far from Sangha uncovered many human remains, textile fragments, as yet unidentified wooden objects and neck-rests. These supports must be discussed here on account of their eccentric form, and also because they belong to the so-called Tellem culture, which may have been an earlier stage of the Dogon. The most usual form is that of a small horse or other stylized animal, whose gently curving back forms the upper surface with a small head at both ends. The supports are two small pillars set at right angles to a kind of footboard. Some of these neck-rests have a piece of bent wood sticking out of one of the pillars which may be a handle. Only discovered a few years ago, the real meaning of these carved neck-rests is so far unknown, possibly they were cult objects for the death ritual.

The problem was solved in a different way by the Zande in the northern Congo. The support, slightly Cat. 85 bent here too, and with a human head on either side, is also the cover of a wooden box. Animal or human caryatids are especially popular in the Congo. The Lunda and Yaka have neck-rests supported by antelopes, birds, oxen or legendary creatures.

There are countless variations on the supports in the form of the human figure. Some have only one, while Pl. 54 others have two or even four figures. They may crouch or stand, with the upper surface resting on their head or uplifted hands.

Whatever the form of a neck-rest, in its natural shape or transformed into a human or animal figure, the Pl. xii finest are undoubtedly those made by the Luba in ★ Pl. 55 Congo. The support, very slightly curved, is now scarcely recognizable because it has become an integral part of the carving. Usually it consists of two seated women facing one another and supporting the upper part on their heads. The position of arms and legs may vary widely, but they always form a harmonious linear

Pl. 54 Yaka (region of Popokabaka, Congo-Kinshasa). Neck-rest, carried by a female figure with a pestle for pounding tubers. Wood, h. 19 cm. Museum Rietberg, Zurich.

Pl. 55 Dogon (Mali). Neck-rest in the form of an animal, probably a grave-gift for the support of the dead man. Wood, l. 27.3 cm. Koninklijk Museum voor Midden-Afrika, Tervuren.

Pl. 56 Lobi/Bobo (Gaoua, Upper Volta). Stool in the form of a club with Janus-head. Wood, l. 55 cm. Museum für Völkerkunde, Basle.

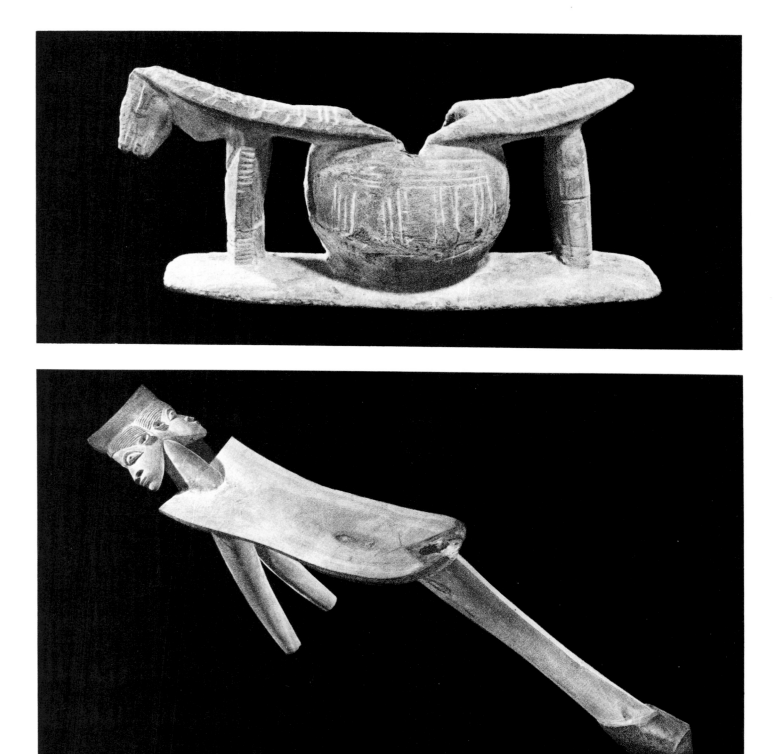

design. The hair-styles display all the variations worn by the women of the tribe, ranging from small ringlets to large fan-like creations. Sometimes these figures are still decorated with strings of old glass beads.

Small stools come next in this group of useful wares. They are found everywhere in daily use, and many are true works of art. Two types can be distinguished, round and rectangular. For everyday use the most simple, functional type was used, perhaps only slightly carved. Cylindrical forms from Cameroun and East Africa are especially well known, where they appear with variations in Tanzania, Kenya and Buganda. The East African types are often carved with very complicated patterns in which the small, bent supports and horizontal ring links play an important part in the whole composition. It is natural that the rectangular plan should take the form of an animal, the four short pillars forming the feet. Similar stools are also known made by the Bobo in Upper Volta, on which, instead of an animal head, a flat, disc-like human face protrudes from the seat. A third type would be more correctly described as a back-rest as there is always some kind of support for the back. These are very similar to neck-rests in shape.

The Makere, Meje and Mobango in northern Congo between the Welle and Aruwimi, make a skilful tripod stool from a thick trunk with six branches. Another type that has numerous variations consists of an oval, slightly concave seat, supported by one or two feet. Sections of a circle and lozenges are carved into the seat. These stools come from the central Congo, the territory of the Bokala and Yaelima and further north from the Bole and Mongo territory. Still another form is found among the Bobo-Gbe or white Bobo and their neighbours in Upper Volta. A longish and elegant form, one half of the narrow seat is borne by three small feet, two of which stand side by side underneath the board. This end is often completed by one or two small human heads. The other, unsupported end can serve as a handle which gives the object a second function as a club. So really it is a club stool, similar to those found among the Lobi. The seats and stools are always carved from a single block of wood and occasionally decorated with geometrical poker-work, incised patterns or heads of nails.

Pl. 56, Cat. 77

From these simple stools the ceremonial seats developed for use only by the clan elders, chiefs and other important persons. Hence they have a function as a symbol of power and will be discussed in greater detail in the social-political section.

Pestles and mortars, bobbins, objects for smoking and drinking, snuff-boxes, powder-boxes, fly-swats, cosmetic boxes and covered jars for keeping dyes, butter and other foods are all things which are perhaps not absolutely necessary for existence but which nevertheless make life more agreeable. All these things were fashioned by African artists into fine works of art, especially pieces having ceremonial significance, for example the small wooden beakers of the Kuba used for the ceremonial drinking of palm-wine. They are small miracles of modelling, testifying to the skill of the Kuba carvers. In their simplest form these beakers are long and barrel-shaped, kept upright by a low, conical foot. Sometimes they look like miniature drums. The

Cat. 80, 92, 93
Cat. 84

outsides are completely covered with geometric patterns of interwoven furrows or lozenges, exactly like the so-called velvet-weave. Also marks of rank of a secret society, animals, or the sun and moon, are sometimes found on these cups. Another form of beaker is in the shape of a face or small base or a stylized human foot. Some have two faces like a Janus-head and these are two cups in one. Even more attractive in shape are the anthropomorphic beakers with a relatively large head and delicate, curved arms and legs. Both male and female figures are heavily tattooed, with the exaggerated genitals of the fertility cults so often found in African art.

Tobacco smoking is really a pleasure, but it can take on ceremonial significance and become an element of the palaver. The imaginative world of the tribe is pictured in finest symbolical and decorative detail on the bowls and sometimes even the stems of the pipes, and it is remarkable how perfectly these miniature scenes of wood, clay or brass are worked.

Snuff-taking is another social pleasure. The snuff is carried in small boxes made of wood, ivory, bamboo, or horn and because these carved boxes are a man's own property he carves his useful box with loving care, fashioning a beautiful object that is pleasing to the eye. The Pende tribe make fine cylindrical snuff-boxes of wood or ivory with a standing figure carved on the lid. More refined are the boxes of the Bena Lulua; some examples, in the usual Lulua style, are in the form of a crouching figure: arms, legs, knees, and elbows are all intertwined while the head rests on the hands. In West Africa among the Senufo and the Bambara the box

itself is often left undecorated, while the cover has a small figure.

Pestles and mortars are essential to grind the snuff and other herbs and spices to a fine powder. They, too, are often carefully carved, frequently as human figures. Manioc and banana pestles are also sometimes decorated with human heads, among the Luba, for example. Flyswats, certainly essential, everyday things, are also symbols of power. Decoration on their handles testifies to a plastic art that has a decided feeling for detail.

Boxes and covered vessels used for storage, for *tukula* powder, for instance, belong to a different category. This brownish-red colouring, made of redwood powder or ochre and palm-oil is supposed to have supernatural powers, and it is therefore not surprising that it is kept in special boxes with symbolic decoration. Once again the varied *tukula*-boxes of the Kuba take pride of place. The flat boxes in the form of a semicircle, or section of a circle, with carved antelope horns on the lid are well-known. Another type is cylindrical and tall and the cover has a grip in the form of two crossed handles. This kind of box is strongly reminiscent of the baskets with handles, even the carved, geometrical ornament is an imitation of weaving.

The Pende keep the *tukula* powder in oval bowls with a single foot. These bowls, decorated on the narrow side with figures or faces, are carried round by certain people at dance festivals, whose duty it is to rub fresh powder into the dancers from time to time. In West Africa ointment- and butter-boxes have a function similar to the *tukula*-boxes of the Congo. Ointment pots of the Baule tribe on the Ivory Coast are usually round. The

* Cat. 84
Pl. 57, 58 a + b

Cat. 91

93

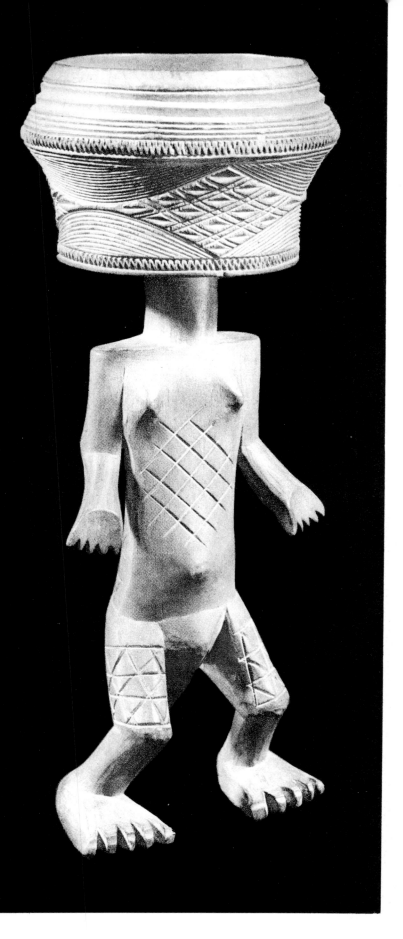

Pl. 57 Mbunda (Congo-Kinshasa). Beaker with a stylized female figure. Wood. h. 20.5 cm. Ethnographisch Museum, Antwerp.

actual conical pot stands on a round disc surrounded by completely carved-out supports. The conical cover with its high rims gives the impression of a step-like construction, on the top of which is a portrait head in the same finely drawn style as we have already seen on the ancestor figures of the Baule.

The Senufo on the northern Ivory Coast carve their butter-vessels into a pompous, but still harmonious shape. The round vessel is carried on the head of a seated human figure with a similar figure on the lid. Birds or animals may be used instead of the human figure, or occasionally a combination of all three, when they take on such a baroque appearance that the actual body of the vessel becomes lost in a complex of mixed figures. This combination of different, clearly unconnected parts of human or animal figures, as well as the elongated human caryatids, form recurrent motifs in the art of the Senufo.

The ritual vessels of the Dogon are very like those of the Senufo in their construction, yet they make a much more powerful, an almost, one might say, aristocratic impression. Probably this is accounted for by their stylized angularity which pares down figures to their absolute essentials. An animal, usually a horse, standing on a heavy base, supports a disc with the round vessel above. The rounded cover is finished with a large figure, perhaps a rider on his horse, or occasionally a kneeling ancestor figure.

Finally the cylindrical bark boxes of the Mangbetu in Pl. XIII the northern Congo, must not be forgotten. They have a slim foot of wood, while the cover on the top of the box is in the form of a human head. The box is there-

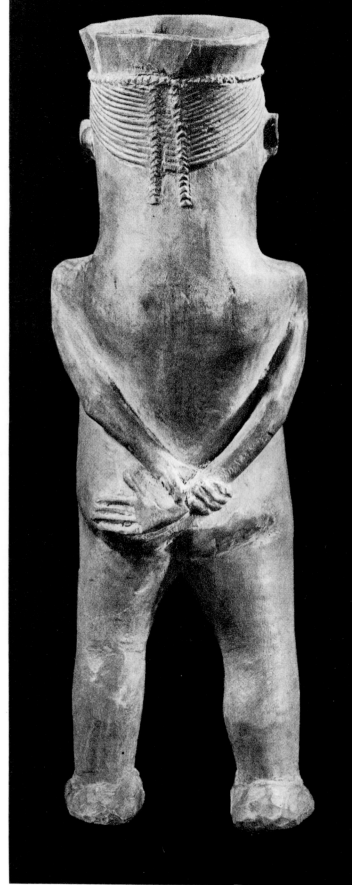

Pl. 58 a + b Lele (Congo-Kinshasa). Drinking-vessel in the form of a human figure. Wood, h. 19 cm. Koninklijk Instituut voor de Tropen, Amsterdam.

fore anthropomorphic. The style of the head is characteristic of the Mangbetu style in general: the head itself is excessively long, an effect that is exaggerated by the tightly curled hair-style. These features are at their finest on the portrait jars for containing palm-wine. Similar vessels are known among the neighbouring Zande tribe.

Weaving bobbins are known only in West Africa, and are part of the vertical belt looms. The long, narrow bands woven on them have to be sewn together later into broader pieces. The two shafts of the loom that keep the warp and weft apart can be moved up and down by a simple rope-and-pulley system. These ropes run over the bobbins hung on a frame. Although they are purely functional objects, small accessories only, they are formed and carved with loving care. The basic shape is always the same—a horseshoe-shaped support into which the bobbin is fixed. But this contraption caught the imagination of the artists. The finest bobbins are made by the Baule, Guro and Senufo peoples, but they are also found among the Dogon, Bambara, Wolof and many other West African tribes. They generally have a human face, miniature mask or Janus-head. Busts and whole figures also exist, and the Baule and Senufo are fond of buffalo heads and birds. The weaving bobbins display in miniature all the styles found on the large masks, ancestor figures and so on and every detail is carved in remarkably fine detail.

We have here only touched on a few aspects of everyday life. A survey of the whole field would be impossible and would turn this book into a catalogue. It has been however my intention to show, by means of specimens, that a large proportion of the objects recognized and preserved as first-rate African art were originally purely functional. They are therefore an essential element in the life of the African and hence often display symbols of the cosmos, though these are no longer recognized as such. Every African culture has constructed its own cosmos, its own view of the world, and the close connection between the sacred and profane world is incessant, for both are inextricably involved in every field of life. One senses the power of the ancestors everywhere and one must therefore be surrounded with ancestor symbols to ward off the threat of evil. This threat is strongest in moments of crisis, such as the transition periods between one stage of life and another, which accounts for the rites de passage, protecting individual and community and bringing them safely through such dangerous periods.

* Pl. 59, 60

DEATH

This mechanism is exceptionally well displayed at the last decisive change in a man's life: his death. For the Pl. 61 African, death is an event of the deepest significance. It is the moment when a man quits for ever his mortal frame. His being, however, the element that made him a living creation, and the soul which animated him, do * Cat. 80 not die. They live on, wander about and threaten the living with their jealousy because they can no longer live on earth. Here too a rite de passage is essential; the ritual of death will prepare the soul for a new existence, for its entry into the kingdom of the common ancestors. If the personality of the dead man was very strong his vitality would be all the more powerful and demand a more comprehensive death ritual. This briefly sketched process of thought is common ground all over Africa. The rituals and customs are however closely allied to individual culture and therefore differ from one tribe to another. Naturally the African feels genuine sorrow on the death of a relative and he expresses his mourning in

the death dances. During this period and for some time afterwards the atmosphere is dangerous for the living and the task of averting possible evil by sacrifice and invocations falls to the priests and other persons endowed with sacred powers.

To illustrate this, we will take one example in detail. This sector of African life has produced certain things which have been appreciated by every art collector for their quality, though now they are only lifeless objects, torn from their living emotional and functional context.

Let us therefore imagine ourselves in the land of the Dogon in the West African republic of Mali. The Dogon are agriculturalists, breeders of small domestic animals. Even today they live in a rather isolated way on the plateau of Bandiagara and at the foot of the steep and craggy cliffs that divide the high plateau from the great flat land of Gondo stretching away to the south. Here, at the foot of the colossal cliffs, the tiny clay villages seem to cling like swallows' nests to their terraces. Above them the fabled conical Tellem structures soar upwards like watchers from the cliff caves. Despite all Western influence, which here has taken the form of cheap imported goods, and despite the powerful pull of Islam, life in these villages still continues as it was centuries ago. It is protected by the laws given by the founders of the villages and in the final count by the mythical culture hero, *Lebe*, the first mortal man. Life is going on as usual when suddenly, one day at dawn, before the first light has touched the horizon, far away in the distance, faint, but clear, there echoes the unnerving sound of drums and clanging iron bells and, in between, the dull sounds of

Pl. 60 Dogon (Mali). Bobbin-holder with a female ancestor figure. Wood, h. 21 cm. Museum Rietberg, Zurich.

shots from old rifles. The death of an adult member of the tribe is being announced. The death music goes on intermittently, echoing from a south-westerly direction; probably the death has occurred at Pege at the foot of the rock face.

A few hours later the news has spread. A man called Apam Saye has died at Pege. He was the father of a family and a man of property. Meanwhile day has come and the corpse, wrapped in blankets is carried by male relatives in silence to a cave not too high up the cliff. There the body is hauled with ropes upwards into the catacombs of the village and placed beside the mortal remains of former villagers. At the same time in the village the male relatives post themselves on the roof terrace of the dead man's house while the widow and daughters receive condolences in another house. The next day, when the sun is disappearing behind the great cliffs, the real death ritual begins.

The drummers place themselves beside the *togu-na*, the roofed-in meeting place of the village elders on a high place at the edge of the village. The small orchestra consists of two large, cylindrical double-skinned wooden drums, the *bui-na* and the *bui-tola*, a round single-skinned calabash drum called *baraba*, and a large iron bell, the *gangana* which is beaten with a rod. Now the musicians start to play and set off towards the square on the far side of the village. Others appear blowing horns and the rest of the male community, armed with old guns, lances and swords, approach from every side. The people press round the square, on to the terraces behind, and on to the roofs of the houses. A group of the dead man's female relatives gathers near his house, which is guarded and furnished with a newly-killed ape that has been set up with its face looking over the square.

As the musicians halt on the way to the village square, the hornblowers describe a solemn circle round a stone called the *anahade dumma* set in the middle. Suddenly the armed men, stirred by the bells and exciting drumbeat, storm on to the square and fight a mock battle. Then a second group of men appears from the direction of the dead man's house. A priest leads them, carrying a pile of the dead man's clothes and sets it down on the stone. On top of this is laid another dead monkey and a rodent. The music starts again and the men dance round the pile of clothes. Suddenly they break apart and one after another throw a stone at a board standing at the entrance of the square. This is followed by a second battle and shots are fired from the guns. During these proceedings the women wail and wave fly-swats and bowls made of gourds. Dancing they draw closer, led by the widow, to the square which has now been deserted by the men. A gripping dance is then executed by the mourning women around the bundle of clothes. They sing their litanies accompanied only by the sound of gourds striking the ground as they bend down.

Then the men repeat their dance, each letting off his gun in turn till the cliff echoes again and again. The noise of the beaten drums, the penetrating sound of the bell and the loud mourning song of the women make an enormous din. And now the women are drawn irresistibly into the rhythm, waving their bowls and fly-swats wildly. It is a proper homage to the dead.

After the climax is reached the hunters and instrumentalists gather and walk several times round the square till gradually quiet prevails. At the end of the death ritual the priest of the *awa*, or mask society, stands up and recites loudly, in the secret language called the *sigi-so*, a song of praise that sounds like a prayer.

The scene may be interpreted as follows: the men who dance and take part in the mock battle are the dead man's relatives. Their songs praise their friend and thank him for everything he has done for them in his lifetime. The mock battles are not only a symbol of the life struggle of the dead man, but also re-enact the battles that the Dogon must have fought in ancient times. Also they demonstrate the power and warlike nature of the adult men. The two dead monkeys are supposed to protect the *nyama*—the wandering soul of the dead man. The stone-throwing has the same purpose; it puts to flight any evil spirits hostile to the *nyama*. The echoing shots of the guns are the tears of the men. The gourds banged by the women despairingly again and again on the ground symbolize the sadness that no more meals will be prepared for the dead man. Later they are actually broken.

After this death ritual there are no more ceremonies for some time, the period of mourning starts and a variety of circumstances will determine when it has to stop and the *dama* take place. For an important person the mourning may continue for as long as two years. In that time the dead man's family must remember exactly who was at the death ritual and what presents were given, for all these people, among them probably many from neighbouring villages, have to be invited to the *dama* when there is a banquet with many kinds of food and *konio*, the millet beer of the Dogon.

Pl. 61 Bobo-Ule (Upper Volta). Buffalo mask, personification of the protective spirit do, used in funeral and agricultural rites. Wood, painted white, black and red, fibres, h. 75 cm. Museum Rietberg, Zurich.

The priest selects a favourable moment for the *dama* and then the preparations for the great mask feast can begin. In contrast to the death ritual the *dama* is celebrated as a true festival. Now at last the *nyama* of the dead man, which has been wandering aimlessly on earth as a potential danger to the community, can make the long journey into the world beyond and join his ancestors for ever. The *dama* (mask feast) is primarily controlled by the *awa*, or mask society, which preserves the sacred masks in a cave far removed from the village.

A *dama* is conducted in the following way:

In the village called Diamini-na, high on the plateau near the cliff, excitement has been rising for some time. Everyone is talking about the great *dama* being prepared for Abinu Dolo. He was a popular man of middle age and a good hunter. Towards evening the day before the *dama* a small group of musicians gathers at the entrance to the village. It consists of two *bui-na* drums and an iron castanet which is held in the palm of the hand and beaten with an iron ring worn on the thumb. At the sound of the first drum-rolls a long line of masked dancers appear in the distance in the direction of the cliff wall. Some distance from the village they gather in a field and introduce the *dama* with their dance. There are many dancers wearing all kinds of different masks. These are about twenty *kanaga* masks (Pl. XIV), four long *sirige* masks, many Peul-women masks, two *na* masks, several *walu* masks, as well as individual ones representing particular people. Every group of masks demonstrates its own style of the dance then the music falls silent and the priest who accompanies the dancers intones a loud prayer in the *sigi-so* secret language. Only then do the dancers continue, goose-stepping their way into the village, where the dances progress around the stone which stands in the centre of the square. The masks are sacred, full of magic power and therefore dangerous for the uninitiated, that is to say the women and children, who are allowed to come to the plays, but kept away from the village-square. They remain in a safe place on the terraces of distant houses, where the power of the masks cannot harm them. The dances go on until twilight. This part of the *dama* could be described as the prologue—excitement, drinking of beer and ecstasy will only reach a climax on the following day.

The Dogon are famous for the great variety of their masks. Occasionally they are used in the death ritual but are chiefly concerned with the *dama* celebrations. All the available masks are never used at one *dama*, because each *dama* requires his own type of mask. And every village has mask types unknown elsewhere. There are also many ancient masks, which have found their way into museum collections, that are no longer used and forgotten. Even more than the figures, the Dogon masks display a simple, elegant style, the chief feature of which is an arrangement of flat planes with sharply canted points that produce a strong *chiaroscuro* effect. Natural forms are totally stylized and reduced to basic essentials. Griaule has written an essay on the masks of the Dogon which is the most detailed account existing in any field of African art. Griaule succeeded, after living for many years with the Dogon, in breaking down the wall of mistrust and thus learning something of the philosophical ideas of the villagers. Their view of the world gives the background of the masks. The uninitiated

look on with astonishment at this other world, created alongside empirical reality, a world constructed on a philosophical system which explains metaphysically the origin of men and things; and herein lie the legends and special features of each mask. Naturally this knowledge, handed down from generation to generation is not available to all. In the case of the masks only the members of the *awa* society are in possession of it, whereas the rest of the men have only a vague notion of the main points of this philosophical system.

Some of the most famous masks are still used at festivals, the *kanaga* for instance. This mask is so well known that it is often used as an emblem of the Mali Republic. It is in the form of a bird of prey. The features are strongly stylized and almost suggest a human face, apart from the clearly defined beak. The mask has a headdress constructed of thin pieces of wood in the shape of a double cross, known in literature as the cross of Lorraine. This cross can be interpreted in several ways. It could mean the outspread wings of the bird, it could also be a human figure as a symbol of creation. Apart from this standard type there are several derivative forms with different names and historical provenance.

* Pl. 62

Another well-marked type is the *sirige* mask. The facial part is like the *kanaga* mask and agrees in the main with most of the other Dogon masks: it is a rectangular face, divided vertically into two deeper set, narrow planes, in which the small triangular eyeholes are set. The *sirige* mask has a giant headdress: a long narrow board, from nine to fifteen feet long, from which several rows of vertical slits in twos and fives have been cut.

Pl. 62 Dogon (Mali). Andumbulu *mask, representing a mythological being created by Ama, before man appeared on earth. Wood, fibres, h. 37 cm. Rijksmuseum voor Volkenkunde, Leiden.*

Pl. XV Dogon (Mali). *Hyena mask. Wood, painted, h. 41 cm. C. P. Meulendijk Collection, Rotterdam.*

This mask represented the 'house with eighty alcoves', that is the *ginna*, the large family house belonging to the clan of the village founder and in the possession of the high priest, the *hogon*. The façade of the *ginna* displays a great number of niches, some say eighty, supposed to be the original ancestors of man. The board above the mask therefore represents these eighty ancestors.

As examples of the almost inexhaustible supply of masks from the animal kingdom we will take the *walu*, representing a horned antelope, the *na*, a cow, the *dyommo*, a hare, and the *yapa*, shaped like a lion. Monkeys, hyenas and many birds appear on the masks.

Peculiar is the *yashigine* mask with its headdress in the form of a woman, which only makes an appearance on very rare occasions. The *yashigine* is a legendary woman, who stole from the men the secret of the masks and therefore had to be initiated into the secret mask society. Since then a certain class of woman has the right to take part in specific dances wearing the *yashigine* mask.

Many of the masks depicting people are not carved from wood, but made of bound fibres, for example the Peul-women mask. The Peul, called also Fulbe or Fulani, have for centuries been the deadly enemies of the Dogon and appear in all the dances. The mask is an exact copy of the hair-style usual among the Peul women: a tall comb and numerous plaits decked out with cowrie shells. To make the mask even more realistic, the dance costume even has a kind of brassière with wooden breasts.

Every mask has its own dance costume made of red, and black fibrous stuff, red anklets and bracelets of fibre and red fibre decoration on the mask itself. The dancer

Pl. xv

must never allow his identity to be discovered, hence the back of the head as well as the face must be disguised.

So let us return from the masks to the village of Diamini-na. On the morning of the second day the musicians gather in the village square and call the dancers. They come singly or in groups, in full dress, collecting from all sides on the square. *Konio* beer has already been circulated to warm up the dancers and, little by little, apparently without definite orders, the dance begins. The two *walu* dancers run as if possessed through the group, striking the earth with their staffs and making fearful awe-inspiring cries as they leap high in the air. They really do look like antelopes.

After a while the scene changes: the tempo of the dance increases and a kind of order emerges from the confused movement. The dancers group themselves according to their masks. First to dance are the *kanaga*. In groups of three they execute in turn their splendidly powerful solo dance, stimulated by the singing of the crowd. All three revolve their cross-shaped masks in a precise but dizzily whirling movement so that they resemble the humming sails of a windmill as they skim the ground. As one group finishes its turn it makes way for the next. The dance continues without a break, only the participants change. When all the *kanaga* masks have finished it is the turn of the *sirige* to show what they can do. There are four *sirige* who execute a solo dance one after another. The drums lead into a slower and more dignified rhythm, then the first *sirige* mask appears on the square. The dancer bends right back till the point of his tall mask touches the ground, then he bends forward in the same way. Then he stands up and with slow, cir-

cular movements swings the long board above the circle of men, who bow to the ground as if struck by a high wind, then spring up again emitting loud cries. It is said that this movement of the *sirige* mask conveys a blessing on the people.

After all the four big masks have danced comes the next scene. The music goes on without a break and if one of the players becomes tired another takes his place with new zeal.

The sun beats mercilessly down as midday moves on into afternoon but the ritual—the *rite de passage*—is not yet finished, for the drums and bells sound ever louder and the singing grows stronger. A new, faster, more urgent rhythm begins and the Peul-women masks appear. The men dance in groups of three or four, a wild, springing dance, emphasizing the rhythm with tin rattles held in their hands. Excited by the atmosphere they grow wilder and wilder ignoring the clouds of dust that rise all round. The dance lasts the whole afternoon, fresh dancers taking the place of those who drop out. Gradually there are signs that the end of the feast is near. The number of watchers diminishes and even the dancers leave when their turn is over. At last the musicians go on their way and soon the dancing place is quite isolated and abandoned. One would never suspect that a *dama* had just been held here.

The *dama* must be briefly explained. Every living creature, man or beast, has his own *nyama*, which is immortal. The *nyama* of the dead man begins its journey to the Beyond during the *dama* and it is susceptible during this time to all kinds of dangers. It is threatened by the uncountable *nyama* of other dead creatures, especially of those animals that the man has killed in his lifetime. The masks therefore symbolically act the part of these animals in order to free the passage for the dead man with their dancing. This is true of both the animal and the Peul-women masks. It has already been explained that the Peul were the Dogon's enemies and the *nyama* of the Peul are still imagined as a fearful danger.

Once the *nyama* attains the Beyond it has nothing more to fear, the masks have fulfilled their responsibilities and can return to the cave where they are kept. The dead man has joined his ancestors at last.

The death ritual of the Dogon described here can more or less be accepted as a pattern for many other West African tribes of the savannah. The similarities are often so amazing that one is forced to the conclusion that elements of an earlier common culture have become intermingled with newer developments. The Bambara, Kurumba, Mossi and Senufo also rely on the masks to protect the dead man's soul on its dangerous journey. And in these tribes too the masks—as everywhere—are the property of the mask society. The masks also have other functions, and play an essential role at the ceremonies of some of the societies. However, since the significance of these societies can really only be explained on the social-political level they will be discussed in the next chapter.

At the death ceremonies in Gabon in the Ogowe river valley, masks are worn representing female ancestors. We are back in a territory where matrilinear relationships dominate and where it would be expected that female ancestors would be to the fore. Nevertheless the female masks are worn by the male relatives of the dead. The masks are greatly sought after on account of their beauty, yet no one knows their exact provenance. They are found among the Pangwe, Lumbo and Kota but originally they seem to have been used only by the Kota. They have a very naturalistically treated woman's face with slit eyes, often resulting in a definite mongoloid appearance. The brows are arched and narrow. The sculptured nose with its delicate nostrils is astonishingly European and even the beautiful arched lips of the closed mouth in no way display Negroid features. The small ears stand out slightly. There is a small wooden collar round the face reaching up into the *coiffure* which consists of one or two thickly constructed rolls of hair on the middle of the head. Between the eyes and the temples is a tattooed relief pattern. The faces of these masks are always painted white, the symbol of death.

If a comparison is made, it will be seen that within this type there are several different kinds of masks. Individual examples from the Kota may possibly have been copied by neighbouring tribes, producing a certain slackening of the original tensely charged style, and the heart-shaped form of the face typical of Kota art is not seen on every mask. Gabon is a peculiar mixed territory, where many different cultures met and were the inspiration for new and interesting developments.

After all the necessary ceremonial rites have been fulfilled and the cosmic order re-established through the death ritual, and when all danger is past, a strong link remains between the dead man and his relations, for life and death are considered as two complementary aspects of one universal existence. The living and the dead are

Pl. 63 Agni (former Krinjabo kingdom, Ivory Coast). Tomb figure. Clay, h. 30 cm. Dr. M. Kofler Collection, Riehen/Basle.

Pl. 64 Agni (former Krinjabo kingdom, Ivory Coast). Tomb figure. Clay, h. 28 cm. Museum voor Land- en Volkenkunde, Rotterdam.

dependent on one another and the dead require regular sacrifices so that their souls may be content and ready to give advice and support. So a figure is made as a memorial and as a symbol of the link with the dead. This is the essential foundation of ancestor worship. At the same time the mortal remains are full of terror; skull and bones are dangerous for the living and must be watched over by a protective spirit.

Many objects of African art display the products of these ambivalent ideas in significant fashion.

Tomb figures made of stone or clay to guard the grave, and often a portrait of the dead man, have been found almost everywhere. *Mintadi* (guards) come from Angola and Loango at the mouth of the Congo. They rely on an old tradition and are portraits of kings and chiefs. Made of steatite, the figures are either seated with crossed legs or kneeling. Many lean their head slightly to one side on one hand, others hold up their head and raise their arms and hands in supplication. The headdress is often decorated with leopard's teeth or claws, and with the insignia of the dead man's rank.

In the district of Krinjabo on the Ivory Coast tomb figures of the Agni have been found. They represent kings and their wives. The three-dimensional heads are finely modelled, their closed eyes giving an impression of a death-mask. Most of the pieces are only heads, though there were also small busts and figures with rudimentary arms. These were usually set on top of reliquaries.

Similar fragments of death figures have been found among the Ashanti in Ghana, also made of clay. The faces, shaped in thin discs, are set slightly backwards on a thin neck. Apart from heads whole figures, seated on stools, are known. Several Congo tribes have made complete altars for chiefs and leaders of the secret societies, and these cover the graves like small houses. A life-size figure of the dead man in clay stands on the grave surrounded by all kinds of cult objects and offerings. The Wangata used to set up large sarcophagi in human form as tomb guardians for their chiefs. The Zande marked the graves with logs crowned with human figures.

Many wooden figures that have been generally classed as ancestor figures should really be counted as tomb figures. Unfortunately the gaps in our knowledge are so wide that it is impossible to define exactly what they were. In the few cases where we have enough information it can be seen that there is indeed a difference between ancestor and tomb figures. The Mayombe, for instance, living at the mouth of the Congo, display, as we have seen, a lively naturalistic style in their ancestor figures. Tomb figures on the other hand are very different—stumpy, with rudimentary arms and summarily sketched features.

Genuine relics are found among the Kota and the Pangwe. Here the bones of important people are thought *Pl. 63, 64 to be especially powerful. They are crowned by the Pangwe and Lumbo with a woman's bust in the same style as their death masks. The powerful men of the tribe maintain contact with the dead by means of these bundles of bones and receive much of their worldly power from them. The same idea lies behind the reliquaries of the Kota, the *mbulu ngulu* mentioned above. *Cat. 56

SOCIAL LIFE : SOCIAL-POLITICAL ASPECT

So far we have only studied the African as an individual, his position in the cosmic system and his relationship with his kinsmen which largely determines his social behaviour. It is also essential to realize that a clear distinction cannot always be made. Many phenomena of the family are themselves linked with others which form part of a larger grouping, a village, a conglomeration of villages, a tribe or a nation.

The microcosm of family groups is repeated in the wider sense. The question of communication between different groups then arises. If it is to function properly there must be rules and laws understood and obeyed by all. It will be clear from the above that the ancestors play an important part here also. In every culture the individual is called upon to participate in the wider framework of social life and he must be prepared for this task. There are several institutions for this purpose, which are so clearly defined as to be sub-cultures in Africa within the main framework. The institution of consecration, or initiation, has already been discussed with a general description of the basic process of education. But that is only the beginning. It is the start of the boys' and girls' social life, where they will play a particular part. Hence the further education is similarly determined and a limited number of institutions are devoted to this end.

AGE-GROUPS, SECRET SOCIETIES, LEGAL POWER, RANK AND STATE-PROCEDURES

All these institutions have some features in common with the general initiation, but display a quite different character on the whole. The knowledge of mythical ancestors and their adventures is here not so important as an intense preoccupation with such individual spirits, heroes or other protectors who have a special connection with the creation myth and the cults of the relevant institution. Like the general initiation a period of trial comes first and the necessary ability must be proven. Peace and war are new elements closely linked with the age-groups; also the idea of justice which regulates the stability of society and finally the element of power. They are the most important forms of expression of the age-groups, secret societies and state organizations.

The age-group institution is found in its purest form among the Hamitic people of East Africa, but is also displayed by the southern Bantu and the Negroes of West Africa. The Masai of Kenya exemplify clearly the role played by this system in the social structure. The boys enter an age-group at circumcision and from then on count among the twelve- to sixteen-year-olds, who, with others, are bound to take part in fighting. The time of circumcision is decided when enough boys are at the right age, then over a period of about four years a whole group is circumcised each year. The circumcised —or *sibolio*—of the first two years form a group together and similarly those of the third and fourth years. Together they form an age-group or *olboror*, each with a name of its own. After the feast that closes the circumcision rites the boys are bald—*barnot*; their heads are shaven, they wear a short pelt and decorate their heads with two ostrich feathers and rub red powder into their bodies. They are given a spear, a shield and a sword and are sent into the bush where they practise hunting and learn the elements of a warrior's life. One of them is appointed leader and they then spend two years in the bush before returning to the community where they undergo some more years of tuition from older warriors.

When the boys have finished their training and are considered fully fledged they join the age-group of the real warriors, or *moran*, and remain in it till the age of twenty-eight or thirty. The *moran* is one of the most important classes in the Masai community. The fierce men in the prime of life who belong to it are responsible for protecting the large herds of cattle from thieves and wild beasts. They form the combat force if there is a war. The *moran* enjoy a number of privileges, but are also bound by severe duties and restrictions. Their arms comprise several very effective weapons: a club, a lance with a very long shaft, a short sword *(olalem)* and an oval shield *(olono)* made of buffalo or giraffe hide. Although the designs on these shields remind us strongly of abstract painting they have a definite meaning, though this is gradually being forgotten. The original, now meaningless, motifs are therefore much altered and varied. Colour is as important as form. The background is mostly painted in white chalk, and the drawing in black (charcoal made of pumpkin rind)—nowadays also blue— and red (fruit-juice or blood). The *barnot*, who are not yet full-blooded warriors are only allowed to have black motifs on their shields. Only the *moran* may use red.

The quartering of the shield's surface and the choice of designs still allows us even today to recognize the arms of the group and the rank and status of its warrior owner. Generally the shield is divided in two sections by a long stripe from top to bottom. This stripe consists of a combination of black and white lozenges or triangles, meant to resemble cowrie shells. The circle sections on either side symbolize places and the same is probably true of the large bow-shaped signs. One of the most important symbols is the one used for bravery, but it does not appear on every shield, for only the *kigeloni*, that is the warriors who lead the vanguard, may carry it. A small red or polychrome symbol on the outer rim of one of the long sides of the shield means that the shield-bearer is exceptionally courageous. But this sign of valour has to be won with the approval of all the *moran* from the same group.

Nowadays little is heard of the great warlike expeditions. Courage is displayed in other ways, such as lion hunting. The men hunt in pairs and the one who can overpower a lion by the tail is then allowed to wear its ✱ Cat. 108 mane like a shako *(olowaru)*. Those *moran* who have not won this sign of their proven courage have to content themselves with a plain leather band stuck with ostrich feathers, framing the face like an aureole.

The *moran* also wear a different hair-style from the Pl. xvi other men. They divide their hair into several long strands, sometimes fastened together at the back of the head and woven into a plait with clay and red ochre. The *moran* live in separate villages or kraals with the mothers, girls and younger brothers. Their leader, called *laigwanani*, has to be an exceptional orator. It is not absolutely essential for him to be the bravest in battle, but he is responsible for administration. He is the co-ordinator who keeps contact with the leaders of the

army and gives orders for strategic movement. He is also the judge within his own group, settling every dispute.

The age-groups of the recruits and warriors together form the standing army. However, at the age of twenty to twenty-five, the *moran* move into the next class. This transition is marked by a great feast called *unoto*. A kraal with small huts, each one belonging to a group leader, is built in the bush and in its centre the women build a larger round hut made of branches and cow dung, called the *esingera*. All the acquaintances from the neighbourhood are invited, a number of sacred cattle are slaughtered and the flesh divided among those present. After this feast the warrior becomes a *moruo*. Only now is he allowed to marry and found a family and in time he may possibly have several wives. He builds his own kraal and changes his hair-style and costume to that of the older men. He is now one of the reserve of the warrior army.

I have described the Masai because their structure explains in a relatively simple way the function and effect of a system that varies greatly in Africa. In West Africa especially the system among the sedentary tribes was so developed that extra functions, of a religious or economic nature were added to the social-political function. A great complex developed, all the parts of which are so inextricably intermingled that it must be examined here as a phenomenon of the social-political life.

In this connection the Masai really produced very little worthy of the name of art, whereas in West and central Africa the opposite is true.

The system finds its expression in societies or leagues of exclusive character. Introduction into such a society is, in principle, open to everyone, but actually depends on personal qualities, sex and social status. It may also be inherited or bought for a large sum of money or goods. The several qualities and rules that were the foundation of every society can be generally recognized, even though it is only possible to formulate a rule by citing exceptions.

The closed society is a community formed with definite purposes, in contrast to natural communities, such as clan and tribe, which are determined by the laws of relationship, and of which one becomes a member automatically at initiation. Generally the individual may choose a society, in contrast to membership of an age-group, where there is no question of free will. The society's secrets must be rigidly kept from non-members. The society is a continuous institution and has its own religious code and place where sacrifice is made. Sometimes there is also a cult house, where the sacred objects and insignia of the society are preserved.

A society receives its new members through an initiation similar in many ways to that of puberty. Here too there is circumcision, ritual death and rebirth of the candidate, followed by his introduction to the society's esoteric secrets. A society may be divided into different grades and a fee, like the entry fee, is claimed from those who want to reach a high position. In this way a man can gain fresh prestige. Every grade has prescribed tasks, accompanied by a costume, masks and insignia. A chief, supported by a council, acts as overlord.

Every society has its own festivals, ceremonies and dances combined with an appropriate lore of secret signs, magical objects, even, sometimes, a secret language. The society is the protector of tribal rites and traditions and is responsible for maintenance of law and order, but it often reveals a tendency to adopt an authoritarian position in the community. The members remain segregated from non-members, they frighten them into submission and even practise a kind of terrorism to attain their ends. A society, whatever its structure, carries on its activities and effects in the greatest secrecy. Originally only those were called 'secret societies', which intensified their irrational and unaccountable actions with the sole purpose of keeping innocent outsiders in a state of fear and anxiety. However the expression 'secret society' is now very generally applied and even societies of perfectly open character and effect bear this title.

The societies are rarely confined to one place and members may come from several different villages over a wide territory. The influence of societies is not limited to one tribe alone but extends over several and they are therefore extremely powerful. According to aim and function the societies can be arranged as follows:

1. Male and female societies of a general nature, which have such widespread intent that they govern almost every aspect of communal life. The best known of these is the *poro*-male society, spread over large areas of West Africa and active even today in Guinea, Sierra Leone and Liberia among the Mande and Dan tribes, and its female counterpart, the *bundu* or *sande* women's society of the Mende. To this class belong also the *simo* of the Baga and Nalu in Guinea; the *lo* of the Senufo and the *komo* of the Bambara in Mali; also the *gelede* of the Yoruba in Nigeria and Dahomey, the *mwiri* in Gabon and the *bwame* of the Lega in the Congo.

2. Many societies comprise a particular guild; people skilled in some craft and forming a social group, class or caste with its own rules, which sometimes distinguish them from others in their own village even outside the confines of a society. Not every craft has its own society, in practice only smiths and wood-carvers. Metal-mining, and above all the smelting and handling of iron is regarded as a magic and dangerous enterprise all over Africa. This explains the ambivalent attitude of many tribes towards the iron-smiths. Iron objects are in great demand, but iron-miners and smiths are feared and spurned. Not so the goldsmiths who are generally held in high esteem, for they work the sacred gold, symbol of cosmic power manifest in the divinity of kings. The wood-workers too bring a formless material to life in human figures and masks, hence wood is regarded as a symbol of the slumbering life-force. From this point of view it is not surprising that the skills associated with the supernatural should be united in a guild.

The Senufo have a caste for the iron-smiths *(fonombele)*, a caste for wood-workers in general *(kule)*, and one for the wood-workers making only figures *(kpembele)*, as well as one for the gold-founders *(lorho)*.

Mask societies, too, such as the *awa* of the Dogon, are relevant. Similar organizations also arise where kings and chiefs, surrounded by a sumptuous court, encourage the production of sacred objects of all kinds.

Groups that devote themselves primarily to economic activities are, among others, the numerous hunting societies, for example, the *tore* of the Mbuti Pygmies in the Congo and the *zuo* society of the Dan. There are also many societies devoted to agriculture, like the *kore* of the Bambara. Finally there are societies whose members take a vow of mutual aid, the *kambun* society of the Bamileke in Cameroun for instance.

The secret societies of the medicine men and priests are quite different. Their most important activity is the eradication of disease and other evils that beset mankind. Incantations and magic preparations are often used as a means of healing.

Some societies concentrate on the study of law and the punishment of wrong-doers, for instance the *egbe* society of the Yoruba of Ekiti in Nigeria, and the *ogboni* society of the western Yoruba, the *ekpo* society of the Ekoi and Anyang in eastern Nigeria as well as the *kue-mtong* and *kom'ze* of the Bamileke in Cameroun. An extreme case of this type is exemplified by those societies which adopt an absolutely anti-social attitude and conduct themselves in opposition to the social life of their own community, or against the European rulers. They specialize in ambush attacks, murdering their victim, or otherwise removing him by poison or magic. These terrorist societies are sometimes widespread and wield impressive political power, as the recent history of Africa has proved. Among these are the leopard society, whose members are found in the Congo, in Cameroun and as far as Sierra Leone, the *mau-mau* of the Kikuyu in Kenya and the *nabingi* in Rwanda and Tanzania.

I have so far only mentioned a few of the best-known examples, and these will be discussed in greater detail below. But there are countless secret societies in Africa,

the function and organization of which are almost completely unexplained owing to their extremely secretive nature. Others, however, are changing, or even gradually losing, their social-political significance under pressure of newer, more modern ideas. Many societies are linked with animal species. Snakes, buffaloes, crocodiles, apes, antelopes and wart-hogs are other symbols beside the leopard. An explanation may be that members of a particular society try to imitate the wounds made with the claws and teeth of a specific wild beast, so as to disguise the hand of man if murder has been done. The phenomenon may also be explained by totemism, the members identifying themselves by magic rites with the relevant totem animal. It is significant that societies often have the same name as animals indigenous to the territory.

I have drawn attention to the two basic elements of African cultures—the extensive system of kinship, and ancestor worship. The societies linked with the two former structures must be considered as a third element. The activities of these societies, companies, or fellowships often find an outlet in the periodic, recurring cult activities which can be extended into important festivals. The benign effect of these festivals is not so important for the society members as for the whole community. Many of these cults are dedicated to the ancestors. It has only been possible to give a bare outline of the whole scene, but, in fact, it is much more complicated and subtle. It is, for instance, rarely possible to discover the original function of a society or to recognize subsidiary functions. The use made of the paraphernalia exemplifies this apparently illogical confusion. They are really strictly linked with certain cults and act as a focal point. Later it will be seen how many cult objects can also be used for other cults.

Leaving the social structure we can now turn to the objects themselves. First the masks: human and animal masks and also some with features of both, which must be carved in conditions of the greatest secrecy and with strict observation of the conventions, if they are to be endowed with proper magic power; masks supposed to have been found in the bush, thus stressing their supernatural origin; masks that inspire profound homage because of their power over peace and war, over the life and death of the innocent as well as the guilty, and by their power to influence the well-being of mankind.

The better a mask fulfils its task, the more power it will have and the greater the honour accorded to it. Successful masks are therefore often very old and have the beautiful patina, so sought after by art collectors, that comes from rubbing with blood, millet paste and palm-oil over a period of many years. If a mask seems ineffective it is destroyed and a new one carved. In this operation magic, which we shall discuss in greater detail later, plays an important part.

Masks provide some fine examples of African art and their dynamic expression and intense effect on the observer are much admired. If we now examine individual masks and their function we must not forget that as non-initiates we really know very little about them. In this respect one must add that the African may give up a certain mask for some reason, but this will by no means reveal to us its whole secret history; on the contrary if a mask is uprooted from its context, we can only have the faintest inkling of its true purpose. It is very difficult, if not impossible, to penetrate further into the world of the secret societies, for their significance is still too great in many African tribes.

The large six-foot *banda* mask is one of the most important masks of the *simo* society of the Baga and other neighbouring tribes in Guinea. It is long and narrow and combines human and animal features. The mouth finishes in a point rather like a crocodile's snout, while the rest of the face is human, with large nose and oval eyes. In the middle of the tall headdress is set a long comb with antelope's ears, and above which are set on either side one or two pairs of long, elegant, curved horns with the points bound together with large, carved spiral ornament. The lively painting in black, white and iron red, gives this mask an expressive force which is intensified in the movements of the dance. The mask is borne horizontally on the head, while a thick crinoline-like raffia cloak covers the dancer to the knees.

The Toma, also from Guinea, possess a mask of the so-called *landa* type, representing a wood spirit of the *poro* society. This mask is also rather elongated with a strongly stylized human face. The otherwise unworked surface of the face has a straight nose, deeply engraved eyes and a round forehead. The details of the Toma mask may vary—especially in the upper part—but the basic shape always remains the same: flat face with an oval chin, no mouth, straight nose and rounded forehead, which is completed by a straight or slightly curved line above the eyesockets. The eyes are indicated by small holes, or not at all.

Pl. 65 Toma (Sierra Leone). Helmet mask of the poro society. Animal head with human features. Wood, l. 86.6 cm. Ethnographisch Museum, Antwerp.

Pl. 66 Mende (Sierra Leone). Helmet mask with Janus face of the bundu women's society. Wood, h. 49 cm. Museum voor Land- en Volkenkunde, Rotterdam.

rows of teeth and huge fangs. The neighbouring *Kissi* have similar masks of which an immense, horizontal headdress mask is the most important. The round eyes, straight nose and huge mouth give a half-human, half-animal impression. The headdress that goes with it is a crown of thick feathers.

The Mende in Sierra Leone provide a dark helmet mask for the appearance of the spirit of the *bundu* women's society after the initiation of the girls. This very finely worked mask is shaped rather like a glass bell. The face itself is relatively small and below the round forehead the eyes, nose and small mouth are arranged in a small triangle, ending in a sharp chin. It has small ears set wide apart at the side. Typical of the style of these masks are the folds on the cheeks and roll of fat on the neck. The hair-style is generally very finely done, and displays a wide variety of styles. Usually there are three or more fan-shaped hair combs, which, with the tallest in the middle, stand up like a crown above the mask. It is an exact imitation of the *coiffure* adopted by Mende women, and can therefore be described as symbolic of the female. On many masks two large back-curving horns are worn over the hair, or sometimes a miniature head repeating the same complicated comb arrangement. There is even one mask in which the head is decorated with a European crown. Oddly enough, also because of the hair-style, this mask closely resembles Queen Victoria. It could be an intentional portrait, because Sierra Leone was a British colony at the time and Queen Victoria a symbol of supreme power. There are also Janus-faced double masks. A slightly different type of *bundu* mask consists not only of a head, but the upper

Pl. 66

* Pl. 65

Pl. 67

The Toma of Sierra Leone have helmet masks for the *poro* society that also combine human and animal features. This manner of depicting spirits whose mythology is often inspired by natural phenomena, appears frequently among the neighbouring tribes of Guinea, Sierra Leone and the Ivory Coast. The front view of these masks of the Toma tribe is similar to the *landa* type discussed above, except that they sometimes have two crooked horns. The side view reveals a horrific jaw with

part of a woman's body with small arms, breasts and two small slits as spy-holes for the benefit of the wearer. The long neck carrying the usual style of head has several rolls of fat.

With the Dan, Gere and Wobe we are on the frontiers of Liberia and the Ivory Coast, a region where masks are strongly developed. These three tribes have produced the main style as well as different sub-styles within each tribe, and mixed styles on the frontiers. The Dan, especially, were so influential that the masks of tribes on their outer frontiers—the Diomande, Tura, Gia and Kru—reveal strong Dan characteristics. The variety of styles that developed, due to reciprocal influence in this relatively small area (not much larger than Holland) is incredible. We are fortunate today in having Vandenhoute's clear and useful classification, the result of extensive field work, which allows us in some measure to classify the numerous masks of this region. Although it is impossible to treat this theme in detail, the salient points may be mentioned here.

First there is the classic Dan mask, which succeeds in expressing the spirit of the human face in a noble form, and which is perhaps the type that combines the essential elements of African art in its purest form. These dark, smoothly polished masks are almost oval, with convex forehead and pointed chin. The nose and protruding thick lips are very naturalistically shaped. The mouth may be closed but if it is open it is in the form of a lozenge. In many masks teeth can also be seen. The masks worn by men have large round eyeholes often with slightly raised rims. While the eyeholes of female masks are usually only narrow slits. The lids may be emphasized by an applied, narrow strip of tin. This type represents the northern Dan style which forms the original nucleus. In the territory where the southern Dan style is found the mask often has a slightly raised, carved line running vertically across the forehead to the upper part of the nose. The dark colour of the masks is attained by insertion in a mud bath. Some masks are partly, or even completely, covered with a layer of chewed kola nut mixed with a red vegetable dye. The male masks may also have moustaches. For the dance these masks are decked out with feathers, glass beads and small brass bells and the dancers wear grotesque costumes of coloured cloth and raffia cloaks, giving them, especially in the stilt dances, an impressive character. Each one of these antropomorphic masks has a name, is used at several rituals of the *poro* society and represents the ancestors in the function of a teacher. At the same time they may represent avengers or village guards. The women's masks are symbols of the fruitful primaeval mother, protectress of pregnant women and children.

The so-called *sagbure* masks, found among the northern Dan and the Diomande, belong to another category. They represent messengers or couriers; they watch over the village and protect it from evil spirits, attacks by enemies and wild beasts and one of their tasks is to give warning of fire in the forest. Among these masks there are some with anthropomorphic features, but the dominant type has an elongated nose and mouth which protrude from the face like the beak of a bird and is therefore sometimes called bird's-beak mask. Certain ∗ Pl. 68 pieces of this kind have a movable lower jaw and a ∗ Pl. 69 thick moustache. Sometimes they are called snap-jaw

masks. Another mask may belong to this type, or it may be the expression of a northern idea in the southern regions. This large human mask has a tall beak-like jaw with carefully carved teeth, under the chin. It represents the protective spirit of the *komo* society among the Mahu or Mau in the region north of the Diomande, and is much feared on account of its enormous magical power. The few examples we possess of this type of mask (Cat. 5) are all bedecked with feathers and grass hair and covered by a thick layer of sacrificial offerings. Individual or collective punishment is in the hands of the powerful and much feared judge mask, which is capable of frightful and cruel deeds when roused. This mask resembles an ape, its forehead is arched and the mouth juts out sharply. Sometimes the lower jaw is movable.

In many of the smaller sub-tribes such as Kulime (Cat. 1), Zanya, Gio and so on, a sub-style is found that has developed from the mixture of different mask characteristics of the Dan, Wobe and Gere. The masks in these styles strongly emphasize the essential features of the human face, even to the point of exaggeration. The forehead is reduced to a sloping surface, almost like a roof, the eyes are missing, although their presence is suggested by the deep shadows; sometimes they are depicted by two large holes. The cheekbones enclose the face like two flat triangles on either side and flank the massive, vertical nose. The mouth often has teeth. The style of the Gere (Pl. XVII) (in Liberia also known by the name Kran) and the Wobe, wherever it appears in its original form, is in complete contrast to the calm, clear style of the Dan. The grotesque masks have animal, not human faces, and especially the wart hog, but at the same time they are so stylized that human features are incorporated with those of animals. In the *poro* society these dynamic masks fulfill a variety of tasks according to their grade. The face is broad, almost square and the essential parts are so carved that the whole mask appears like a composition made up of several horizontal layers. The lower edge of the forehead is strongly emphasized, the eyebrows stand out like horizontal discs and the remarkable eyes are of a shape that can best be described as castanets. The nostrils of the large, jutting nose and the horizontal thick-lipped mouth are broad. A row of little metal plaques form the teeth. The lips are occasionally accentuated by a layer of red material. Pointed or blunt tusk-like protuberances border the edge of the mask. The cruel and supernatural appearance of this mask is strengthened by excessive decoration: bunches of feathers on the head, and round the face a circle of little bells, cartridge-cases and other metal objects and added to all this a moustache and beard of hair or fibre. A variation of the type has conical, tube-like eyes. These so-called *te-gla* masks have a mainly political significance. There are masks with two or even three such pairs of eyes and others on which the lateral protuberances take the form of inward-curving, pointed horns. These too sometimes have a movable lower jaw.

We must now turn our attention to another tribe living to the north of the Dan on the northern Ivory Coast—the Senufo, producers of a rich variety of masks used in the activities of different secret societies and especially the important *lo* society. The masks were also used for the ancestor cult and death ritual of their members as well as many other ceremonies, but the details of their function are not exactly known. One receives the impression that a mask may have several functions, and that the mask appearing in several subsidiary groups under different names is one and the same, and that societies other than the *lo* use them. However, the masks can be grouped together by shape so that a rough classification is possible. All the sub-tribes of the numerous Senufo people are renowned for the richness of their art, but the district of Korhogo in the middle of Senufo territory seems to have the greastest variety. The large masks of the *lo* society called *kponiugo* and *waniugo* may be considered first. These strongly sculptural masks are worn horizontally and one should really see them from all sides to be able to appreciate the powerful expressiveness of every detail. The *kponuigo* is a buffalo head Cat. 19 with human face and long elegantly curved antelope horns. Two huge, crooked fangs protrude from the wide-open mouth furnished with big teeth, and the upper jaw is pierced by two large boar's tusks, which point either upwards, forwards or backwards. This strange creature carries another smaller animal on the top of its head—a chameleon, snake, hornbill or other kind of bird and sometimes even a combination of all ★ Cat. 2 these beasts.

The *waniugo* mask differs from the *kponiugo* by a kind of bowl worn on the head to contain the *wa*, a magical substance that assures the success of the ceremonies. This mask is linked with the mythological world and symbolizes the original universal chaos before the appearance of the creator. It may also take the form of a Janus-head with two great incisors. In Europe it is known by the name 'fire-spitter. In the *gbon* cult the *waniugo*

Pl. XVII Gere or Kran (Ivory Coast). Secret society mask. Wood, painted, h. 26 cm. Dr. M. Kofler Collection, Riehen/Basle.

masks have to combat the demons and soul-eaters that threaten the village. During the ritual, which is always held at night, the masks are made to spew out sparks and fire. The costume that goes with it, and which is also worn by the accompanying dancers, covers the whole figure like a loose hanging sack. It is sewn together from strips of material in patterns of squares, lozenges, triangles and circles made by the reserve process of dyeing.

The Nafara of the territory of Sinimatiale, northeast of the Korhogo, use a mask resembling the type mentioned above that may be a simplified version. The small, round head with long, slim, ribbed antelope horns and broad jutting mouth is very charming. It forms a part of the *kagba*, a kind of saddle-shaped construction of vegetable stuffs fringed with raffia along the bottom. On one end at the top of this 'roof' construction the mask is fixed horizontally, from the other end hangs a thick fringed tail, the whole representing a mythological animal, which is moved below the 'roof,' i.e., the body, by a standing man. The *kagba* is so holy, that only members of the *lo* may look at it; it is the symbol of the *lo* society and closely linked with its higher grades. Also from the same region, and similarly constructed to the *kagba*, is the *nassolo*. It is, however, larger and the body of the animal seen in section is not triangular, but round. The outside of the body is painted with large circles and triangles in white red and black and the ornament is similar to that of other *lo* groups. The *nassolo* which means buffalo-elephant, needs two people to move it. It also is a general symbol for the spirit of the *lo* society.

Pl. 68   Dan (village of Ze, Ivory Coast). Tamboge ancestor mask, used by the leader of the initiation. Wood, feathers, h. 25 cm. Ethnographisch Museum, Antwerp.

Pl. 69   Dan (Ivory Coast). Mask of a female ancestor, with a bronze bell. Wood, h. 26 cm. L. van Bussel Collection, The Hague.

Another type, the *korobla* mask is also in the form of an animal. It is a helmet mask found in many regional variations, though they all lack the horns and the bowl for the *wa*. The functions of these masks seem to be very different, depending on the character of the society where they appear. The *korobla* is used at the death ritual in the *lo* society, while in the *dieli*, a union of tanners and leather-workers, it is the focal point of the initiation rites. In that case it represents a baboon; the head is round and the snout sticks straight out with large, flat jaws, and the unbroken row of upper teeth contrast with the singly carved ones of the lower jaw, which look like small pillars. A long, narrow rib divides the surface of the face in two, forming the nose at the same time. The round eyes are often small and frequently lacking altogether, though sometimes they are larger and covered with brass sheeting. The ears are oval. There are many variations of this basic form, but they are all easily identifiable as baboons. Now and then holes are bored through snout and head to hold feather plumes. There are Janus-masks here too. A thick collar and coat of fibre completes the costume.

Like all the other holy masks the *korobla* dances in a secluded place called the *sinzanga*, where all the society's manifestations take place. Other animals, besides baboons, hyenas and wart-hogs for instance, occur among the *korobla* masks. The wart-hog, beside the typical animal characteristics of large mouth, long narrow ears and wild boar's tusks has in addition the face of a man with a small mouth. These masks too often have little figures of animals such as a chameleon or hornbill as well.

Completely different, not only in form, but in their whole character, are the small face masks known as *kpelie*, *kodelie* and *kulie*. These finely decorated and often beautifully polished masks show the Senufo artists in a different light. All grotesque and horrific elements have gone and their place is taken by a dignified, stylized human face, which contains several different symbolic elements.

The *kpelie* mask is usually oval and the face stands out in sharp relief above the surface. The brows are arched crescents above the narrow slit eyes, and a small open mouth with pointed teeth lies below the long thin nose. The downward pointing ram's horns on the head are a recognizable characteristic of many *kpelie* masks and Pl. 70 the two appendages hanging on either side of the chin called 'legs'. On either side of the temples are rectangular or semicircular flat pieces of metal or other ornament, which perhaps are meant to represent a greatly stylized *coiffure*. Most important, however, are the figures on the head. The *kpelie* is an ancestor mask which is used at the ceremony of the *lo*. Although the occasions on which it is used may differ, it always represents an ancestor closely connected with the society's origin. In the higher grades of the society it stands primarily as a symbol of the metaphysical world in which the imperfection of human existence is strongly emphasized. The figures worn on the head depend on the group to which they belong, in the manner of a coat of arms. The best-known emblems are: a comb, the symbol of agriculture, a bird, especially the hornbill, linked with the smiths, a bundle of palm-nuts, symbol of the wood-carvers, while small human figures are apparently connected with merchants. When they appear in public the *kpelie* masks are often furnished with antelope horns, whose magic power increases the holiness of the mask. The rest of the costume is a kind of collar or cloak made of long fibres, a knotted robe decorated with black lozenge shapes and, as an attribute for the dance, a bunch of red fibres.

The *kpelie* mask also exists in other forms. Among the Kufolo it has two faces and symbolizes the union of male and female. There are also some metal masks made by the *cire perdue* method. Some very old ones are known, but usually their authenticity is very doubtful as so many are made for sale. The same is unfortunately true of many wooden *kpelie*.

Some examples exist of *kpelie* with a human face that ends in a long pointed bird's beak. They seem to be restricted to the north. Especially interesting are the transitional styles with combinations of different characteristics, for instance the face masks from the north, ornamented with strips of metal, clearly influenced by the Bambara.

In the south-east on the other hand in the country bordering the Baule, the so-called 'legs' and heraldic figures are missing. Instead the masks carry buffalo horns as is usual in the country of the Baule, or ornaments which give a characteristic hair-style. Here the slit eyes are not straight but curved giving the impression that the mask is looking downwards.

There remain several other types though they are really more like superstructures, than masks. They are large and more or less rectangular, sometimes rounded, boards with a small basket under one end, and this the dancer fixes on his head. The board may be plain or decorated with black and white checks. Generally the central part is cut out into stylized fretwork pattern of a lizard. This figure is stylistically sometimes surprisingly similar to the human figures on the *kanaga* masks of the Dogon and especially so when the tail of the lizard is lacking. These masks, too, belong to the sphere of the *lo* society and are carried by the initiates in the ceremony of the *kwonro* grade which is the stage directly before full membership. In one more richly worked type horizontal fretwork bands of stylized human figures, riders and hornbills are cut in the board. On both front and back is an animal's head with long, smooth or Pl. 71 ribbed, almost circular, horns crowned with a mythological figure.

Finally another type must be mentioned although it is very rare and is scarcely ever found in collections. Its area of distribution among the Senufo is relatively small, being known only among the Kiembara in the region of Korhogo. These are masks made in pairs, male and female, of the helmet type with a superstructure. The mask is in the shape of a helmet and has a large, rectangular spy-hole. The superstructure consists of a tall very stylized human figure with short, powerful legs. The elongated, cylindrical body is carved horizontally in ribs and carries on without a break into the neck which bears a massive head. The female figure is recognizable by its breasts, the male carries a quiver on its back. These masks are called *deguele* and belong to the higher grades of the *lo*. They may only be worn by certain people. They appear at the death ceremony of important members and are thought to be the materialization of metaphysical ideas from Senufo mythology. They are not in themselves gods but are considered as culture heroes from the mythical origins of man. This is symbolized by the quiver, whose arrows give rise to lightning, and thus to fire. The *deguele* accompany the soul to the beyond.

Northern neighbours of the Senufo are the Bambara. We have already seen that in the border regions their style has something in common with that of the Senufo, otherwise however they form a group with a self-sufficient concept of art nearer to that of the Mossi and Bobo. At first glance the art of the Bambara may seem coarse or to say the least not very refined, for the shapes are almost clumsy and lacking in detail. Yet it is exactly this crude arrangement of planes that endows the art with its great harmony.

Once again the best examples of this art are found among the masks of the secret societies. The *komo* society is found everywhere and apart from fulfilling many tasks in the community, it is open to all. The focal point of all the ceremonies of this society is a mask representing the archetypal smith, the bringer of culture, who gave men the knowledge of many things essential to their existence. The mask is worn horizontally on the dancer's head. It is a stylized portrait of an animal head with long, narrow, flat jaws. Small alterations in the basic shape result in other kinds of animals. It is however in some cases difficult to recognize the animal for the foundation will be completely covered with a substance made of clay, blood and magic ingredients. From this conglomeration different horns protrude from both ends while the upper surface is decorated with plumes and porcupine quills. Other excrescences consist of birds' skulls, modelled out of the same material and also stuck with feathers. The irregular shape of the mask embraces the elements, earth, air and water, and it is said to control the rhythm of the cosmos. Its rather repellent appearance scarcely allows it to be classed as art, yet it emanates considerable formal power. Its inherent and exceptional powers arise from its magic nature and it is therefore dangerous and has to be kept in a clay hut which serves not only as a dwelling, but also provides the sacred place where sacrifices to the mask are made.

The masks of the *komo* society are similar in type, though they are rather bigger and have long narrow ears and an animal on the head. They are also completely covered over with a particular substance, yet the essential form remains clear, because it has neither protuberances nor horns.

The masks of the *n'tomo* society belong to a class with human faces. The *n'tomo* is an organization of boys who have not yet been circumcised and who have no rights of entry to the adult societies. *N'tomo* masks are more finely made than the animal masks. They are longish, oval and have a kind of frame made of a row of long, vertical points. Sometimes in the middle of this row there is a female figure, or an animal figure in front of it. The forehead of the mask is round, while the rest of the face is rather flat. The straight nose and pointed mouth are carved in high relief. The small, round or angular eye holes are set very high, right under the ridge of the forehead. In many cases, if not always, the masks are decorated with cowrie shells sometimes mingled with small red *kisi* fruit stones, stuck on to the

face and frame so as to cover it almost completely. Other masks are decorated with pieces of tin.

The Marka, a people living in the northern Bambara territory of San have a slightly different style. The faces of their masks are long, growing narrow towards the base, and the decoration consists of beaten metal with incised geometric patterns. For decoration too, small nailheads are beaten in rows into the metal. Sometimes thin metal tubes may hang in front of nose and eyes.

Two types of mask of the Mossi from Upper Volta may be recognized in the territory not under the dominion of Islam. Both masks are very abstract in shape and belong to specific societies but very little is known of their spiritual background. The mask of the *wango* society represents an earth spirit and is therefore a fertility symbol. The actual face of the mask is a small flat oval plane, across which a zig-zag crosspiece runs vertically as an indication of nose and mouth. Two triangular sections are attached to this crosspiece and form the eyes. The vertical line of the crosspiece is continued over the forehead in two jutting horns and a pair of slightly turned-out ears, for the mask is supposed to represent an antelope. On a large board-like structure behind the horns there is a large female figure—a symbol of fertility. The mask is sometimes decorated with geometric patterns in white and reddish brown. The other type has a long, stylized face with a round forehead. The same crosspiece and spy-holes are also found here. The superstructure consists of a tall, board-shaped comb, which may be plain or incised. Lozenges and triangles in white and reddish brown form the pattern.

The Bobo, neighbours of the Mossi are, like the

Dogon, Bambara and Mossi, creators of an abstracted, stylized art that we shall encounter again among the Kurumba and people of northern Ghana.

The Bobo fall into three subsidiary groups, which differ sharply both culturally and artistically. Here the helmet masks of the Bobo-Fing—sometimes called the Black Bobo—in Upper Volta, must be mentioned. At first glance these helmet masks resemble the Mossi masks with the board-like superstructure and white, black and reddish brown colouring, but on closer inspection a number of clear and definitive differences appear. There are human faces with a comb, straight, sharply cut noses and protruding mouth. Sometimes the top of the head has yet another superstructure made up of different creatures like birds and chameleons. The whole mask is covered with bands of incised lozenges and triangles painted black, white and brownish red. Another type of mask called *kele* came originally from the society of the iron-smiths and displays a stylized human face, which is longish, angular and has a small rectangular mouth. It is divided by a long narrow nose. To left and right of the upper part of the nose are small round spy-holes, the round forehead crowned by a narrow board-like structure about as long as the face and decorated with incised triangles. The abstracted form is emphasized by the large triangles painted on the face.

The masks used by the societies of the Guro and Baule of the Ivory Coast at their ceremonial dances show a very different style. We have already seen something of the plastic art of the Baule in the portrait busts and ancestor figures and in small everyday objects. The

same delicacy and immense care for the smallest detail is also evident in the masks with human faces, though the animal masks display a completely different style. The black, polished human masks with slit eyes shaped Pl. XVIII like coffee beans, fine straight nose and delicate oval or rectangular mouth, always have an expression of restrained dignity and composure. They are generally richly tattooed with different patterns according to the clan. The hair is finely arranged in a roll reaching across the forehead from one ear to the other. The face is often framed by a zig-zag border. Many of these masks have a symbol on the head, in the form of a geometric ornament or a bird, sometimes two birds facing one another, or a combination of small horns. The masks are black or brown and polished, though details such as mouth, eyes or bird's beak may be painted in red and white.

The masks of this type known everywhere as *mblo* belong to the societies with social-political tasks in the village. But the exact standing and function of many masks is not known although we realize that they are an expression of a mythological world picture, representing primaeval beings imagined as the world's creator. For instance there is the sky god, Niamie and his opposite number the earth goddess Assie. The wind god Gu who turns the world by his breath; Guli is the spirit of the dead and Gbekre the monkey serves as a judge of the dead, while the ram is a spiritual creature linked with the sky.

Double masks with two faces side by side, known as *kloro*, symbolize the male and female principle, that is the union of Niamie and Assie, heaven and earth.

The animal masks forming the other class of mask

have been mentioned already. In contrast to the masks in the form of the human face these are helmet masks worn horizontally on the head. They are larger and more massive and the fine detail is sometimes replaced by polychrome painting. Buffalo masks representing Guli, a powerful spirit that protects men from enemies' bullets, ambush attacks and from the effects of evil demons are very important. The Guli masks can also be separated into numerous sub-divisions. One of these has human features. The muzzle of the buffalo head is angular, the forehead rounded; round, protruding eyes are painted white with black pupils, while the human nose is long and narrow. The head has two broad, short horns curved almost into a ring. The mouth has carefully carved teeth. This mask is also called *egbwe* and is used at fertility rites within the society.

* Pl. 72

Another type with a spherical head and rectangular mouth represents Kakagie the son of Niamie, a spirit of the dead. The small round eyes are set wide apart and divided by a group of broad stripes leading from the forehead to the mouth. The horns are straight, with inward-turning points. This type of mask is painted in polychrome and some Janus-type examples are known.

The *kple-kple* forms yet another class of buffalo mask. It is a disc-shaped, very stylized face with pear-shaped eyes, the tips of which point downwards. The half-spherical pupils are often inlaid with glass splinters. The mouth is horizontal with pointed teeth. The horns spring from the centre of the skull and describe an almost complete circle. The *kple-kple* always appear in pairs, one red, the other black.

There are also elephant and antelope as well as buffalo masks. With these the dancer always wears a cloak composed of many layers of vegetable fibres.

These mask styles, indigenous to the Baule and summarized here, can nearly all be found among the neighbouring Guro, whereas the Yaure, a sub-tribe of the Baule, show clear indications of a transitional style. It has been made clear with other plastic forms that the Baule and Guro styles are difficult to separate. This is also true of the masks, especially in the borderlands. The Guro style, however, has one or two distinguishing marks: the face of the human mask is usually longish while the forehead and bridge of the nose form an elegant S-shaped profile. The tattoo pattern cut in relief on forehead and cheeks is a repetition of the short protruding tattoo marks on the men's faces, and another characteristic of many Guro masks is the broad, wooden collar that serves as a fixture for the raffia cloak. There are polychrome, as well as black and brown polished masks. There is a much stronger tendency than with the Baule to add animal features to the human face—elephant's ears, or a superstructure in the shape of a cockerel's or other bird's head. There are also human masks with long horns and a superstructure in the form of one or two human figures.

The *je* must be mentioned among the animal masks. They have the shape of a buffalo head with broad, flat horns and an open mouth. Then there are the antelope masks owned by the *zamle* society, the significance of which is military. The polychrome mask gives another example of the elegant line running from forehead to nose and the small slightly open snout ends in a point, while delicate horns point upwards. The elephant masks of the Guro are, like the human masks, slim and long.

The Yoruba in Nigeria must next command our attention. This large race which displays an extraordinary artistic unity despite its tribal divisions, is distinctly separate in many ways from the people so far discussed. The social-political structure of the Yoruba is like a pyramid or triangle, with the highest authority at the apex and in the Yoruba it is embodied in the *oni*, the king. The *oni* resides in his palace in the holy city of Ife and is honoured not only as a political ruler, but principally as the representative of the Oduduwa, the ancestral father of the whole Yoruba people, whose divine power he wields. The myth of creation relates that Oduduwa gave each one of his children a crown decorated with strings of glass beads and sent them away from Ife to found kingdoms for themselves. This legend therefore explains the origin of the other Yoruba kingdoms, today numbering about fifty. Their *oba*, or kings, belong to the clan of the founder who came from the family of Oduduwa. These kingdoms are, in the narrowest sense, city states and together form several provinces: Oyo, Egba, Ijebu, Ife, Ondo, Ekiti, Kabba, etc. A part of the Yoruba people lives on the far side of the border in Dahomey, that is in Fon territory. Fon and Yoruba have influenced each other in several respects.

Right through the pyramid there runs a vertical structure based on the principle of the secret societies. The active political power of these societies is very far away from the divine power of the kings founded on traditions and mythology, which, in fact, is only a symbol for the unity of the people. The *ogboni* society to which the elders of the different cities belong, is the actual holder of state power, for its members are all chiefs who hold the administration of the cities in their hands. These chiefs represent different ranks according to hereditary titles of their clans.

It often happened that an *oba* took away the titles and functions from a chief's clan in order to bestow it on another, yet the real power still remained in the community of chiefs. The *ogboni* societies are still very prominent in Yoruba territory where they dominate the judicial settlement of village disputes. In general they restrict themselves to controlling the daily life of the villagers and local administrators. The *ogboni* societies use no masks in their cult, but their meeting-house is the sanctuary for a series of other objects, worshipped as sacred pieces. Among these are some drums, called *agba*, which are very old. The largest is more than three feet tall and is carved with symbolic figures, one of them being a stylized human figure personifying the guardian of the *ogboni* house. Little is so far known about the meaning of the ornament on the *agba* drums and even the members of the society itself understand very little now of the deeper significance of these symbols.

Another attribute connected with the *ogboni* cult is the *edan*. The *edan* are bronze figures about eight inches high, and set either on a staff or a bell. They present a couple, man and woman, who are often bound together by the heads with a chain. The style of these figures, cast by the *cire perdue* method, is very remarkable and departs in many respects from the style of the wood-carvings: the faces are often broad and flat, the slit eyes have a horizontal coffee-bean shape, and the nostrils of the narrow straight nose are flared and flattened. The wide

mouth has narrow lips and the chin sometimes has a beard-like ornament. The body is elongated with strong emphasis on sexual characteristics, while arms and legs consist of thin, bent sticks. Besides these *edan* there are other larger, bronze figures in a similar style, but little can be said about them for we only know that they belong to the cult objects of the *ogboni* priesthood and that they are connected with an earth cult. Their style presupposes them to be the last remaining examples of an undoubtedly earlier and higher stage in the art of bronze-casting.

Two of the many societies that hold power in the Yoruba tribe are particularly widespread: the *gelede* cult society and the *egungun* society.

The *gelede* has developed especially among the western Yoruba and is also represented among the Yoruba in Dahomey. This society works for the good of the community and organizes a ceremonial mask feast and dance every year. When these dances are performed in public they are purely for entertainment. The dancers, appearing in pairs with identical masks, often represent women and wear women's clothes to which large, wooden breasts are attached. The *gelede* masks are helmet masks worn over the head. The simplest (Cat. 8) portray a human head with full cheeks, receding forehead and a large round back of the head. The large almond-shaped eyes have holes instead of pupils and the lids protrude slightly. The broad, flat nose has flaring nostrils, while the lips are full and fleshy. These masks nearly all have three horizontal or vertical tattoo marks on each cheek and occasionally three similar stripes can be seen on the forehead. The ears lie flat against the head like

question-marks and the hair-styles reflect all those current
among the Yoruba women. Apart from this basic type
there are numerous *gelede* masks with superstructures,
where the imagination has been given free rein. No
other African sculpture displays such a lively imagination as these mask structures: complicated scenes are
built up with several figures; giant figures with movable
arms, hunters, judges, riders and also animals, such as
the panther or birds and other creatures. The snake, unknown in the Nigerian Yoruba masks, appears rather
frequently in the Yoruba masks of Dahomey, which
must undoubtedly be due to the influence of the Fon,
for the widespread snake cult practised there probably
gave the land its name: *Dan*—snake, *homé*—within,
hence 'within the snake'.

The scenes are usually inspired by themes from the
rich mythology, yet there are also secular scenes, representatives of the Portuguese or other Europeans wearing a peculiar kind of helmet, for example. Some masks
also exist protraying Hausa or other peoples of Nigeria.
The imaginative resources are endless and new ideas
inspired by everyday events constantly appear. In these
masks, where the spontaneity of the pure folk art of the
Yoruba is at its best, the dynamic power of the form is
enhanced by colourful painting. The *gelede* masks of
Ekiti in the north-east of Yoruba territory are interesting in this connection. They are used for the *epa* cult, a
feast held every two years and intended to ensure fertility of the land and the well-being of mankind. The
superstructure of this mask is higher and even more
complicated, if possible, than the *gelede* masks discussed
above; it consists of several rows of human figures,

arranged in a circle round a central figure personifying
a particular founder of the clan, who is often presented
as a mounted warrior—*jagun-jagun*. If it is a symbol of   * Pl. XIX
fruitfulness the scene is one of children surrounding the
mother of the clan. These masks may be as high as three
feet and sometimes weigh nearly one hundred pounds.

The other widespread society—unknown among the
Dahomey Yoruba—is called the *egungun*. Closely connected with the ancestor cult, its members appear as
masked dancers at the death ritual, personifying the
egungun, the soul of the dead, which takes possession of
the dancer's body. In the northern Yoruba towns a
general death festival is held in honour of the dead clan
chiefs and founders. The *egungun* dance in processions
through the town, finally gathering together in front of
the *oba's* palace. They wear long colourful clothes,
covering the whole body, even the hands and feet, and
standing out above the head like a stiff, ruffed collar.
Helmet masks are used for this costume, similar to those
of the *gelede* society, but simpler and with smaller superstructures made in the shape of the clan insignia of the
dead. Another mask of this type is without parallel in
Africa: it has two superimposed faces, the outer one of
which is movable so that it can be opened, revealing the
inner, true mask.

The Bini, too, neighbours of the Yoruba, who live
around the capital, Benin, have mask societies. We
know very little of these masks, but they must be briefly
mentioned here although they are very rarely seen in
collections. As is the case with the Yoruba, the wood-
carvings of the Bini show signs of an independent folk
tradition, that is quite separate from the court art known

to us principally through the famous bronzes. A relationship between folk art and court art is rarely discernible. The form of the Bini mask follows the curving shape of the tree trunk from which it was cut and the face stands out strongly in relief from it. The eyes, beneath heavy lids, have slits while cheeks and forehead sometimes have vertical bands of tattooing. The headdress is round. Occasionally these masks have several rows of notched coral beads similar to those seen on the bronzes. The masks are painted blue and reddish brown; the face is white.

Societies flourish especially among the Ibo, Ibibio, Ijo, Edo, Ekoi and Anyang in south-east Nigeria near the mouth of the Niger and over the border into Cameroun.

The Ibo of modern Nigeria are in many ways the counterpart of the Yoruba. They too are a large people consisting of many tribes inhabiting the territory from the delta to the Cross river in the east. Among many of these tribes, the Afikpo for example, the system of kinship is doubly unilinear, that is the individual is a member of a group stemming from a clan founder on the male side and at the same time he is a member of another group descending in line from a female clan founder. One result of this sytem is that related individuals may live far apart, resulting in an extensive distribution of certain cultural practices. This is indeed the case with the Ibo. Related tribes have not only influenced each other, but also, by contact, the neighbouring peoples. Many of the well-organized societies differing in name from place to place have only a local significance and restrict themselves to regulating the life of the village. The

Pl. 73 Idoma (south-east Nigeria). Mask used at the death ritual. Wood, white with black accents, h. 28 cm. Museum Rietberg, Zurich.

Afikpo also maintain a system of age-groups, each one of which has its responsibility within the framework of the village. The Ibo also have women's societies besides those of the men.

Many types of mask are used for cults among the Ibo. One group are the *mmwo* or spirit masks, incorporating the spirit of the dead man or woman. It covers the whole head of the bearer and the face of the mask is very narrow with a high, round forehead. The small slit eyes, delicately pointed nose, sunken cheeks and protruding lips, sometimes revealing the teeth, remind one forcibly, with their white colour, of death masks. The superstructure may consist of a pair of broad buffalo horns with narrow inward-turning points and sometimes there are two pairs of horns, one behind the other, in front of a tall, narrow comb running from back to front down a central parting. Apart from these large masks there are smaller ones with no superstructure covering only the face of the wearer. Male masks of this type usually have the same features as the female but are far more expressive and threatening with their large mouth and long, pointed teeth. Their superstructures may be very complicated and, apart from other mythological symbols, are sometimes furnished with a pair of ram's horns, symbol of the thunder god. The *mmwo* masks nowadays serve as a form of entertainment apart from their use in the death cult.

Contrasting with these very fine masks there are many grotesque helmet masks made to be worn horizontally on the head. They personify different spirits in the forms of monkeys, goats, or sharks, to mention only the easily identifiable motifs among many other legend-ary creatures. These *ulaga* masks were taken over with the relevant cult from the Ijo, who live to the south of the Ibo in the delta of the Niger and have numerous water spirits which are represented by the large masks of the *sekiapu* society. These, too, are horizontal helmet masks, half-human half-animal monstrosities and furnished with huge cylindrical teeth or with a hippopotamus jaw, with sharply jutting protuberances. Other related tribes, for instance the Abua in their *egbukele* society, also worship water spirits. The dancers invoke the spirits as they wade through the river holding the mask close to the surface of the water.

The masks of the Ibibio, situated to the east of the Ibo, display the same resourcefulness of style as other peoples of eastern Nigeria. The large number of variations, which makes it so difficult to classify any typical style, undoubtedly originated in the free exchange between peoples. In the Ibibio tribe the *ekpo* and *idiong* societies use masks. The *ekpo* society, which devotes itself, among other things, to medicine, owns the so-called sickness masks—portraits of spirits held responsible for certain illnesses, such as the hideous and contagious tropical diseases like leprosy, framboesia, or gangosa, the horrible consequences of which are reproduced with great realism. There are other masks too for expelling different kinds of demons. They are no less horrific in effect, having an arched forehead, half-closed eyes under heavy lids, pronounced cheekbones and a broad mouth that is occasionally furnished with a movable jaw. A sharp contrast to these masks, which in general have a black patina, is presented by a group of masks and superstructures used for the cult of a female divinity. They are

personifications of a fertility goddess connected with water, whose symbol is a snake. The pose of this polychrome figure with delicate features and bearing a snake in upheld hands, is reminiscent of similar Cretan pieces.

The most important of the different tribes living between the Cross river and the border of Cameroun are the Ekoi, Anyang, Banyang, and Boki. Here too the influence of the *ekpo* society is dominant in everyday life. Its members wear large helmet masks in the practice of their duties, supposed to be the personification of former members of the society. Variations in the shape of the masks indicate seven different grades in the *ekpo* Pl. xx society. They are faces realistically portrayed, sometimes as Janus-heads with two or even three faces, and covered with antelope skin. The light-coloured ones with open eyes are female, those of a dark colour and closed eyes, male. The different faces of a mask look out in all directions for they govern the past and future and are omniscient. The eyes are sometimes inlaid with metal and the teeth are made of wooden sticks. The hair is indicated by numbers of small wooden pegs. Sometimes there are also two twisted and notched antelope horns. The circular motifs on the temples are marks of rank within the society. Some small masks covered with skin are made in the same style as these giant helmet masks.

Tribes with a completely different style inhabit the wide grasslands of Cameroun, a style that displays a complete unity despite a combination of different single elements. This grassland style is found among the Tikar, Bali, Bamum and Bamileke, the Bamenda, Bekom, Bafum and Bamessing. They all have a king and his court as a focal point and this had a powerful influence

on the development of the plastic arts. There too, however, the secret societies dominated social life and were known by different names: *majong* among the Bamileke, *ngumba* among the Bamenda. Membership was limited to the chiefs and elders of the village, whose eldest sons occupied a lower grade of the society and as *chinda* (servants)—a form of secret police—carried out the orders given by the society leader. The masks belonging to Pl. 76 these societies have several functions within the framework of their activities and they are kept in the society's religious house. These masks have several peculiar characteristics, which are also found in the sub-styles: they are large wooden masks with round faces, eyes set wide apart, with accentuated, round pupils. The thick nose has broad nostrils and the mouth, nearly always open and furnished with large teeth, seems to be smiling. The cheekbones may be pronounced, but more often we find huge, round, sometimes quite grotesque cheeks. The ears are semicircular and protruding. Some rare old masks are covered with copper sheeting, the head being decorated with glass beads or woolly hair. On others the hair is carved into the shape of broad roll-shaped chignons. The most striking masks however are those with a tall superstructure. This consists of several fretwork figures carved in wood, human figures occa- Pl. 77 sionally but more frequently animals or heads of animals, probably to be interpreted as clan symbols. The leopard is the royal symbol whereas the python with two heads is the special symbol of the king of Bamum. Other reptiles such as lizards, chameleons and crocodiles also appear. Six or eight broad notched rays from a circle, Cat. 95 represent a spider stylized into a geometric pattern.

Similarly ape and buffalo heads may be arranged in superimposed rows so that they are no longer important as single motifs, but form a rhythmical element within the framework of the whole composition.

Another mask worn by the Bamileke in the *kom'ze* society is of special interest. It is a helmet with holes for mouth and eyes which is drawn over the head. It has two large, circular, protruding ears and below the mouth continues in a long extension reaching to the knees. It is made entirely of material and completely covered with glass beads arranged in circular motifs.

Among the animal masks the large elephant masks of the Bali and Bafum should be mentioned. With stylized heads and large bowl-shaped ears, the tusks and long straight trunk are developed into a harmonious composition. Elephant masks play a part at death rituals within the society.

Another example of the integral part played by the mask within the activities of the secret societies is the Lega in the north-east Congo. We know that the lives of the Lega or Rega tribe are wholly dominated by the *bwame* secret society, which is organized in several grades. Each one has its own initiation feasts with dances, songs and cult objects, and of these the masks are especially important. Beside the dance masks worn in front of the face there are some small ones attached to the side of the head or to the shoulder, held in the hand, or spread on the ground during the ritual. A large part of these ceremonies is dedicated to the ancestor cult. The masks, collective clan property, are called *idimu* and are usually no larger than eight inches. Smaller masks may belong to individuals and are then called *lukungu*. They may be

inherited by a relative having the same standing in the secret society as the owner. The masks of the two highest grades are made of ivory and are called *lukwa-kongo*. Similar masks, but of a lower grade, are made of wood. All these masks are powerful symbols of the vital force. Although little is known as yet of the Lega these masks have been sought after for years but unfortunately many fakes are also to be found in collections.

Probably the clear, stylized, powerful form gives these masks their appeal. The concave face rises to the Cat. 13-15 pronounced eyebrows set off against a rounded forehead, and ends in the jutting jaw and chin; the oval mouth is slightly open, while the narrow eyes and delicate nose stand out in relief from the heart-shaped face. The general impression is of a death mask, an idea reinforced by its white colour (kaolin). These masks also frequently have a knotted raffia beard.

In discussing the nature of the secret societies I have concentrated on the masks, which justify special attention by their importance, but it should not be forgotten that many other objects play their part in the cults of the secret societies. Several objects are worthy of consideration on a level with the masks as they represent a highly developed African style of art.

Among them are to be found figures, staves, drums, flutes, dance costumes and attributes as well as ornaments. These pieces, like the masks, are essential components of the society; they are the material expression of a unified world of ideas. Hence their form and style often displays the same characteristics as the masks because they symbolize the same ideas. Whenever this is

the case I shall refer to the earlier discussion and delve into the deeper significance of the objects only when they are different. Once again I shall begin in the west.

The Baga possess sacred wooden vessels called *anok* or *elek*. This vessel serves as a base for a pillar-like neck, on which a head is placed, either obliquely or horizontally. The back of the head is extended, hollowed and carved with fretwork, while below the human forehead and nose the chin turns into a long, pointed beak. This vessel belongs to the *simo* society. Within the hollowed head it contains the magic element that represents the clan's protective spirit at the death ritual. Another cult object worthy of note and which is predominantly found among the sub-tribes of the Landuman, is a very beautiful carved wooden snake. The triangular, flat head with round eyes develops harmoniously out of the curves of the body, enlivened with large, red, black and white triangles. The whole figure is about six feet long and when it appears with the fibre cloak made to go with it, and borne by several people it seems like an enormous primaeval apparition. It is a symbol of fertility unifying water and earth, and is the spirit guarding the initiation ceremonies of the *bansonyi* secret society.

I have already mentioned a bird that appears as a detail on the masks in the Senufo tribe. It is the hornbill, *setien*, traditionally one of the first creatures on earth. In the ceremonies of the *lo* society this bird appears as a single figure and is called *porpianong*. It is a large wooden bird with strongly stylized features: a rectangular board forms the wings from which the round body emerges; the head, on a slim neck, often has a kind of cockscomb while the long beak curves inwards to touch the body again. The legs of different length stand on a small pedestal. Sometimes these birds are painted with red and white lozenges, triangles and points. During the ceremonies they are worn on the heads of the dancers.

Cat. 65 One peculiar piece is the so-called bronze 'ring of silence' decorated with the head of a buffalo. Such examples as we possess exhibit the same degree of technical ability displayed by the Senufo in metal-casting. These rings were formerly worn by the novitiates immediately after their reception into the *lo* society. The new members wore the rings in their mouths when they returned to the village wearing this symbol of silence to prove that the newly acquired secrets of the society would be safe with them.

Pl. 70 Mythological dance staves are known among the Bambara and the Dogon. They are made either of wood or bronze with an elegantly curved handle in the form of an animal's head, sometimes that of a horse. The Dogon staves have a human figure, or a pair of twins, *nomo*, brother and sister, who lived at the beginning of the world.

Musical instruments will be discussed in greater detail in a later chapter, but those that play a special part in the cults of the secret societies and are sacred objects as well as musical instruments must be mentioned here. The most important of these are wood or ivory trumpets decorated with mythological themes or crowned with a human head, and usually blown tranversely. They are found all over Africa from east to west, but by far the finest pieces were made in ancient Benin.

One very small object has become a collectors' piece —the diminutive wooden hammer used by the Baule

to strike their iron bells. The actual hammer head is bow-shaped and furnished with a small striking pad. It is decorated with geometric patterns and a human or animal head.

However the most important musical instruments are the drums, and these are held to be exceptionally sacred by many secret societies. They are endowed with magic power and the older they are, and the more sacrifices have been made to them over the years, so much greater the awe in which they are held. Often a male and female drum furnished with easily recognizable sexual characteristics will be kept as a pair, in Dahomey for example. In the Baga tribe the drums of the *simo* society were supported by male or female figures. Very finely carved, they form the most important part of the composition. The relatively small drum stands on a richly carved pedestal borne on the head. The body of the drum is incised with geometric motifs or rosettes and the skin is stretched across by means of wooden wedges driven into the body. Some drums are also known which are supported on the back of a stylized horse. The sacred drums of the Senufo, called *pliewo,* can be recognized only by the stylized feet on which they stand as symbolic of the male body. Others are borne by a seated female figure. The bodies of the drums are decorated with mythical animals, snakes, lizards, hornbills and riders in relief. Similar drums are found among the Baule.

In Congo and Angola too the societies use special drums for the initiation rites. They are held obliquely between the knees and struck with the hand. Frequently they are double-skinned drums, more appealing by their form than geometrical carving. The *dinga* drum of

the Pende for example, which is beaten during the circumcision ritual, is shaped like an amphora, except that the wide neck is covered with a tightly drawn skin. The drummer sticks his legs through the large carved 'handles'.

The function of some figures brings them also within the realm of the secret societies. For instance, the *lilwa* society of the Mbole in the northern Congo possesses long thin female figures with extended arms and legs and a flat, round, heart-shaped face topped by an arched forehead enclosed by the hair in a semicircle. The narrow, slit eyes and small mouth give the face the look of a dead body, an appearance emphasized by the yellowish-white colouring. It is indeed intended to represent a dead, more particularly, a hanged person. A whole series of these figures is known and they are supposed to be people who were hanged for their betrayal of the secrets of the society. Nevertheless the powers of these men are supposed to have been transferred to the figures, which now appear as protectors of the society. They have become, like the rings of silence of the Senufo, though in a rather different way, symbols of the vow of silence laid on every member of the society.

Of the great number of cult objects produced by the Lega one must mention the very stylized, cubist wooden or ivory figures which form part of the rites of the *bwame*, as do the masks similarly formed. The bodies of these figures are generally distorted, the arms may be missing or very summarily indicated. The body seems to emerge like a pillar from a heavy foot. There are Janus-headed figures and variations with a second or third face at shoulder-height. Others stand with raised

Pl. 80 ; Cat. 50

★ Pl. 79

★ Cat. 111

Pl. 79 Senufo-Niene (village of Touvere, Ivory Coast). Pliewo *drum of the* lo *society. Wood, animal hide, h. 87.5 cm. Ethnographisch Museum, Antwerp.*

Pl. 80 Mbole (Congo-Kinshasa). Female figure. Used at the initiation rites of the lilwa *society. Wood, with a white face, h. 69 cm. C. P. Meulendijk Collection, Rotterdam.*

arms or with their chin in their hand. The style is similar to that of the masks described above. These objects rank as insignia for the higher degrees of the *bwame*.

DECENTRALIZED POLITICAL POWER

Let us now turn to the other important aspects of political power: its development in Black Africa and its function in the traditional community.

It should be made clear from the outset that the institutions of political power in administration and government are always founded on the ancestor cult and kinship system, although African development has resulted in great extremes, ranging from the absolutely decentralized autonomous power of the chiefs to the strongly centralized state having an absolute ruler at its head. The simplest political structure is found among the Bushmen. Here the extended family, consisting of blood relations, relations by marriage and their children, forms the smallest unit. It is an autonomous group of hunters, knowing no chief as such. The leader is usually the eldest, but may, in certain circumstances, also be the most successful hunter. Inheritance plays no part and economic ties replace a social-political structure.

The nomadic cattle-raisers like the Hamito-Nilotic tribes of East Africa have extended the simple structure of the Bushman's society and produced more differentiated patterns. Here the family groups or *lineages* extend to include exogamous clans; every clan has a leader who inherits his position, while the oldest, and therefore most important, clan provides the chief. This overlord

is not only the political, but also the religious head of the whole people and his position is passed on to his eldest son. In places where clans move over very extended areas, there is a system for naming a representative in his place.

Among the sedentary peoples such as the south Bantu, who are bound to the land by agriculture, cattle-rearing or a combination of both, the clan relatives may be scattered over distant villages. Thus a village may represent a family group, whose overlord is also the village chief. A clan is formed from several such villages. The ruling family, whose chief governs all the other clans, and is therefore in fact the tribal chief, belongs to the oldest clan, from which all the others are traditionally supposed to have arisen. The same pattern is more or less repeated in the purely peasant peoples of the Congo and West Africa, though certain differences must be noted: for instance, despite clear tribal formation and cultural as well as linguistic unity, there is frequently no question of centralization, for here the villages are autonomous self-contained little worlds, recognizing their own village chief, a member of the founder clan, as the highest power. The unifying element is not a living personality, but a culture hero, who is regularly feasted and honoured. His traditional descendants also become part of the ancestor cult. Built into this very varied structure will be found the ancestors of several distinct *lineages* and they are often more important for the small nucleus that forms a village community, than the far-distant and faint figure of the primaeval ancestor. The secret society is another factor and the two systems together often ensure that the officially recognized chief, who comes from the most influential clan, is also the leader of the society. When a family group of this kind grows, winning power and favour, one result is the development of a class wielding considerable power through the strictly oligarchical system. A subsidiary phenomenon arises in the buying and selling of titles and positions because relationships and rules of heredity no longer satisfy the needs of reversion. Systems of this kind can of course be infinitely refined and varied. For instance, an oligarchic family from the oldest and officially most important clan may so improve its original position that its ancestors enjoy national honour and may be actually elevated to the position of gods, on account of their importance in the social-political order. A large pantheon of divine ancestors develops whose direct descendants represent the religious power on earth.

This outline of the main features of African social-political systems is necessarily sketchy. Actually it is all much more complicated and many-sided, but a wider ranging discussion would be out of place here since we are not writing a study of African sociology. However, these short notes will supply the necessary foundation for the discussion which follows enabling us to see the pieces in their proper context.

We now come to the regalia, symbols of power, and cult objects, properly described as the material symbols of the power lent to mortal man by his ancestors. These are sacred objects, literally the representatives of those people who are entrusted with power. The system did not develop everywhere in Africa in definite stages and it should not be assumed that peoples with a relatively simple administrative system must necessarily pass through every intermediate stage to achieve such a varied and complicated system as is known among other African peoples. This is absolutely not the case. There are examples where people with a more highly developed social-political system forced its way into the territory of a more simply organized tribe and impressed its own system upon them; but this must be considered an external influence, for most of the systems we know are thoroughly independent and also of equal standing within the framework of the whole culture, however 'primitive' individual systems may appear.

It is not surprising therefore that some cultures have a richer collection of cult objects than others and that artistic quality is also variable. The sedentary communities obviously had better opportunities to develop the material side of this aspect than the nomad peoples for whom cattle were all-important. The following examples have been chosen then according to classes of objects rather than in strict geographical order. We must start again with the omnipotent ancestors whom I have already described—albeit rather generally—in the preceding pages.

The Dogon people enjoy absolute decentralization of political power. The villages are autonomous, having their own chiefs who are members of the oldest *lineage* of the most important clan.

Nevertheless the Dogon have a strong connecting link in the *sigi* feast, which takes place every sixty years. Behind the feasts lie ideas similar to those that have formed the social-political structure of the Dogon people. Primaeval man, according to the creation myth

Pl. 81 Luba (Congo-Kinshasa). Arrow-rest. Detail. Wood, glass beads, overall height: 86 cm. Museum voor Land- en Volkenkunde, Rotterdam. (Cat. 82)

of the Dogon, was immortal and instead of dying changed into unearthly creatures, the *yeban*, who are represented as snakes. This was the fate of the last eight immortal ancestors, who lived before the time of mortal man. The eighth ancestor had a son called Lebe, the first man. When he died he was buried and others came after him. When the time came for men to leave the land of paradise called *mande*, they wanted to take with them the remains of the first man. But when the grave was opened there was a live snake inside instead of the expected corpse and this snake went with the Dogon on their exodus to the north. When they reached the tall cliffs they founded the first southern village, Kani Kombole, and here Lebe disappeared into the ground. Then the Dogon spread out all along the cliff and raised altars to Lebe who would one day return to earth. The last important village of the Dogon, situated in the far north on a lonely mountain top is Yugo Doguru. This village is a sacred place and the first preparations for the *sigi* feast begin there. Then the feast spreads outwards and southwards to the other villages. The *sigi* feast is a memory of Lebe, who introduced death in the shape of a snake.

Death caused fundamental changes in earthly life, for new arrangements had to be made to fit the facts of its presence into the world order of the eight ancestors. The most important of these new arrangements was, and still is, the *sigi* feast. The central point of the festival is a giant mask carved from a tree trunk in the form of a flat snake. This mask serves as a sanctuary for all those fundamental ideas that came to earth with the first dead men, and is therefore a symbol of the unity of the Dogon people. Every village makes a new portrait mask of the snake every sixty years.

A further example may help us to explain the visual presentation of the dominance of a particular clan, in this case the *ekpu* figures of the Oron clan from Calabar in east Nigeria. This clan, belonging to the Ibibio tribe, used to represent its chiefs as ancestor figures. Some of these carvings are still in the possession of the original families. They are carved from logs and the body frequently still shows the round and bullet-like protrusions of the raw wood. The upper part of the body is narrow with straight arms, the belly, however, very rounded. Many of these figures have a long, thin stylized beard hanging down as far as the hands, while a conical or cylindrical headdress reveals their rank as chiefs.

A similar idea is behind the ridge figures formerly seen in large numbers on the roof-ridges of the chiefs' houses in the Suku, Holo, Mbala and other related tribes of the Kwango-Kasai area in the Congo. Nowadays they are only to be found among the Pende. They are figures of women supposed to be the wives of the chiefs. In their right hand they hold an axe, in the left a beaker. Other female figures were set up, carved either as a whole figure or emerging in vague form from the pillars of the palisade before the house. This palisade encloses a small space, or lobby. The figures are called *tungunlungu* and are the exclusive attributes of the leading chiefs. The Pende are matrilinear so the female figures probably represent the clan mother figure.

The chiefdoms of clans in the middle Congo are clearly defined, the leading chiefs ruling like kings over their small territories. They are quite different from most of the West African peoples, whose secret societies have taken over responsibility for most social-political tasks, for here the chief is absolute, and even the supreme judge.

The Pende and several of the neihgbouring tribes such as the Mbala, the Pindi, Suku and Yaka, and to a lesser degree, the Jokwe, use special staves in legal disputes. Whenever a quarrel between two clans is to be settled, the two official speakers for prosecution or defence carry a staff and these, known as *mihango* by the Pende, give the speaker the support of the clan ancestors in his difficult task, and he is at that moment the representative of their supernatural power. There are examples crowned with a male or female figure, others show a plain head with a body in the form of a broken lozenge. Another variation has a thickened top like a goitre and in that case the human figure or small head will be carved in high relief out of this thickening.

There are also other staves which have a limited function: for example the chief's staff found among the Jokwe, Pende, Lunda, Luba and Songe, but also in the Dan tribe in West Africa. These sceptre staves represent the power of the chiefs and whenever one appears it is shown the same reverence as the chief himself. They generally have a human figure representing the original clan father or mother. They are exceptionally fine examples of the best African carving. Staves of the Luba tribe are mostly decorated with female figures. Their hands are laid on the breast and strings of beads often slung round the hips. The details of hair-style, features and scarification marks are executed with minute care. It is relevant to mention here the implements used by the

Luba for the preservation of regalia. They too are staves with females figures but the figure has a three-pronged fork sticking out of the head, on which arrows, bows and other attributes of the chieftain, worn on ceremonial occasions, are hung. These finely-carved staves are provided with an iron point for sticking in the ground.

The Jokwe carve human figures in the same style on their chief's staves as their ancestor figures, with hands touching the navel and a tall hair-style arranged in loops. There are, however, also staves with only a small head instead of the whole figure. These are found not only among the Jokwe but also in other Angola tribes, such as the Ngela, Lunda, Luena and so on. On the female heads the variations in hair-style are particularly remarkable. The dignitaries' staves of the lower Congo have quite a different appearance. They are decorated all round with human figures and with power symbols such as drums, trumpets and ornaments made of cowrie shells. Typical examples come from the Kakongo and the Mayombe, but also from West Africa, where the Atie of the Ivory Coast carve certain animals—symbols of their tribe—on the staves. These animals are sacred to a political totem group and may be neither killed nor eaten by its members.

The symbols of the chiefs' dignity also include parade axes and daggers or other ceremonial weapons. Because of their function they differ from the real weapons which inspired them in the changed form and rich decoation which demand great skill both from the woodcarver and the smith.

The crescent-shaped axes of the Pende were formerly used as power symbols when the human sacrifices were beheaded on the appointment of a new chief. The wife of the chief is still shown with this kind of axe in her hand. The art of the Congolese ceremonial weaponmaker was highly developed in the Kasai territory and once more it was the Songe who acquired the greatest skill. But beautiful ceremonial weapons were also produced in other parts of Africa, in Nigeria, Ghana and on the Ivory Coast. The handles of the daggers end in a human head and the metal blade is so fixed as to seem like a long tongue hanging out of the mouth. Metal and wood ceremonial knives are also attributes of the rulers. Their fretwork blades are often carved with grotesque forms.

Other material expressions of power and might are the stools or seats, even thrones, of the chiefs which should be differentiated from those used everyday. The chiefs' stools lay impressive emphasis in their symbolic decorations on the connection between the sacred power of the original ancestors and that of their earthly representatives. Usually the stool has a flat, circular or rectangular seat which is supported by different kinds of motifs, and the range of artistic solutions to the problem in view of its limited function is surprising. Usually the supporters are in the form of human or animal figures. There seems no end to the imaginative range of the sculptors so that it is very difficult to classify them schematically. A few examples must therefore suffice. Animal figures show quadrupeds such as lions, leopards and elephant, buffaloes, apes and fabulous beasts with human faces and these are especially loved by the Fon in Dahomey, but also in Cameroun and several Congo tribes such as the Luba and the Pende. Besides animals

* Pl. 81; Cat. 82

* Cat. 83

* Cat. 106, 107

such as birds, lizards and snakes, human figures, supporting the seat like caryatids, also play a large part. The seats of the Luba tribe are usually borne by a single female figure and this caryatid has developed over the course of time into the most important part of the whole seat. The actual seat is reduced to a minimum; it rests on the head and on the hands—raised sideways—of the woman, who may be portrayed standing, kneeling or squatting on her heels. The Luba also made seats with two caryatids standing together. All the minor tribes of the Luba used several variations of this basic scheme and those of the Master of Buli, with their strongly individual style, deserve especial notice.

These chiefs' stools, when not in use for official ceremonies were kept under the guardianship of the chief's first wife. Guarding the chair was an honourable task. Jokwe and Pende showed a great preference for crouching figures with knees drawn up. They sit on a disc-shaped base with elbows resting on their knees and hands on the head over which a similar disc-shaped seat rests. The Jokwe have a tendency to overdecorate their seats with large round-headed brass studs. Some Pende seats are borne by three outward-looking crouching figures. The link with the ancestors is finely expressed in some of the Dogon stools; the seat is borne by eight Pl. 82 figures representing the eight immortals who arranged ★ Pl. 83 the world before the birth of the first mortal man. Sometimes these figures are fitted in twos into the slightly curved pillars.

A further development of the simple stools described above is a back-rest or superstructure having a similar function. The Pende, for example, make stools with a conical foot and a figure of a warant or desert lizard. A large human figure is set on either side of the flat seat; one is a seated man wearing a chief's cap and the other a seated woman. The necks and torsos of the figures are especially powerfully carved because the man who uses the stool puts his arm round the neck of the figures and rests them on the upper part of the body.

A similar idea, differently executed, is found among the Jokwe and, due to their influence, also the Pende. The traditional seat has, in this case, a board-shaped fretwork carving as a back-rest and this is crowned with human figures. The seat has a completely different appearance among certain peoples of East Africa, for instance in Tanzania, and this has spread back to the Congo. A chief's throne of the Nyamwezi tribe has a disc-shaped seat borne on three small feet, and having a tall, semicircular back-rest, on the outside of which a large figure of a man with bent arms and legs is carved in high relief. The hands and head of the figure extend beyond the sides of the back-rest. A similar design is known to the Luba, though it is quite different from the anthropomorphic chairs. The cylindrical chair has a semicircular back-rest in this tribe also, the outside of which is completely covered with notched ornament. Over this a large snake carved in relief winds its way upwards. The chiefs' stools of the Kwele are the same shape.

European influence inspired seats exactly like our own. The African carvers copied the technique as well as form, for the chairs were not carved, as traditionally they would have been, out of a single piece, but are constructed in several sections. Examples of these chairs have been found in Senufo and Ashanti territory but also in Angola and the Congo, where they inspired a new syncretic art among the Jokwe and Pende. These chairs are carved with or without arm-rests. Back-rests and stretchers are decorated with original carving, with themes including European figures beside indigenous protective spirits. In the middle of the top crossbar at the back there is a round face carved in relief having the traditional Jokwe hair-style. A standing or seated figure is often placed on the supports of the arm-rests, but the richest work is usually on the stretchers: genre scenes and episodes of daily life, musicians with their instruments, nobles in sedan chairs, or people holding gourds of palm-wine. If Europeans are depicted they are often covered with white kaolin. They appear with bicycles or motor bikes and sometimes as soldiers. Such pictures of Europeans on an African chief's stool may seem very strange, but there is a plausible explanation: in these regions the Europeans always appeared as the representatives of a political power far greater than that possessed by indigenous rulers. They brought bicycles, guns and other unknown, unimagined things, linked in the mind of the Africans with the European power, which were therefore accepted as symbols of power and given the same standing as traditional symbols. This happened not only in the western Congo, where white influence had long been intensively at work, but also in Nigeria and Ghana where conflict with the Portuguese led to a remarkable degree of artistic syncretism.

CENTRALIZED POLITICAL POWER

So far we have discussed almost exclusively the effects of decentralized power, which is generally in the hands of people described as chiefs, with power usually only over their own clan. Now we must further examine the powerful organizations that extend beyond the single clan, embracing several together in sub-tribes and these, ultimately, in large tribes or peoples. We shall also discuss centralized power groups with an absolute ruler at their head, who—exactly like the chiefs—receives his power from the ancestors. The difference then is only one of degree, the principle is exactly the same, except that everything is more sharply defined, even in art. The organizations of state power developed independently throughout Africa's past. Many kingdoms disintegrated completely after a period of prosperity, as for instance the medieval kingdoms of the Mali and Songhai, the Congo Zimbabwe, Luba, Lunda and Zulu states. Others still held together until this century and only collapsed when modern political pressures became overwhelming: the Mossi kingdom under the *mogho naba* in Upper Volta, the Tutsi of Rwanda and Burundi under the *mwami* and the Ganda under the *bwaka*. Others still exist today, yet politically speaking they are no longer of consequence. They signify rather a sacred element in which the sense of national unity of the people is founded. Such are the emirates of northern Nigeria; the kingdom of the *asantehene* of the Ashanti in Ghana; the Yoruba kingdom under the *oni* in Ife and the kingdom of Benin under the *oba*; the kingdom of the Fon in Dahomey; the Sultanates of Cameroun; the kingdom of Bunyoro in

Pl. 82 Dogon (Mali). Round stool, supported by four pairs of ancestors. Wood, h. 28 cm. Dr. M. Kofler Collection, Riehen/Basle.

Pl. 83 Kwele (Congo-Kinshasa). Chief's chair with four heart-shaped faces, two of which can be seen to be women. Black wood, white painting, h. 98 cm. Museum Rietberg, Zurich.

155

Buganda and the kingdom of the Kuba under the *nyimi* in the Congo.

In all these cases power has been consolidated in a strict system of ceremonial procedure followed rigidly by the king and the aristocracy which consists of his relatives. This system is confined within the palace walls and often results in the formation of a miniature city within the city proper. Here, around the person of the divine king and his family, the various ceremonial cults are carried out, far removed from the common people for whom the king represents the divine ancestors. It should not, however, be concluded that the king is himself divine. He also is mortal, but as a direct descendant—patrilinear or matrilinear—of the sacred founder of the kingdom, he possesses the divine power which enables him to provide a good and happy life for his people. But if the king falls sick his country is threatened with evil.

It is very difficult for Western man, accustomed to democratic ideas of government, to understand the structure of the African state. We can, of course, appreciate the material products of a culture based on these principles, but the emotional significance and symbolic power which they had for many thousands and indeed still partly have, is very alien. This is not to prevent our recognition of the quality of the works of art that have fallen into our hands. They are the products of a court art, created by the very best available craftsmen. This is one of the few places where traditions can be traced over long periods, for the objects that served for the glorification of the ruler and his family were preserved in the palaces for centuries. Such pieces have only recently emerged from the closed circle of the court, to find their way to Europe or America.

A knowledge of this tradition may help to deepen our understanding of the background of African art. The objects, however significant they may be for us, are, however, not all, for the genealogies of the ruling families are also of great importance. These genealogies, carefully preserved and handed down from generation to generation, recount the miraculous story of the tribal founder and the history of his descendants, in the direct line. Trained professional singers regularly relate the epic deeds and heroic achievements to the common people. Thus, by emphasizing and legalizing their mythical ancestry the dynasty ensured its position, extending and consolidating its religious and political might far beyond mere local significance. The members of the dynasty successfully created a state that governed a whole people. These are described as kingdoms. It is not very important that many details of transmitted history do not agree too exactly with sober reality, for the religious, mythical view of the world is rigidly ordered and in itself logical. After all, the early Christian legend is a question of faith too, and this is worth remembering as we examine the following category of objects.

First the so-called figures of kings made by the Kuba in the Congo. A genealogical line of one hundred and twenty-four kings is supposed to have reigned since the foundation of the kingdom. Of these many, especially in the early period, must be legendary. They come from the sub-group of the Mbala (not to be confused with the other tribe of the same name living in another part of the Congo) who joined with several other tribes, among them the Ngongo and Ngendi, to form the Kuba federal state. The state is held to have enjoyed the greatest period of prosperity under the ninety-third king, Shamba Bolongongo (1600-1620), who was a peace-loving ruler and forbade the use of the fearful *shongo*, a throwing knife. It was he who began the pro-

* Pl. 84

duction of raffia-work, *musese*, introduced the smoking of tobacco, and a board game called *lela* with twelve divisions, which was to supersede the game of dice. It is said that this prince was the first to have his portrait carved in wood. The portrait has been preserved, and it displays all the characteristics which appear again and again on later pieces, and which may be taken as essential marks of the Kuba style. The prince is depicted sitting with crossed legs on a rectangular base, his hands resting on his knees. He wears the royal headdress decorated with cowrie shells around a straight border and a belt with cowrie shells around the waist. In his left hand he holds a royal knife, the handle pointing forward and the horizontal blade towards the back. The portrait figure carries an emblem that is closely connected with the reign of the prince and hence has become a symbol for the prince himself: this is the *lela* board game, placed on the pedestal in front of the figure. This portrait was the model for all those subsequent kings, which are all done in the same style. Consequently, although each one was supposedly a portrait from life, they became stereotyped and cling closely to a tradition which imposed itself unwittingly on the sculptor's hand. The number of authentic royal portraits among those that have been preserved is not exactly known. Some think only nine, others suggest twelve or nineteen figures. It is certainly

possible that the figures were copied and accepted as authentic by collectors.

The one hundred and seventh Kuba king, Misha Pelenge Che, whose reign is placed in the second half of the eighteenth century, carries a drum as a personal emblem. The one hundred and eighth, Bope Pelenge, has an anvil—Kata Mbula, the one hundred and ninth (1800-1810) is again portrayed with a drum and Mikope Mbula (1810-1840), the one hundred and tenth, has a small female figure as an emblem, undoubtedly representing a freed slave whom he married.

Tradition has it that the portrait of the ruling king was carved while he was still alive and kept hidden. When the prince felt that his end was near he had himself shut up with the portrait so that it should take up his last breath. In this way the portrait figures became the guardians and intermediaries of the sacred power which was taken over by the successor to the dead ruler. The sacred fount of life endowed by the ancestors never went astray.

In essentials the Kuba produced court art, though its characteristics spread well beyond the court circle. Reserved for the kings, and therefore a symbol of great power, were the seats, in the case of the Kuba, stools with a disc-like seat and foot and a central supporting pillar slightly waisted in the middle. Several board-like convex carved supports between seat and foot give the stool a delicate elegance. The royal drums too played an important part. They were held in awe as especially important symbols of royal dignity and handled with great reverence. They are slim, single-skinned drums with a cylindrical body, tapering off towards the base

which ends in a round flat foot. Sometimes the body of the drum is broadened out like a swelling directly below the tightly-drawn skin, or occasionally it may be conical, with the broad lower end resting on a pedestal, which has the form of a stool with a central pillar and several bent supports roundabout. The drums have a relatively small vertically notched handle on the upper part and sometimes also a human face, furnished with a hand on the lower part. The body of the drum is partly or completely covered with geometrical patterns, clearly inspired by the ornament of the raffia-work.

* Cat. 103, 104

Similar drums are known to the Lele, whose art is strongly influenced by the Kuba: these Lele drums also display, as well as the crocodile figures and human faces, the beautiful linear designs of the weavers' patterns.

Drums are also attributes of royalty in the East African lake kingdom. At the Tutsi courts of Rwanda and Burundi several sets of large cylindrical drums are preserved. The traditional rhythms beaten on them with sticks are incredibly complicated. The drums are only used on special occasions which concern the *mwami* or his family. The same is true of the royal drums belonging to the Bunyoro and Ganda.

Royal kingdoms developed also in the grasslands of Cameroun. The central power lay in the hands of the king, but it was moderated by the decentralized claims to power of the secret societies, always controlled by a relative of the king. Among the kings, known as *fon*, Nyoya of Bamum recently attained considerable fame. The grassland cultures are all very similar and the same unity is apparent in art, allowing an overall picture of the area to be formed. There is, however, considerable variation

in detail, because the artists enjoyed great freedom in the individual interpretation of traditional themes. The art of Cameroun is also primarily a court art with the glorification of the king's position as its aim. This is clearly seen in the architecture of the houses, which form a palace complex and especially in the house of the ancestor cult. The doors are covered with fine rich carving and the accentuated door-frames consist of heavy straight posts and rather narrower crosspieces that serve as lintel and threshold. The posts are carved with human figures one above the other, often interspersed with animal figures in lively compositions displaying an exceptional sense of rhythm. The crosspieces are generally less richly decorated, perhaps with a row of human faces, stylized crouching figures or animals. The pillars forming the façade of these houses, look as if they were supporting the roof, but they serve chiefly as decoration. They too are completely covered with carved figures. Figures, standing one above the other, are sometimes carved in three dimensions, sometimes as Janus-figures, while the pillars are vaguely reminiscent of American Indian totem poles. Together with the doorposts they form a harmonious unity, that gives the buildings an impressive appearance. The themes depict important events in the reigns of a certain *fon*, and occasionally he himself is portrayed with his chief wife, surrounded by power symbols such as the leopard and the python. The pillars may illustrate a whole family tree, matrilinear or patrilinear, as may be. In the ancestor-, or cult house the objects which are symbols of royal power and also play a part in the ceremonies of the ancestor cult of the ruling family are preserved. There are near life-size ancestor figures, seated or standing, arranged in a long row. These represent the portraits of dead kings, their mothers and wives, the latter depicted as pregnant or suckling a child. Other equally large figures are the *chinda*, servants. At official feasts they are placed on either side of the throne. They hold everyday objects such as the king's arrows in their hands, or, in an expression of homage, cover their mouths with their hands. These figures show a peculiar decorative technique popular and common in the court of Cameroun: inlaywork. The older figures still found from time to time among the Bamum tribe are thickly inlaid with cowrie shells, while later pieces have applied work of imported beads or rather small glass rods. Gourds may be completely covered with beads in a similar fashion. Such gourds are royal attributes and are used for drinking palm-wine; they have a long neck and are furnished with a broad, cylindrical foot. Tradition demands that every royal gourd should contain a bone from the skull of a dead *fon*, and hence they are sacred objects. The bead decoration of blue, white and dark red is infinitely variable and combines into *fasces*, zig-zag lines, herringbone and circular patterns. The stoppers of the gourds are carved with chameleons, hornbills and buffalo heads. The thrones of the *fon* also deserve special mention. They are true thrones with rich decoration revealing the highly developed art of the wood-carvers. Every ruling *fon* has a new throne made for him, but the queen mother and all officials who represent the king also have the right to possess a throne of their own. The thrones of dead rulers are sacred objects preserved in the ancestor house. These thrones are carved out of a single block of wood and resemble a round table; the seat is round and flat, supported by numerous outward-looking figures standing on a low, disc-shaped base. Sometimes there are leopards or snakes between the human figures or occasionally lizards, apes and buffalo heads. Some thrones are supported by two, even three rows of figures one above the other, others rest on one or two large carved animals and have a back-rest in the form of a human guardian. Others again are completely anthropomorphic; they are carved in the shape of a large, seated human figure bearing the actual seat in its own hands.

Cat. 101, 102

These three basic forms may appear in several variations and the style of decoration is variegated too, but the most remarkable are probably the thrones covered all over with glass beads. In later times copies of European chairs were also carved, or stools imported and covered with glass beads to fit in with local tradition.

Finally we must mention the great royal drums which are made especially for the coronation of every *fon*. They consist of two horizontal slit drums each carved from a single tree; their ends depict the *fon* and his predecessor, or they may be in the form of a leopard or chameleon. Some examples of the Bamileke tribe end in a powerful abstract elephant head, whose large circular ears and horizontal tusks create a remarkably fierce expression.

The style of carving found in the grasslands of Cameroun must also be mentioned here. The plastic style of the Baule has been described as containing the best elements of African art and has been taken therefore as the most suitable introduction to the study of African art. The opposite is true of the art of Cameroun. Scarcely any other style of Africa—possibly with the exception

Pl. 85 Ife (Nigeria). Portrait head. Clay, h. 23.5 cm. 13th century. British Museum, London.

Pl. 86 Ife (Nigeria). Portrait head of an oni. Bronze, h. 35 cm. 13th century. British Museum, London.

of the Yoruba—has so exploited the repetitive element in design as to lend the whole composition a strongly rhythmical impression. African art in general is characterised by three-dimensional carving, but the Cameroun is exceptional in building complex designs out of essential details, an artistic approach which one would expect to find in Asia or Oceania, rather than in Africa, though by this I do not wish to infer any possible connection between these continents.

It has already been seen that in the art of the Kuba the dimension of time—history—plays an important part in royal art. This principle is even more clearly seen in the court art of the West African kingdoms. First the Yoruba: as we know the Yoruba country consists of numerous small kingdoms, whose rulers, *oni* or *oba*, inhabit palaces in the capital city of their kingdom. All these princes trace their ancestry back to Oduduwa, the Yoruba culture hero. Oduduwa founded Ile Ife, the holy city of the Yoruba; and it is ruled by the *oni*, whose omnipotence as sacred ruler is still recognized by all the minor princes. Nevertheless in the fifteenth century conquerors from Nupe in the east with new strategic weapons such as horses, managed to subdue the land. They founded a secular government under their *alafin* in Oyo in the northern Yoruba country. Surprisingly enough they completely absorbed the Yoruba culture in the course of time.

Mythological and historical events are so closely linked in Yoruba history that the appearance of certain forms of art and techniques that have astonished the modern world pose many as yet unsolved questions.

Frobenius, William and Bernard Fagg and Willet have clarified many problems by their research. Unfortunately it is not possible to discuss the subject in detail here and the reader is advised to turn to the specialized studies. Our main interest is the function of court art in the Yoruba tribe and we must therefore look towards Ife where the finest works of art were produced. Even today new and exciting finds can sometimes be added to those pieces which have been handed down from generation to generation as possessions of the *oni*, and thus objects of the state cult.

The terracotta heads of the thirteenth century date Pl. 85 from the greatest period of Ife. These nearly life-size memorial heads—formerly parts of complete figures— were made from moulds. The remarkable realism of the heads has led to the assumption that they were probably memorial heads of kings and their families. Since the discovery of these naturalistic reproductions of the human face, so unusual in African art, a good many opposing theories as to their origin have been put forth. Some look to Mediterranean and Egyptian influence, other suggest a local African development from the earliest Nok culture which flourished in northern Nigeria, between the fifth and first centuries B.C. on the plateau now known as Jos.

Whatever the true answer the naturalistic reproduction of the facial features was, already by the thirteenth century, a characteristic of a definite style, displayed not only in the terracotta heads but also in the bronzes, found in Ife. The bronze-casting technique, the level of which was never again attained either in Ife or anywhere else among the Yoruba, was of an astonishing technical skill. Traditionally it dates from the reign of the third *oni* descendant of Oduduwa, Obalufon II. The faces of the bronze heads are incised with fine vertical ridges with small holes about the mouth and chin, perhaps for holding coral beads. There are no known bodies to these life-size heads; they probably had wooden bodies and were set up as symbols of royal dignity. Masks have also been found in the same style and there was a discovery not long ago, in 1957, of the bronze figure of an *oni* in full regalia with headdress, necklace and carrying royal attributes. A double figure is also known which probably represents an *oni* with his wife. Cult objects were found beside the figures, among them a small bronze ritual cup. It consists of a round vessel supported by a cylindrical pillar on a round, flat foot. A bow-shaped handle sticks out of the pillar supported by a miniature stool; above it on the wall of the vessel is the head, carved almost in the round, of a queen, while her body is presented in relief all round the cup. It is an unusually beautiful object, its form being derived from the *apere*, the ritual stool made either of quartz, stone or bronze. Other things discovered were heavy bronze armlets and staves.

Many of the pieces found are now in museums in Nigeria, Europe and the United States, yet there are still some which are held in awe beside cult objects of later periods. The highly-developed court art of Ife makes it understandable, that even the smaller rulers who were related to the royal house should copy the style of life of the *oni*. As representatives of the *oni* they still reign today under various titles such as *alaye* (Efon), *owa* (Ileshi), *ewa* (Ado), *ogoga* (Ikere) *alafin* (Oyo), or *alake* (Abeokuta). Their power has scarcely any real significance now, yet they are symbols of the well-being of the people and therefore the annual ceremonies connected with them are still carried out regardless of the modern ideas of government which have established themselves. Of all royal and sacred status symbols the crown decorated with beads and the glass bead veil covering the face are certainly the most striking. There are also other crowns, hereditary pieces, or presents, all of which have special functions. The traditional power of the *oni* and the related rulers is only a faint shadow of the splendour of earlier times, yet many of the smaller kings have succeeded in constructing famous palaces and bringing honour to their line through the court artists. And although the famous bronze-casting technique of former times was lost, wood-carving took its place in a style reminiscent of folk art. Some of the sculptors who worked for a royal court are even known by name. They made giant figures, portraits of the princes and their wives in wood and no detail bearing on the status of the ruler is ever neglected. A frequent motif of court art is the rider with a lance or gun, and a sword, who is known by the generic name, *jagun-jagun* mentioned earlier; he is supposed to represent Obatala, one of the apotheosized Yoruba ancestors.

The palaces were also furnished with carved wooden pillars, that supported the overhanging roof of the inner court. Row upon row of men who have played a part in the history of the ruling family are carved on them. They are colourfully painted figures but, although very fine, they lack the monumental vitality of the pillars of Cameroun. On the other hand the very few carved doors that have been preserved from the palaces

Pl. 87 *Yoruba (Nigeria). Sacrificial bowl for the river-* orisha: *osun, carried by a* jagun-jagun *horseman. Wood, h. 76 cm. Early 20th century. Museum Rietberg, Zurich.*

are very pleasing. Lively scenes in bas-relief draw on events which must have made a deep impression, such as the appearance of the first bicycles; occasionally they depict such legendary scenes as Obatala as a rider. Comparable are the pictures on the doors of the palace at Abomey, capital of the formerly notorious Fon kingdom in Dahomey. The scenes are, however, not so richly carved as on the Yoruba doors, but present individual symbols; ceremonial swords, axes, guns, the sun and moon, snakes curled up with their tails in their mouths, or lions.

The traditional power of the *oni* was effectively limited by the sudden changes of the last century, yet the last *oni*, Adesoyi Aderemi, unhesitatingly took up a ministerial position in the new government when Nigeria became an independent state in 1960. The destiny of the neighbouring city state of *oba* of Benin was different. The history of the Benin kingdom and its divine rulers also rests partly on mythological events, but here we are on firmer ground than at Ife. European history informs us that in 1472 the Portuguese Sequeira discovered the city of Benin and it was the Portuguese once more in 1485, under the leadership of d'Aveira, who made the first European contacts with Benin. In the seventeenth century other Europeans took the place of the Portuguese, and it is from the contemporary reports of the Dutchman Dapper of 1668 that we receive an impression of the glory and richness of Benin's prosperity. Its last secrets were only surrendered several hundred years later, when after a punitive expedition by the English in 1897 the capital city went up in flames and the *oba* Ovoramwen was exiled. Benin's art treasures, pre-

served for centuries within the palace walls, were brought to light and came to Europe as the spoils of war, where people gazed with wonder at these incredibly splendid pieces, more beautiful than anything ever before seen from Africa. The highly developed *cire perdue* casting technique and the fine ivory-carvings made such a deep impression that it was simply not believed that technical skill of this standard could possibly be inherently African. Almost at once theories evolved by which the art of Benin was ascribed to an external origin. In contrast to the art of Ife Benin was represented by a relatively large number of pieces, probably about two thousand. Scholars were at last given the chance to form some kind of chronology with material examples to study. But it was not so easy; Africa did not want to give up her secrets without a struggle and although many scholars attacked the problem intensively they came to different conclusions. Even today much remains unclear, but it can be said that William Fagg's chronology, which recognizes three periods, is undoubtedly a good starting point for further research. In this work it is only possible to examine the objects and the interested reader is again advised to look to specialized studies for more detailed information.

The greater part of the pieces from the palace are in the *cire perdue* technique. The rest are ivories and a few wood-carvings.

The technique of bronze-casting is supposed to have come from Ife. At that time Benin was subject to Ife and the *oba* were descendants of a son of the *oni* of Ife. Oguola, the sixth *oba* of this dynasty, is supposed to have asked the *oni* to send him a master craftsman who could teach the art of bronze-casting in Benin. And the *oni* sent him Igu'egha, who taught the Bini their craft. This must have happened towards the end of the thirteenth century. Igu'egha was made a culture hero by the bronze-smiths after his death. This story is a legendary explanation of a phenomenon which played an important part in the enhancement of the king's house, and fits well into the framework of traditional African history, but it must be made clear that no relationship has ever been certainly established between the bronzes of Ife and those of Benin, the true origin of which is equally mysterious.

The finest bronzes were made in the course of the fifteenth century and belong to the first period. They are æsthetically fine, hollow-cast portrait heads executed in realistic style with very thin walls—only an eighth of an inch thick. The hair is built up in several overlapping, horizontal steps and in each one the hair is ordered in regular vertical strands. Above the eyes are four perpendicular swollen scarification marks. A broad collar patterned in coral beads forms the base of the head. A little later, in the early sixteenth century, a portrait head representing the queen mother was made. This was the first time that the *oba* Esigie introduced the title of queen mother for his mother Idia. Her portrait shows a headdress with a tall point made of a wide-meshed network of semi-precious stones and corals. The same scarification marks and broad coral neckband are present here too.

Although a certain naturalism is present in these heads they differ from the very individualized Ife heads in their rigid stylization which became even more marked in later times.

★ Pl. 88, 89

Pl. 88   Benin (Nigeria). Bronze plaque with a warrior in full armour, h. 40 cm. 17th century. Museum Rietberg, Zurich.

Pl. 89   Benin (Nigeria). Bronze plaque with two warriors. H. 51.2 cm. 17th century. British Museum, London.

Dating from the middle of the sixteenth century to the beginning of the eighteenth are bronze plaques with representations of kings, warriors, servants and foreigners cast in high relief. From Dapper's descriptions we learn that the wooden pillars of the palace at that time were covered from head to foot with these plaques. Two hundred years later, at the time of the punitive expedition, none of them were to be seen. The plaques were no longer used and were stored, along with many other old works of art, in the storehouses of the palace. On the oldest of them, Portuguese soldiers are frequently seen armed with helmet, cuirass, halberd and gun. The seventeenth-century plaques represent the people of Benin. The smallest details have been preserved in the

bronze and these plaques are like a richly decorated picture book, providing many details of clothing, appearances, weapons, musical instruments of the people, not only of the Benin kingdom, but also sometimes of other tribes of Nigeria. There are heroic and hunting scenes, ceremonial and ritual events that took place in the reigns of different rulers and were immortalized by these decorations in bronze to the glory of the dynasty. Other plaques have leopards, crocodiles and mud-fish. To the second or middle period, which lasted till about the middle of the eighteenth century, belong also the heavy heads, to which large carved elephant teeth are attached. This type was introduced by the *oba* Eresonye about 1740. The heads have tall coral collars reaching to the lips and a small cap woven of coral beads, from which long coral ropes hang down on either side of the face.

Decline set in during the third period that ended in the late nineteenth century. Power of expression weakened and finally gave way to soulless copying. About 1816, the time of the *oba* Osemwede, the head-dress was enriched with two wing-like additions and the broad neckbands were placed on a flat raised ring. Pl. xxi

There are many other artistic products besides the most imposing bronze pieces we have just mentioned: figures of the *oba*, of warriors and riders, or cult objects for altars or to be borne along in processions during dances and ceremonies. Cocks decorated the altars of the queen mother or those of the mothers of high dignitaries. On ceremonial occasions water was poured over the *oba's* hands from vessels made in the form of a ram or a leopard. Snakes and birds embellished the towers of the palace and small ornament masks were carved hang- Pl. 90

ing on the belt. One object, known as the "altar of the hand" is rather peculiar. It is a small, cylindrical altar shrine, covered with human and animal figures in varying arrangements and furnished at the top with a rectangular opening intended for the reception of offerings.

Ivory carvings are far less well represented than bronze-casting. A few rare pieces have been preserved from the sixteenth and seventeenth centuries, of which two small masks have become world famous. One of the masks has a wreath of small Portuguese heads, one of which is broken off, as a hair ornament. Around the neck is a coral necklace. The other mask could be a double mask, and it too has a wreath of seven Portuguese heads, alternating in this case with heads of different form, one of which is missing. Unfortunately the collar,

167

which displays a further eleven Portuguese heads is also damaged. In style these masks are similar to the bronze heads, They are a symbol of divine kingship, which is also true of the ivory leopards, known in several small, and two larger examples. The two larger leopards are constructed of several pieces of ivory and made to stand alone. Long armbands were also made of ivory, decorated in bas-relief and motifs include Portuguese riders, snakes, leopards and mud-fish. Ivory also served to make staves, fly-swats, and trumpets. Smaller decorative elements, ridges or notches, are often emphasized by inlays of brass nails or brass strips. The question as to the function of Benin art can be easily answered because creative art was exclusively done for the *oba*. All these objects were power symbols, in which the idea of the divine ruler was embodied. They supported the sacred power, symbolised in the person of the *oba* and responsible for the well-being of the people. The theory that a work of art only realizes its full value in its proper cultural context is truer of Africa than anywhere else, for many of these pieces have very little æsthetic appeal when observed coldly in the showcases of museums. They could only develop their true power as a focal point on the altars and shrines in the midst of the bloody sacrificial ceremonies and surrounded by an atmosphere charged with the overwhelming power of the sacred ancestors.

The Bini could not easily forget their splendid past and soon after the English punitive expedition they elected a new *oba*. The present *oba*, Akenzua II, a grandson of the exiled *oba*, tries, as nearly as possible, to follow the way of life of his predecessors. He does everything

to breathe new life into the old arts and crafts and is, up to a point, successful. In Benin today bronze-work is being produced and although the quality is only moderate, there are exceptions which give hope for the future. And when the *oba* carries out his religious duties as the centre of a small so-called 'kingdom', through the coral beads and ceremonies with queens and courtiers in full parade there shines the memory of the glory of former times. A last example of sacred kingship is offered by the Ashanti kingdom in Ghana. The Ashanti have been able to preserve their traditions better even than Ife and Benin. And the symbolic effect of the sacred power is clearer, as it is far more powerful than the ancestor cult and justifies the description of divine power. This might is drawn from the sun and the moon, its symbol is the golden stool, in which is enshrined the unity of the Ashanti people. This is not to say that the ancestors play no part at all: on the contrary, here too linear descent is decisive, for of all the seven matrilinear clans which make up the Ashanti, there is only one which provides the kings or *asantehene*. He is at the head of a confederation of states each one of which is ruled by an *omanhene*, forming the Ashanti state. The kingdom was founded in 1701 by Osei Tutu with its capital at Kumasi. The legend runs that Osei Tutu was once seated beneath a *kumnini* tree when in an extraordinary way the powers of nature were let loose, the air filled with dust and thunder, and a stool covered partly with gold having two bells floated gently down from heaven and came to rest on Osei Tutu's knees. This stool which is so sacred that it must never touch the earth, contains the *sunsum*, the collective soul of the Ashanti people. So the

* Pl. 91

golden stool is a symbol of power, riches and health. There are many other stools beside this great national one. In the Chapel of stools blackened stools of earlier rulers are preserved, and sacrifices regularly made. The new *asantehene* at his ordination sits briefly three times on the stool of his predecessor—a ceremony which symbolizes the uninterrupted line of royal power. Stools belonging to the *omanhene*, and other important political or religious figures who are honoured as representatives of the ancestors, have a similar significance.

* Pl. 92

The basic type has a rectangular seat, a cylindrical hollow supporting pillar carved in fretwork, and a flat base, its form following that of the seat, though it may be smaller and round. The edges of the seat are slightly turned upward. Apart from this basic type there are naturally numerous variations. Sometimes, for instance, the central pillar has four thinner ones beside it, or the upper surface of the stool can be adorned with metal sheeting. In these ancestor stools—one assumes in the central pillar—the *sunsum* is preserved. No one ever sat

Pl. 92 *Ashanti (Ghana). Ancestor stool with a central pillar used as a seat for the* sunsum. *Wood, h. 54 cm., l. 70 cm. Museum voor Land- en Volkenkunde, Rotterdam.*

Pl. XXI *Benin (Nigeria). Portrait head of an oba. A large, carved elephant's tusk was inserted in the head. Bronze, h. 52.8 cm. Early 19th century. Rijksmuseum voor Volkenkunde, Leiden.*

on these stools. There were chairs called *asipem* modelled on the European shape for that purpose, and actually used as thrones. They are decorated with brass nails in patterns forming royal symbols. Even the golden stool (it is made of wood and only sparingly decorated) has its respective *asipem* which is decorated with gold nails and gold sheeting.

The Ashanti are matrilinear, and therefore the queen mother, the *ohemaa*, plays an important part. She is the true owner of the state, and therefore the *asantehene* of the Ashanti, the *omanhene* or petty rulers are all ordained by her. She is seen as the daughter of the moon, and silver is her attribute. Her son, the ruler, is the son of the sun, and his metal is gold. The sun is an everlasting, dynamic, life-giving principle which is the centre of the universe, and its powerful rays reach every corner of the sky. The *asantehene* is the representative and incorporation of this source of power on earth, and therefore the life-giving centre of the state. The life-power, called *kra*, is found in every man; yet it is manifested most strongly in the king. When the king dies, or rather when he sets off on his last journey, then his *kra* returns straight to the sun. Formerly the queens, the whole court, and all his slaves, had to follow the king into death to accompany his *kra* on its long journey.

Gold, symbol of life and exclusive privilege of the kings, made from the very beginning a great impression on European visitors to the Ashanti kingdom. The description 'Gold Coast' is relevant, for gold was held to be the sacred life-giving principle, and only kings were allowed to weigh out the gold-dust required by the goldsmiths for cult objects. To weigh the gold, small

gold weights were used, a whole series of which is today in the possession of the *asantehene*. Gold for trade with foreigners was apportioned with similar weights made of brass. Gold was needed for ritual purposes, not only in the form of dust, but also carved into all kinds of cult objects—insignia and decorations expressing religious and symbolic values. Fortunately many of these objects still have a role to play in state ceremonies, though, unfortunately, we cannot describe them here in detail. We will only establish that the basic symbols are often the sun, the moon, or some other royal emblem, and that behind the many symbols are religious and philosophical theories about the *kra* and other metaphysical concepts.

A different symbolism however is to be found in many objects, the proverbs for instance that are so

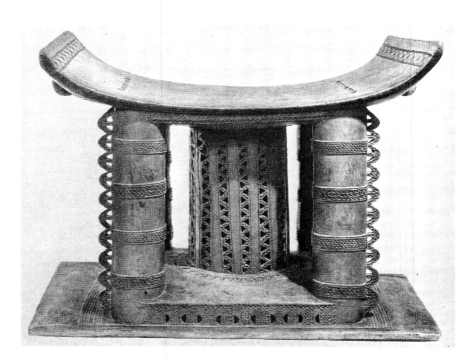

Pl. 93 *Ashanti (Ghana). Ring in the shape of the* betene *palm. Gold, h. 4.5 cm. Rijksmuseum voor Volkenkunde, Leiden.*

Pl. 94 *Baule (Ivory Coast). Door, probably from a clan shrine. The buffalo mask is associated with the sky god Niamie. Wood, with traces of white painting, h. 130 cm. Museum Rietberg, Zurich.*

popular in many parts of Africa, and this is where we must look for the meaning of the crocodiles, cockerels, doves, lions, and so forth which appear as small figures in gold or gold inlay on the scabbards of ceremonial swords or on the staves and state umbrellas of dignitaries. The same spirit inspired the clay reliefs on the palace walls of the Fon rulers in Abomey, although they are completely different in conception. These widely differing polychrome scenes may be regarded as puzzle pictures or picture stories. Their content, however, is not of a profane nature, but serves only for the glorification of the royal heroic deeds. The same interpretation can also be applied to the bronze plaques of Benin.

The soul-discs, called *akrafo-konmu*, are remarkable objects. They were insignia of the leaders or soul-bearers—persons, therefore, who had the right to represent the *omanhene*, whose *kra* was handed over to them at certain ceremonies. The gold soul-discs are decorated with incised ornament, showing clearly the motif of the sun. This gold jewellery is an example of the high quality of goldsmith's work; there are Pl. 93 hair, neck, and breast ornaments, rings, armlets, decorative pieces that were fitted to the sandals, and golden masks.

Bronze was worked at the court also, and the bronze-smiths trace their descent from the same Igu'egha of Ife who was supposed to have brought the technique of bronze-casting to Benin. The Ashanti made ceremonial pieces almost exclusively—bells, covered bowls, vessels, lamps, and jugs. But their bronze-work is not able to arouse the same admiration as the Benin bronzes. An exception may be cited in the bronze vessels known as Cat. 63 *kuduo*—tall-sided vessels cast by the *cire perdue* process, and having a flat or slightly rounded cover. Usually they are supported by a circular base, swelling slightly outwards, and furnished with vertical supports. The walls of these vessels are occasionally decorated in relief on old pieces, but more commonly they have a linear, incised design in the shape of the religious symbols mentioned above. The covers often have carefully executed three-dimensional groups of men or animals—a leopard attacking an antelope, a procession of musicians, and so on. The *kuduo* were used at purification rites. Filled with gold dust and other vital ingredients they were also buried with the dead. Several vessels of this type were found in the former mausoleum of the Ashanti kings in Bantama, not far from Kumasi.

Pl. XXII Ebri (left), Baule (right) (Ivory Coast). Two gold masks, carried by the kings on their swords, h. c. 7 cm. Museum Rietberg, Zurich.

173

We have not yet mentioned the *kente* cloths which were the privileged possession of the *asantehene, omanhene*, and the queen mother. These long cloth bands, leaving one shoulder uncovered, are still greatly treasured today. However, because the traditional rules are somewhat less stringent than formerly, the *kente* cloths are now worn as a kind of state dress and status symbol by other classes of officials. The cloths are sewn together from long, narrow bands of material, into which at regular intervals stripes of red, brown, yellow, and green were woven horizontally.

The Baule, Agni, and Abron, like the Ashanti, belong to the larger ethnic group of the Akan, and some elements, summarized briefly in connection with the Ashanti kingdom, are common to all. Shortly after the foundation of the Ashanti kingdom, after the death of Osei Tutu, a war of inheritance broke out between Aura Poku, a queen mother, and her brother, Dako. Aura Poku had to flee and, with her attendants, reached the Ivory Coast, where she founded the Baule kingdom which, like the Ashanti, is based on gold. The Baule also made fine gold weights and highly developed goldsmiths' work. Good examples are provided by the gold pendants in the shape of a human face or a ram's head, all cast by the *cire perdue* method.

The Baule carved the emblems of members of their ruling house on their doors. The position is absolutely different, however, from those of the Yoruba, for the Baule doors show only one or two central motifs which give a definite rhythm to the whole surface. For instance, one palace door has been preserved on which two elephants are carved, one above the other, expressing the desire for power and long life. The upper elephant is supposed to stand for the rule of the queen mother Aura Poku, and the one below for her grandson Kuaku Anugbele. Other Baule doors are decorated with Pl. 94 mythological themes, such as fish or rams.

★ Pl. xxii

ECONOMICS

A large part of the plastic art of Africa has been discussed from the social viewpoint—something which should cause no surprise, since relationships between men are grouped in every culture under the social heading. These are processes of developing communications between the individual and society without which no culture can continue. An essential element of communication with a group is the individual's ability to express himself, an ability (when certain claims and factors are realized) to make himself understood. When such social contacts have once been taken up, the process can theoretically take on every imaginable form within the framework of a given culture, and may, in certain circumstances, also manifest itself as art. That kind of process arising out of the development of any given expression, which may be realized somehow as a recognizable work of art, is present in every culture.

In Africa the stress was laid on wood sculpture, which was created as an expression of social relationships. If, on the other hand, we examine the works of art connected with economics, it is immediately apparent that they are much fewer in number.

The hunt, with which we must begin our discussion, has by its very nature little to do with art, however important it may be for the economy of certain cultures. I have briefly described above several African hunting communities, and suggested reasons why art plays such a minor part in them, although there are a few exceptions which should be cited.

Rock-paintings, which were mentioned earlier during the historical introduction, really belong to this group, and here the astonishing fact must be recorded that the splendid talent of the painted hunting scenes (whether the prehistoric scenes in the Sahara or the later ones of the Bushmen) has never reappeared among the Negroes of any other region, nor has it survived among the Bushmen. It is extinct. Rock-painting was clearly so closely linked with the magic hunt rituals that it could have arisen only in the specific circumstances of those communities, and it would be interesting to look for parallels in those hunting communities which may have been responsible for the cave-paintings of southern France and northern Spain. That, however, would be to overstep the bounds of this work.

For many Negro peoples hunting, accompanied by some form of agriculture or horticulture, is an economic necessity. In such cases hunters, under the leadership of the most successful man, are sometimes organized into a kind of guild, which is divided into grades in exactly the same way as the secret societies, with rights, responsibilities, and tests. To this class belong the dances with animal masks which were executed before the hunt as a magical condition of success. It is a situation we find among many of the woodland people of West Africa, the Gere, Wobe, Dan, Bete, and Guro, and among others, the Nupe and Afo in north Nigeria, and the Jokwe and Ngola in Angola.

Fishing is the basis of the economy with other peoples, such as the Genia in the Congo, the Bozo on the Niger, the Ijo in the delta of the Niger, and the Nago peoples who live in the lake-dwellings near Cotonou in Dahomey. The hunt, of course, is also used by agricultural peoples as a supplement to their vegetable production.

Hunting magic, which is supposed to guarantee

follow more easily. These wooden bells are carved out of one piece into the shape of a thick hollowed disc. On one edge is fixed a loop and opposite there is an opening from which hang two or three small clappers. The surfaces of the disc are generally convex. Much care is usually expended on the production of the bells which are decorated with finely carved human faces or intricate geometric patterns. Hunters' pipes of wood or ivory are also found in the Congo, generally left undecorated but of fine shape.

In the field of agriculture and farming we are, so far as art is concerned, once more on well-known ground. The earth, provider of rich harvests but also, in times of drought, the cause of empty storerooms and famine, is to the African farmer plainly a symbol of female fruitfulness, and when the rain falls it represents the male life-giving principle. Life has constantly to be renewed, the rhythm of the seasons signifying death and rebirth. Man must actively intervene in these events, and he therefore invented an official who is known by different names—Master of the Land, Father of the Land, Lord of Earth. According to tradition the bearer of this official position is a descendant of the first man, who made the land arable and founded the first village. He occupies the position of high priest, decides the time when work in the fields is to be done, and carries out the ritual of the earth cult. He calls for rain when drought prevails, and sends it away if it lasts too long. All these important duties give the Master of the Land a very high position, equal in rank to the village chief and his eldest son. He is the spiritual leader and preserver of tradition.

This phenomenon is widespread among the peoples

success, appears everywhere in many different forms, and obviously animal figures play an important part. Usually they are crudely fashioned from some kind of organic material, as for instance the wax lions used by the Jokwe for hunting rituals. The Lunda, who also live in Angola, possess a finely carved wooden piece of hunting magic in the form of a rider (plainly a European) seated on a cow. For many Congo peoples the dog is an essential companion to the hunt, and he has a wooden bell attached to his neck so that the hunter can

of west Sudan—the Bambara, Dogon, Kurumba, Mossi Tallensi, and so on—but it is also found among the Bari and Latuko in the White Nile territory. Among the Dinka the chief of the clan is at the same time the official rain-maker of the whole people, and the same is true of the Shilluk, who are also Nilotes. Among the Shilluk a divine kingship also developed. Their kings are descended from the culture hero Nyakang, whose spiritual power is passed on to the new ruler at his coronation. The great rain ceremony used to take place in Fashoda,

and at the same time similar ceremonies were carried out by the king's representatives in the neighbouring provinces. It was Nyakang who caused the rain to fall from heaven.

The *hogon*, high priest of the Dogon, inhabits a special house known as the *ginna*. It differs from the usual houses by its façade, which has earned it the name of the 'House with eighty alcoves'. Nearby stand the *hogon* granaries, where millet from the *hogon's* fields is stored. This harvest, used for the first sowing of the following year, brings blessings, and it is therefore sown to the accompaniment of special rites. The granaries of the *hogon* are larger than those of any other village dwellers, for they ensure that there will always be enough food for everyone. The granaries, like all the buildings, are made of clay, and their walls are decorated with breasts formed of clay, or large Lorraine crosses like those on the *kanaga* masks. The granary doors—now almost all replaced by plain boards—used to display peculiar carvings. The finest doors are probably those on which conical female breasts are surrounded by row on row of stylized human figures (Pl. 95). These figures represent the eighty ancestors of mankind. The doors have bolts in the form of a sliding bar, as found all over West Africa. The lock itself is always artistically carved, perhaps in the form of a lizard or a bird, or shaped like a *walu* mask showing the heavenly twins or some other mythical creature. The doors of the *ginna* were often richly decorated, usually with events from the story of the creation in which the eight Dogon ancestors form a focal point.

The same themes are found on the doors of the Senufo shrines, but the style is completely different. Senufo

doors display a circular motif in the middle, perhaps representing the navel of the universe, but possibly the sun. From this circle four shafts run outwards diagonally across the door, while above and beneath this central part are mythological symbols—tortoises, crocodiles, hornbills, chameleons, *kpelie* masks, and human figures (riders or hunters). The locks resemble those of the Dogon, but are in the typical Senufo style. The Bambara sometimes made locks in the shape of a woman with a characteristic mitre-like headdress.

We have already described many of the masks in connection with the secret societies, but there are some additions which, although part of the organization of the secret societies, are yet so closely linked with agriculture that they fit better into this chapter.

In Guinea the Baga use an enormous fertility mask called a *nimba* for their agricultural ceremonies at seed and harvest time. It is carried in procession twice yearly, and the women throw rice over it. When a *nimba* falls to pieces from age it signifies a good omen for a long life and many children. The *nimba* is a helmet mask, and its narrow semicircular head is fixed on a slim neck. The face is dominated by a giant sharply hooked nose, the eyes are round with raised rims, and the diminutive mouth has protruding lips. The ears are formed by a semicircular ridge, and a short comb runs from the middle of the head back to the neck. The tattooed surfaces at the side of the face are covered with a waffle pattern arranged in rows. The upper part of the body ends in four supports which fit on to the dancer's shoulders, and he looks out through a spy-hole between the heavy breasts. The mask is completed by a long raffia cloak.

This mask also includes the male principle, because the eyes and nose, seen from the front, could be taken for the male genitals. Variations of this *nimba* mask have the same construction, but are carved much more realistically in the shape of the human figure. They are remarkable for a very small head borne on an excessively long neck. The mask, however, may be just a headdress in the form of a woman's torso with an intensely expressive face, deepened by large round eyes with black pupils, and plaits of human hair hanging down behind.

The Bambara's link with the earth is revealed in very impressive ceremonies and dances, and for these severely stylized antelopes or antelope heads are used as masks. These headdresses are connected with the circumcised youths, who together form an age-group called *soli*. The age-groups are combined into larger units, *flan ton* or *flan kuru*, and these combine again into field groups, *chi wara to*, who come forward every year when work begins in the fields, or when a new piece of land is to be cleared. While the young men stand in a row breaking up the earth with hoes, spurred on by the rhythm of the drums, two dancers wearing the antelope headdress stand by to oversee the proper progress of the work. They wear a long raffia cloak and lean on staves. Their dance imitates the high, impulsive leaps of frisking antelopes. They are supposed to represent a *chi wara* (work-wild animal), that is a working animal, for this dance is a memory of the culture hero who taught mankind with his claws and a stick how to cultivate the earth. The dance of the *chi wara* pair (there is always a male and female animal) is not only an invocation of the earthspirits, which may have their peace disturbed by

* Pl. 96; Cat. 105

Cat. 34

* Pl. 97

* Cat. 12

* Pl. 98

Pl. 97 Cameroun. *Buffalo mask with an iron hoe in the mouth. Wood, black and white painting, h. 67.5 cm. Museum voor Land- en Volkenkunde, Rotterdam.*

Three main styles can be distinguished. The first, horizontal style is a relatively naturalistic representation of the antelope—long horns with gently curved ends and narrow ears extending from the pointed muzzle. Sometimes the head of the animal is replaced by a stylized human face with a straight, flat nose and rounded forehead resembling the animal masks. The tall, straight neck is carried on a relatively small body. The tail usually has a slight upward curve, but it is sometimes only indicated by a loop. Female animals often carry their babies on their back or neck. In other examples the body is entirely neglected, leaving only the head and powerful neck. A strange thing about this horizontal style is that the head and body are never carved from one piece, but the head is fastened to the body with large nails.

In the second, vertical, style (Cat. 10) the body and legs are reduced to a pedestal from which the elongated neck, muzzle, and horns stretch upwards. Here too the female beasts carry their young on their backs, whereas the male *chi wara* of this style features the body only as a decorative part of the composition, but in this case the neck is emphasized by a flat, widely spreading mane. The curve of the neck is repeated by the fretwork zigzag lines or triangles indicating the mane. The head with pointed muzzle and the straight horns stands upright, while the points of the horns curve slightly backwards.

The third style is probably the most remarkable. It is a purely abstract work of art in which the faint curves of the body, the pointed lines of the horns, and the sharp outlines of the legs together express a vitality and movement seldom seen in African art. It is only on

the agricultural activity and therefore have to be placated, but it is also a fertility ritual invoking fertile crops. The *chi wara* also appear at agricultural matches between neighbouring villages.

From the artistic point of view the *chi wara* represent different groups of styles. They are probably the finest examples of stylized African art, for with a delicate play of line the sensitive carvings display the natural beauty of the living antelope.

closer inspection that one sees that the whole composition is really an antelope supported by another antelope, a chameleon, or a tortoise. *Chi wara* are also known in this style when they have one or several standing or seated human figures on the forehead or back.

These three styles were originally limited to certain regions, but some elements of design were exchanged between them. For this reason, and because the place where a *chi wara* was found is not necessarily the place where it was made, the classification of pieces in collections is by no means easy. The Kurumba of Upper Volta, for example, also produce a mask headdress in the form of an antelope head. But in this case the whole approach is more naturalistic, although there is some stylization. The powerful neck supports a head with a pointed protruding snout, and this line extends upwards, beyond the long sharp ears, in a gentle curve ending with the vigorous towering horns. These finely-shaped antelope heads are colourfully painted with large triangles in white, brownish-red, black, and light blue, and the triangles are filled in with rows of spots. The headdress represents Yirige, the culture hero, who drove away evil spirits at the first tilling of the land. He also appears at the death ritual following the mourning period, and with the same task.

The Bobo-Ule, or Red Bobo from Upper Volta (also known as the Bwa and not to be confused with the Bobo-Fing mentioned earlier) have animals on their helmet masks, and these are of the first importance for agricultural rites. In this case the buffalo is the important culture hero, and it also symbolizes the link with the earth. The bird-spirit masks are very striking; they are in a style which could be described as Cubist, for they are constructed of angular and rounded planes, which are once more painted with circles, triangles, lozenges, or checkered patterns in black and white. The buffalo masks exude especial power, their triangular open mouths on angular snouts protrude far beyond the face. The large, bullet-shaped eyes are ringed with concentric circles, while the heavy, flat horns turn almost full circle. The vigorous weight of the whole thing is emphasized by the black and white decoration. The owl mask has a flat, round face out of which stare large eyes framed in concentric circles and its gaping beak forms a protruding rectangle or a diamond shape containing huge teeth. Above the face of the mask is a large board-like headdress. It is divided into geometrical planes by sidelong, symmetrical and deep notches of different shapes, also painted in black and white. Out of the narrow base of the headdress springs a large bent hook or spike which, like the beak, is painted red. A handle for the dancer to hold is carved into the chin of the mask. A variation of this is the mask with the horizontal wing-like board on either side of the face. It represents a butterfly, and in imitation of the insect's flight the mask is shaken up and down around the axis of the face during the dance. All these masks are worn with a large fibre mantle.

In central Nigeria also—among the Tiv, Jukun, Chamba, and other tribes—we find the religious link with the earth, and seed and harvest rites associated with it. Buffalo masks are also present, for the buffalo is considered to be the protective ancestor of earth. Generally, these masks are very abstract in style, the composition comprising two elements only—the large, flat nearly closed circle of the horns, and the small, angular jaw.

Cat. 20 Among the Chamba the buffalo, or wood-cow as it is called, is given anthropomorphic features. The surface of the face is rectangular and carries two vertical, only slightly curved horns. Two small spy-holes are pierced in the powerful, round forehead, with the small nose as the only relief on the flat face below. Every year there still takes place among the Tikar of Cameroun and the related peoples—Bamileke, Bamenda, Bamum, and Bali—a ceremony which is supposed to guarantee the fertility of the fields and also of men. This feast takes place at the end of the dry period, and it is celebrated with mask dramas, sacrifices, and the drinking of palm-wine. Here, too, we find buffalo masks, but in this case they are large wooden masks more or less realistically carved as buffalo heads. In the typical style of the grass-

Cat. 21 lands the head has large, almond-shaped eyes, an open mouth full of teeth, and large nostrils. The horns are relatively small, but are close together and bent inwards. Some examples of this kind are covered all over with glass beads. As variations we find masks with a human face, round cheeks, and buffalo horns. The buffalo masks are still in use today as part of the agricultural ceremonies, although originally they were, like the antelope and elephant masks, used in connection with the ritual of the hunt.

The belief behind these feasts is that the dispenser of fruitfulness and nourishment dies every year. Hence the link with him has to be renewed annually, so that he can be reborn and the earth be fruitful. The king, as representative of the divine power, is the focal point of the ceremonies, and sacrifice, and the drinking of palm-wine symbolize his relationship to his people.

Apart from masks many other objects are connected with the different agricultural ceremonies, and I must here lay stress, once more, on the fact that their functions may actually be manifold, for the pieces belong to the community store of cult objects, and may be used for this or that purpose according to need. Surprising to us, but easily comprehensible in African philosophy, is the close connection of the earth with death, but here in a negative sense. The earth must constantly be purified, not only of the spirits of nature everywhere active, but also of the souls of the dead who have not yet embarked on their journey into the beyond. Pieces thus closely connected with the earth I have arranged under the economic aspect. We must begin with the so-called rhythm pestles, or *deble*, of the Senufo. These are long poles carved out of thin tree trunks, on which the lower, shorter portion remains unworked. The upper part is in the form of an elongated male or female figure with arms so wide set that they can be grasped as handles for the grinding. The members of the *lo* societies beat the *deble* rhythmically on the ground during the different stages of the death ritual, and also at the annual first tilling of the soil.

The Senufo, like the Bambara, also have agricultural competitions between the young men of neighbouring villages. There are contests in hoeing the new fields. The victor receives a staff crowned with a female figure, called *daleu*. It is connected with the field rites and the earth, for the female figure embodies the earth mother. The staff is also an attribute of the *lo* society, to which the competitors must belong. Among the cult objects we

find the same figure again, seated on a small stool with a covered vessel on its head. There are staves, similar to the *daleu*, on which perch one or two birds with outspread wings. Smaller figures of flying birds are fixed to the wings of the large ones with iron pegs. These staves are carried as prizes in the competition, and are set up in the fields.

★ Pl. 101   Many carvings which are not obviously ancestor figures are part of the earth cult, and they are found all over the savannah of western Sudan. They are generally only crudely carved human figures—men, women, and riders—or animal figures, that are kept on the altars of the earth-priests alongside a variety of iron or bronze pieces. Being fertility symbols, especially of the fertility of the earth, they are never described as ancestors. They

Pl. 99, 100 are solely magic objects which the priests know how to handle. They will be discussed in greater detail under the religious aspect, but it is possible to anticipate a little.

It has been mentioned in passing that the Dogon are guardians of the Tellem culture, whose material remains were found in the conical clay constructions on the cliff face, and were ascribed by the Dogon to a people they called Tellem, traditionally supposed to have occupied this territory before the Dogon. Whatever the truth may be, it is a fact that these remains were found with human skeletons in the towers which had obviously served as tombs. Apart from human figures, neck-rests, fragments of textiles and finely knotted plait-work, vessels of clay, bronze and iron armlets and spear- and arrowheads, also came to light. The wood-carvings of African art were discovered relatively late, and it was only after the Second World War that they came in large numbers to Europe and America, where they were quickly acquired for collections. The Tellem figures represent a definitely archaic style. Head, body and limbs are indicated only in rudimentary fashion and, as a result, the cubic or cylindrical shapes are very impressive. They are mostly covered with a thick, irregular incrustation which obliterates the detail. Some of them hold their arms vertically upwards. There are also double figures of this kind, while others ride on a scarcely recognizable animal. Single animals are also known. All these figures are clearly distinguishable from those of the Dogon, although there are some Dogon figures which have this thick crust. Another category combines both Tellem and Dogon characteristics in its style, and must therefore be placed chronologically between the two. That would agree with the Dogon's assertion that they once lived together with the Tellem, before the latter finally left the district. The buildings in the lower caves of the cliff face could also fit into this interim style, for they certainly display a mixture of elements from the round towers and the angular, many-storeyed buildings. At present we know very little of the Tellem and their culture, despite the fact that a scientific expedition was made a few years ago to study the question. One thing is certain, the objects attributed to the Tellem belong to a culture which has nothing to do with the culture of the modern Dogon. The Dogon regard the Tellem objects —especially the figures—as magical, powerful things, which the priest used with their own objects to make rain magic, but they have never been claimed as ancestor figures. The animal carvings serve as guardians of the millet fields and are supposed to ensure a good harvest.

Pl. 99 Senufo (Ivory Coast). Quadruped with horns, used at the rain ceremony. Wood, 1.32 cm. L. van Bussel Collection, The Hague.

Pl. 100 Senufo (Ivory Coast). Figure of a rider. Wood, h. 36 cm Dr. M. Kofler Collection, Riehen/Basle.

The connection with the earth is expressed among the other peoples of West Africa with great spectacular feasts—feasts that could frequently be described as demonstrations. They include the whole state, and fundamentally are nothing more than general homage to the divine power of the king, the general provider. On these occasions subjects filled the royal granaries with a proportion of their harvest—enough to last a whole year. Here there is an economic factor in the role of mainstay to religious-cum-political power.

The Mossi celebrated the feast, now abandoned but formerly called the feast of the *soretasgho*, that is, the 'feast of the completion of the way', in the course of which agricultural products from the whole territory were brought to the *mogho naba* of Ouagadougou, the supreme ruler of the Mossi kingdom. Another form of tax was connected with the annual feast of the royal ancestor called *basgha*. The district officials with the right to attend brought cattle, money, and other things as presents. Similar institutions are known to the Agni people (for example, the Baule), and the Akan (the Ashanti, for instance). Here the yam is the most important crop. The big *odwira* festival of the Ashanti was originally a purification ceremony for the dead, and especially the royal dead, and it was accompanied by human sacrifice. It has altered its character over the years, and today is celebrated more as a New Year feast and harvest thanksgiving. The first yams are offered as a sacrifice with palm-wine and slaughtered sheep before the royal tombs and stools, and later the crop is divided among the people. Only after the ceremony is over can the yams be eaten by everyone, and the *odwira* ceremony is often therefore called the yam feast. After the end of the war against the British in 1896 the feast was no longer held in Kumasi, though in all the other Ashanti states it is still the most important of the whole year, and is a time when all the splendour and glory of the insignia and regalia of the *omanhene* and their courts are on view.

The Yoruba, too, have a yam feast, but in this case it is linked with other ceremonies, and in many places the ceremonial consumption of the new season's yams is no longer celebrated. In eastern Yorubaland, in Owo, some wooden carvings from the first yam feasts are still preserved. They stand on the ancestral altar of the king. They are human heads having long ram's horns and a round neck resting on a flat, circular base.

The old beliefs linger on among the Bini of Benin in the *igue* feast which, as part of a series of annual ceremonies, culminates with the ritual of renewal and rejuvena-

Pl. 101 Dogon (Mali). Hermaphrodite figure of a rider. Wood, h. 36.5 cm. Old Dogon. Musée de l'Homme, Paris.

tion of the divine power of the *oba*. Forehead, hands, and feet of the *oba* are anointed with a salve prepared from roots, seeds, and herbs, the fruits of the earth. The Ibo of Onitsha province east of Benin have a similar custom. The Ibo culture is usually very sharply distinguished from the Bini, and is nearer to the cultures of the Ibibio and Ijo. The Ibo groups were, however, always open to outside influence, so that Onitsha has become an interesting example of culture transference. At the head of the small Onitsha kingdom is the *oba*, representative of sacred power for his people. Together with the idea of a god-king, Onitsha took over from Benin the whole complex of ceremonies connected with it, because at that time Benin's influence was very strong. Parallel with the *igue* is the *ofala* feast that manifests two different aspects—the *obi* makes a ritual withdrawal to the altar of his ancestors to renew contact with them and with the earth, and at the same time the *ofala* is also a yam feast, celebrated as thanksgiving for the new harvest.

The other Ibo tribes also cultivate the yam as one of the most important crops, and it is a focal point of their annual harvest thanksgiving feasts. The yams are stacked on a tall scaffold, and mask dances are held. In the northern districts the white female masks mentioned before are then brought out. The eastern Afikpo wear *maji*, or knife masks, at the harvest dances. These are strongly abstract polychrome masks with tube-shaped excrescences, arranged one above the other. The mask has a sickle-shaped headdress, representing a yam knife. The Kwale-Ibo model clay figures as protectors of the yam fruit.

I have very briefly summarized the spiritual background to the many farming symbols as an expression of the link between man and earth. Man appears simultaneously as the agent and beneficiary of the supernatural powers. In our descriptions we have already touched on an essential feature of religion, but in the chapter devoted expressly to it I shall go into the subject in greater detail.

The Nilo-Hamites, east and south Bantu peoples, and the Hamites of the Sudan (who are mostly cattle rearers) show scarcely any artistic expression in the form of wood-carving. Fertility magic for cattle is found everywhere, yet it is rare for it to be manifest as art in any form. The Shilluk mentioned above, whose economy rests as much on field-crops as upon cattle-rearing, form very attractive clay fertility figures. They are called *deang*, and represent oxen modelled with great plastic sense with a powerful body and large horns. Similar cattle and other clay quadrupeds are found among the Sotho in South Africa.

A special position is claimed by the rare iron sculptures that were found in 1867 in the palace of the ruler of the Karagwe. These are buffalo and antelope figures with delicate, slim bodies, legs, and horns. Their stylized form is peculiar to the iron sculpture of Africa.

RELIGION AND THE SUPERNATURAL

The art of Africa has been studied so far as an expression of earthly human interrelationships, but in this chapter we come face to face with a different dimension—the religious or supernatural aspect.

It is not easy to define the concept of religion. Individual religious systems are much more easily described. One thing, however, is common to all religious systems —they are concerned with the expression of a natural, profane, or earthly order and with a supernatural, sacred, or heavenly one. This difference between sacred and profane is present in every culture, and can be described as the foundation of all religions. The ideas, opinions, and methods connected with it form a definite system based on a philosophical religious approach explaining universal questions, such as the reason for man's existence, the power of nature, and life and death. The philosophy gains shape with the development of a mythological system.

Apart from theoretical explanations of philosophical systems, every culture has developed ideas and ways of managing the practical aspects of life. Here, sober rational thought is put to one side, and its place is taken by faith. Faith really means a projection of metaphysical problems on to an omnipotent but distant power, which frightens men, but which they nevertheless try to approach. This ambivalence creates an atmosphere of holiness around the idea of an all-powerful god. Hence the sense of awe, worship, and dependence. Men try to make contact with the divine through particular actions. The most personal of these is prayer, from which direct success is expected. Rituals were created to ensure regular contact between the sacred and the profane, for

example, the constant reiteration of a particular myth.

Sometimes a myth has to be dramatized to maintain the cosmic system—for instance, parts of the myth of creation are enacted at regular intervals, being in this way ritually and symbolically repeated. This is the explanation of many different sacrificial deeds. When religious services are for the good of the whole community, then a priest or priestess leads the ritual. The priest, due to his position and his personality, fulfills the necessary conditions for contact between sacred and profane, but it is he, above all, who knows the myths and who also possesses the greatest wisdom.

In many cultures the priests have developed a complex and exclusive theological system from their intricate knowledge, and this is widely divergent from the simple understanding of the myths by the people. The priest may also take the part of a doctor or medicine-man in cases where a sickness can be traced to supernatural causes and where the cure must be sought in sacred ritual.

Magic is quite different, for although it appertains to the supernatural, it has nothing whatever to do with religion. The priests sometimes may use magic in their rituals, but generally magic is connected with the occult, and is evil and mysterious. It is entirely in the hands of the magicians or witch-doctors, whereas religious offices are part of the public cult.

Some expressions, concepts, and objects have already emerged in connection with religion, whose function was more intelligible if looked at in a different cultural context, and so I must once more emphasize that, in reality, several aspects work together, and are therefore difficult to separate. If the picture presented here seems unduly schematic it is only because the central points can thus be extracted and analysed.

We shall therefore concern ourselves with the religious function of African art. It must be reiterated that the religious aspect is present everywhere in African cultures, and it is not therefore easy to separate from other aspects as it is in modern Western culture.

Everywhere in Africa we encounter the belief in a supreme power, an omnipotent god on whose supernatural power man is wholly dependent. The Bushmen call him Khu or Kaang; the Hottentots, Tsui-goab; the pygmies, Tore; and the north Congolese, Nzambi. The god of the Masai is Ngai; of the Zande, Mboli; the Dogon worship Ama; the Ashanti, Nyame, and the Yoruba, Olorun. Most of the peoples feel that the supreme being is far away, and not clearly intelligible. Generally he is connected with the sky and the sun. There are also earth-spirits which, in contrast to the masculine gods of the sky, are female. Many tribes also worship a series of less elevated creatures connected with natural forces, such as water, rivers, thunder, rain, forests and holes in the marshes. Apart from the world of supernatural creatures described here as spirits or gods, there is also the world of ancestors. The ancestors are much closer to man, and directly influence his life. The reason many myths are so complex is because the supernatural world of spirits, and that of the ancestors, is inextricably mixed. It occasionally happens that the first ancestor drives out the supreme being and takes his place, a transference of values carried out by the southern Bantu for instance. In certain hunting peoples of East Africa the first ancestor takes the form of a hunter who descends into the underworld and brings back the benefits of culture for mankind. Also the universal trickster figure, a divine scoundrel and betrayer, who upsets both gods and men, appears in Africa, for instance among the Yoruba tribe. Wherever there is faith in higher beings sacrifices are made at special places, either in the forest, the fields, or in the centre of a village community. Such places are recognizable by stones, trees, or balls of clay, or they may be graves, ancestor houses, or rivers. The central point is always an altar with cult objects. In West Africa, and also in the Congo, the building of altars is widespread and well developed, but the kind of cult varies greatly. We have already discussed the secret societies and agricultural communities, where certain bush- and earth-spirits are presented as masks. Higher beings, described here as gods, are never pictured as images in Africa, for they are so distant and so comprehensive in their nature that they are not to be imagined. There are, of course, exceptions—for instance, the Yoruba, who have developed a pantheon out of a mixture of gods and ancestors but do not make a personal image of their supreme god, Olorun. They represent instead only the *orisha*. It is a temptation to translate the word *orisha* as god or divinity, but it would not be correct. *Orisha* is the expression of a religious idea, for the Yoruba believe that Olorun can pass on his divine powers to other creatures. These creatures—intercessors, mediators between god and man owing to this transference of power—are the *orisha*. There are numerous *orisha*; four hundred at the very least. Their portraits decorate the altars of the temples consecrated to

them. An *orisha* may be an influential ancestor, a clan founder, a river-spirit, or the leader of an army. In short, any personality which incorporates an aspect of divine power, and obviously, on this basis, the number of *orisha* is almost without end. However, they are mostly only local, although some are honoured over a wide area. Only a few are common to all the Yoruba tribes. Every *orisha* has a special characteristic, and the enormous multiplicity makes it very difficult, if not impossible, to identify an *orisha* whose history is not known. Only the most common can be given a specific name. The style of the *orisha* figures resembles that of other wood-carvings, and some of the most important *orisha* are discussed below. The myth relates that Olorun, god of the sky, commanded sixteen subject gods to create the world, and to fill it with life. Obatala, known also as Orishanla, received the material to do it—a gourd filled with earth and a five-toed hen. On his way down from the sky, however, Obatala drank so much palmwine that he fell into a deep sleep. Thereupon Oduduwa came and took the gourd and the hen, and travelled down to the first sea. He scattered the earth on the waters, and the hen scraped it into a heap, and thus the land was created where Ife now stands. Then the other gods came, and let themselves down on a chain into the land of Ife. Once again Obatala drank too much, and thus created the cripples, the lame, and the hunchbacked. Soon a war broke out among the gods, and Oduduwa was the victor. He became the first ruler of Ife, and hence the first ancestor of the Yoruba.

There are numerous variations on the general creation myth of the Yoruba, and, depending on the local interests of a dynasty, the story may deviate greatly from the original pattern. Obatala is always closely connected with the act of creation, however. We have already encountered him as a hunter on a horse armed with lance or gun. His wife, an *orisha* of the earth, is always surrounded by many children.

Ifa is the personification of the divine omnipresence and the cosmic order. Linked with him is the *ifa* cult, constructed round the *ifa* oracle. This oracle is often consulted before a war, a long journey, or the birth of a child. The oracle must be interpreted by a priest, for the system demands an apprenticeship lasting many years and is so complicated that one might almost describe it as a science. The oracle boards are part of the cult, also a vessel for the preservation of palm or kola nuts, and a pestle with an ivory or wooden bell called *iroke*. The oracle board is rectangular, square, or round, and the wide border is always decorated with fine carving. The interwoven wavy bands and small head of the *ifa* are nearly always present besides other geometric or figurative ornaments such as birds or humans. The bowls containing the kola nuts are among the finest products of the Yoruba wood-carver's art. The rather small bowls are carried by very naturalistic figures, often even groups of figures—mother and child, riders, hunters, and animals of all kinds. They are painted in bright colours as is usual in Yoruba art. The nuts are sometimes preserved in covered vessels. Other bowls may serve at the same time as oracle boards—for example, round vessels with tall, steep rims, decorated in high relief with birds, tortoises, and human figures. The interior is divided into several compartments for the preservation

of the kola nuts. The cover is the actual oracle board, which fits on the vessel with the underside upward. The Yoruba from Dahomey have a rectangular oracle board that is supported by a row of human half-figures. On both ends of the board are seated figures with conical vessels in their hands. The cover, fixed with a hinge to the vessel, is also conical and has a bird at the tip. The pestle is in the form of a small staff on which a female figure is kneeling. She carries a bell in the shape of a beaker on her head, and its sides are decorated with complicated intertwined wavy bands.

The oracle is consulted in the following manner: the priest or priestess takes sixteen nut kernels and throws them several times on to a flat plaque covered with cassava meal. The ringing of a bell invokes the god. The stones form a pattern as they fall on to the plate, which is then referred to a certain verse from the *odu*, the old ★ Cat. 75 mythical poems, recited by a priest. Then the combination is interpreted according to the question.

Another very important *orisha* is Shango. He also is one of the first ancestors, like Oduduwa—a son or a grandson (this has never been agreed) of the founder of Ife. Shango, sometimes also called Oronmiyon, left Ife with a military expedition and founded Oyo, and as we have already seen, Oyo, under the *alafin*, became the secular opposite to Ife. Tradition pictures Shango as a cruel ruler, and today he personifies thunder and the storm. His attributes are *oshe*—wooden staves held by Pl. 102 the priestess during the ceremony. These staves carry a human head or a complete human figure with a double axe at the head. The double axe is strongly stylized, and is somewhat reminiscent of a broad hair-ribbon tied in a bow. The figure may be either part of the handle or it may stand on the double axe. The axe is a symbol for the stone 'thunderbolts' which are in fact relics of the Neolithic period. These thunderbolts are supposed to drop from heaven during a storm and, like the lightning, destroy houses deserving of Shango's wrath. The thunderbolt must be found by the priest before the evil can be banished. The form of the double axe is related to the curved ram's horns, for the ram is Shango's sacrificial animal, and symbolizes lightning by its sudden, powerful attacks. Shango has two wives, Oya and Osun, and both are worshipped as river-*orisha*.

In the *orisha* known as Eshu or Elegba skill and execution have found their personification. This is a typical 'trickster' figure—a divine cunning betrayer—but he represents also the peacemaker between heaven and earth. He is comparable with Mercury in the Classical world. The Eshu-priestesses are to be seen seated in the entrance to the markets, for the market-goers offer them money for protection against quarrels and brawling in Cat. 40 the market-place. Eshu is sometimes depicted seated, wearing a pointed cap and playing a flute.

Several other *orisha* ought to be mentioned. Ogun is a war god, and is worshipped by the smiths. Olokun is the *orisha* of the sea; Oku of agriculture; Obatala because of his mythical actions is the protector of the misshapen, while Osanyin watches over medical science. Ibeji is the giver of twins.

There are many other *orisha* and every one has its own altar, its own sacred place, and priests who by regular ritual observance preserve the balance of supernatural forces. Many Yoruba villages and towns still celebrate

the annual 'feast of the figures', when all *orisha* figures in the temples and on the altars are ritually purified and newly painted, then carried in procession to the marketplace before the royal palace, or—in the villages—in front of the house of the highest authority. There the less important *orisha* pay homage to the highest ones. Nowadays Islam and the Christian religion are ousting the old traditions.

We have described the Yoruba first because in this tribe the apotheosis of the ancestors in myth and then their introduction into an all-embracing religious system is especially clear. This pantheon of gods is not however confined to the Yoruba. It is also found among their neighbours, the Bini of Benin, and the Fon of Dahomey, who have developed a similar structure, and also the Ashanti and (slightly less clearly marked) the Baule.

The chief god of the Bini is Osanobua (also called Osa) who is the creator of the world. The present day *oba* dynasty of Benin, however, does not stem from him. The *oba* are descendants of Araminya, son of an *oni* from early Ife, although there are individual altars on which Osanobua is formed in clay. The eldest son of Osanobua is Olokun, who is associated with water, and especially the sea. Many altars are dedicated to him today, and he is invoked for the gift of children and of wealth. The portrait of Olokun with his wives and children is made of clay. On the old Benin plaques Olokun can be seen as an *oba* in full dress, with coral robe and crown. To right and left he is supported by a servant, and, in the place of legs, two elegantly curved leaping mud-fish spring from his robe. It is difficult to

Pl. 103   Baule (Ivory Coast). Figure of the ape god Gbekre or Mbotumbo.
Detail. Wood, overall height: 66 cm. Dr. M. Kofler Collection, Riehen/
Basle.

interpret this figure, but when we think of the significance of the sacred kingdom we may assume that the
oba has here adopted the form of a god.

Nana-buluku is the creator of the world of the Fon.
Male and female principle are united in him for, from
him stem *mawu*, the moon and female principle of the
West which governs the night, and *lisa*, the sun and
male principle of the East which governs the day. Sun
and moon are conceived as twins from which fourteen
lesser divinities spring which are generally described as
vodu. *Vodu* may be translated as god or gods, though it
is actually not the same thing. One important *vodu* is
Gu, associated with iron and war. Usually he is felt as a
good power, helpful to men, and yet he is especially the
patron of the iron-smiths. Age is both the hunter and
protector of wild animals; Aido-wedo or Ji is the primaeval snake which plays a part in the worship of
Xevioso, the thunder-god, who is comparable with
Shango of the Yoruba. Xevioso is the heavenly judge
who brings both rain and drought. The priestesses of the
thunder cult carry axes with a handle ending in a ram's
head with open mouth. The brass blade is fixed in the
ram's mouth. It is a broad, crescent-shaped blade engraved with two snake figures—Aido-wedo. These are
supposed to bring thunderbolts to earth. The rest of the
blade is carved in fretwork with two fishes, inhabitants
of the sea reminiscent of Xevioso in his marine aspect.
A crenellated, meandering line, symbol of lightning,
runs from the head of the ram along the blade. At the
back of the shaft, below the ram's head, is a short,
nearly triangular blade symbolizing the thunderbolt.

The snake, Aido-wedo, has a marine as well as a

heavenly aspect. It is connected with the rainbow, and is depicted in circular form, tail in mouth. The Fon worship yet another snake, Dan, as the centre of a widespread cult. Dan is linked with fertility and birth, and plays a general role in human affairs. Apart from gods associated with heaven and water, there is yet a third category representing the earthly powers, and these gods are worshipped in the *sagbata* cult.

The Fon have taken the *ifa* oracle cult over from the Yoruba and they call it *fa*. The complicated divination system has remained exactly the same, and the attributes, too, are unchanged. It is, however, remarkable that the kola nut bowls are often borne by individual animal or bird figures, and here also the snake swallowing its tail appears. I have already remarked that the snakes appearing on the *gelede* masks of the Yoruba in Dahomey derive from the art of the Fon.

The Fon rarely portray their gods, nor are there here (in common with the rest of Africa) any portraits of the supreme god, for he is said to have withdrawn after the creation of the world and never made another appearance, so that no portrait could be made. We shall return later to the figures found on the altars of the Fon, but two of the most remarkable figures, larger than life-size, must be mentioned here. These arrived in France in 1894, the year after the collapse of the Fon kingdom. Both figures represent Gu, the *vodu* of iron and war. One of them is constructed entirely from iron pieces, bits of railway line, nuts and bolts, metal-sheeting, etc. It is dressed in a short bell-shaped robe, and * Pl. 103; Cat. 31-33 the thin splindly legs are visible below standing on a round iron disc. On the head is a disc decorated with

spearheads and iron stakes. The other figure is formed of brass sheeting. It stands with straight legs placed side by side, the arms bent, and in each hand is a ceremonial sword with a fretwork blade decorated with circles and triangles. These two figures are unique in the history of African wrought metal-work. They look so strange in the framework of African art that they could more easily be taken for modern Western sculptures.

In the complicated religious system of the Ashanti, Nyame is the highest god. Nyame is both male and female, the great mother, creator of the world, the moon who is represented on earth by her daughter, the queen mother. Nyame in his male aspect is the provider of the sun and the father of earthly kings, the *asantehene*. The symbols of Nyame—spirals, triangles, pyramids, numbers, circles, palm-leaves, and so on—have been observed before as decoration on royal attributes, indicating very clearly the close relationship between the divine state and the religious system of the Ashanti. Asaase afua, a daughter of Nyame, is the goddess of the good earth, of fertility and procreation. Her counterpart is Asaase yaa, who represents sterility and the underworld. Her symbols are to be found on gold ornaments and weights; for instance, snakes and scorpions are death symbols, but if a recumbent cross be added to it, rebirth after death is indicated. The powerful river-god Tano is everywhere greatly respected.

The Baule possess a figure with the head of a monkey representing one of the humbler gods. It is called Gbekre or Mbotumbo, a god with several tasks, for he is both judge of hell and helper of those in need, pro-

tector of the living against their enemies. He is also an agricultural god, playing his part in the harvest ritual. Gbekre is pictured standing with lightly-bent knees and arms, holding in his hand a small alms bowl. The monkey's face, with low forehead, round eyes, and long muzzle is vigorously done. The Gbekre figures are often covered with a thick crust of offerings. They are found in many collections, and comparison of different examples makes one realize how strongly the individual expression of the artist can make an impression on a figure even when, as here, it is a question of a defined and narrow theme set by tradition and style.

Apart from his relations with the supernatural world arranged, as it were, in a settled pantheon, mankind also tries to make contact with the lower supernatural powers—in other words, with the many different kinds of spirits that beset mankind but which can be helpful towards him. The Africans erect altars, chapels, or cult places for these spirits also, and they make offerings to ensure that help will be forthcoming. There are invisible natural spirits, with common collective names known only locally, but which are classified and arranged as a rich part of the whole creed. Outside Africa these spirits are known by the vague and inadequate description of *juju* or *grisgris*.

At this point the concept of magic begins to play a part and merits our attention. By magic certain actions are understood which, as long as they are carried out in exact accordance with the rules, must necessarily bring success. Looked at formally, these actions are a special technical process. Supernatural power is used, but it is not considered sacred. The priest, as has already been pointed out, may use magic as an integral part of his religious activities. Here, though, it is a question of public magic used for the benefit of the community and recognized as such. It can be called good, or white, magic. Black magic, on the other hand, is conducted in secret; it serves individual interests only and is anti-social. Black magic is controlled by magicians and witch-doctors.

Magic can be divided into three types:

(1) Imitative magic: the desired procedure or aim is enacted in the ritual. For instance, a model is made of a person one wants to kill; it is pierced with a spike causing the individual to die the same death. It is accepted now that the hunting scenes of the prehistoric cave-paintings, where the painting of the successful hunt was supposed to bring actual success, must have had similar magic intention.

(2) Sympathetic magic: substances with magical properties are used which guarantee the desired result. Also fetish amulets and protective figures of all kinds are used.

(3) Contagious magic: in this case substances have to be taken from the body of the person who is to be influenced, hair, spittle or excrement for example.

Apart from religion, which establishes contact with the supernatural, and magic, which tries to attain its ends by the application of supernatural powers, there is a third possibility for controlling the occult—divination, which attempts to interpret the will of the divine power. There are two principal kinds of divination: in the one a specific object is used whose utterances are ordered not by the person carrying out the ritual, but

Pl. 105   Lower Congo. Mirror fetish in the form of a seated human figure. Wood with traces of white painting, glass, iron and textile, h. 42 cm. Ethnographisch Museum, Antwerp.

by fate or luck; in the other kind a contact with a divine spirit is sought, who then takes possession of the person and speaks through him. All these forms of magic and divination are known in Africa. And it can be said without exaggeration that magic plays a large, if not overwhelming role in the traditionally-minded African communities. That is a statement of fact, and should not be taken as critical judgment, and we learn with continual astonishment that the practice of magic and magic ideas are still very widespread in our Western culture. This brief introduction leads on into an examination of the objects with relevant functions.

The Ibo of south-east Nigeria set up richly decorated altars to the nature spirits called *alosi*, on which are placed dozens of wooden figures. The altars are found all over the country and are greatly respected. The *alosi* are responsible for sickness and death, but they also punish men who do not fulfill their promises or who have committed perjury. By making sacrifices to the *alosi* the priests try to expel the threat of evil. A particular *alosi* is invoked by the priest if a quarrel has to be settled for which the village judge has failed to find a solution. Many *alosi* altars brought repeated successes in this field and thereby achieved a certain fame. A wooden figure was put on the altar in gratitude, but it is never a portrait of the *alosi*, but is said to be one of his 'children'. The more powerful and successful the *alosi*, the more 'children' will be found on his altar. In the northern Ibo territory especially, in the district of Udi, the altars have a fascinating appearance. The human figures are rather crudely carved and painted in bright colours; standing or seated, they have children or weapons beside them and are always wonderfully eloquent. There are important government officials seated in a brotherly way beside policemen or European governors, while in between will be found an *ikenga* figure, also donated by a grateful worshipper. An *ikenga* is a protective household god. The little figure sits on a stool, with a sword in the right hand, in the left the head of an enemy. Two thick ram's horns curving backwards grow out of the head of the *ikenga*, though sometimes their place is taken by large headdresses composed of many animals. Only the father of a family may possess an *ikenga* and it is supposed to bring him success in all his undertakings. When he dies his *ikenga* has to be destroyed.

The Fon of Dahomey also have figures made of wood that are protective and supposed to save the house from all kinds of bad influence. They are called *bochi*. They are coarsely carved male or female figures, connected with numerous different spirits, believed to be present everywhere. The *bochi* are part of a group known as *gbo*. *Gbo* are magic objects, although in fact anything can become magic or be used for magic actions: horns, vessels, iron staves, jaw-bones, animal feet, lance-heads and so on. Magic objects of this kind are found everywhere in Africa and are often worn as amulets on the body. Such are the small ivory masks of the Pende, the miniature wooden masks of the Dan Cat. 67, 68 and also the wooden masks, which the Gere hang over the lintel of the door below the roof. The collector of African art generally takes little interest in all these things connected with magic, because they are usually unattractive, if not actually ugly and repellent, and are

better suited to purely ethnographical collections than the art collector's cabinet.

Since the arrival of the Portuguese in Africa such magically charged figures have been called fetishes. Fetish is derived from the Portuguese word *feitiço*, which simply means: something made, something manufactured. Since then this rather misleading idea has been applied to all figures to which a magic quality can be attributed. The magic power is contained in a specific substance, which is added to the figure.

We have already encountered a fetish in the Tellem figures of the Dogon. A few more examples will be cited here to clarify their rather horrid character, so very different from ancestor figures.

Black magic fetishes of the Senufo are called *kafi-gueledio*. They are carved in wood and wrapped in a sack leaving only the legs free. The sack is tied round the neck forming a ruff for the head. Sometimes iron rods or pieces of wood are fixed to the floppy sleeves with feather crowns on the head. The piece of cloth is completely encrusted with offerings and the whole figure is hung about with little bundles and antelope horns each of which contains a magic substance.

The clay modelled heads of the Kran in Liberia belong to the same class. They are not actually figures, but horrible, skull-like objects called *gasua*, decked out with pigs' tusks and different animals' teeth. The teeth are stuck in pairs above the eyes and mouth, with the points turned inwards. The mouth, too, has large teeth and a row of small horns stands up like a crown of thorns on the forehead. The effect is completed by a huge bunch of feathers on the head. Said to be especially effective are the magic *yanda* figures of the Zande in north-eastern Congo. In his detailed study of them Burssens clearly explains the role played by magic in the *mani* secret society. The *yanda* figures may be made of either wood or clay, and although they are anthropomorphic, they comprise only head, rump and legs.

The arms are altogether lacking or indicated by small stumps. The form is very archaic, though there are variations in detail such as the shape of the face, hairstyle, nose, mouth and legs. Sometimes the figures are decorated with necklaces of tiny beads or chains of brass rings attached to the ears. There is also a group of small human figures, though they are scarcely recognizable as such. The head has degenerated into a cone-like stump and the conical body finishes in a point. The stump-like legs of the clay *yanda* figures are turned forwards, giving the impresssion of a seated figure. Although the marked abstraction of the human figure may have an astonishingly powerful effect, the real power of these objects lies in the magic charge they bear. *Yanda* figures are the property of the leaders and members of the *mani* sect and no one else has the right to possess one. Their magic power may be applied to various purposes: the success of the hunt, healing the sick, settling quarrels and in a general way against magic and harmful influences. * Cat. 74

The same idea is contained in the remarkable fetish figures of other Congo territories. In particular the mirror and nail fetishes, known under the general Pl. 105 name, *konde*, and found in all the tribes of the lower Congo and Loango. The Mayombe make human figures in the style described above, though occasionally these will have a small box on the torso. The box Pl. 106 a + b is furnished with a mirror in front and contains the magic substance, which is often increased by the addition of little bundles, feathers, iron rings and so on. * Pl. 104 Whereas these figures—either seated or standing—are Pl. 107 usually beautiful and attractively made, the nail fetish figures of the Kakongo make a completely different impression. They are large and also carry a small box with a mirror on the torso, but are stuck all over with nails and iron staves, so that the wood of the body can scarcely be seen. The more iron on these fetish figures the greater their power, for iron is considered to be heavily charged with magic. Their menacing appearance is occasionally increased by their holding weapons in upraised hands. Animals may also be used as fetish figures: standing or seated dogs, sometimes with a head at either end of the body, leopards with the small box on their back and covered all over with studs. The fetish figures of the Teke have a human shape and the magic substance is placed in an extension of the rump, cloaked on many figures by a ball of clay. The fetish figures of the Songe, also Congo peoples, have horrible features. They are standing, human figures carved in the well-known Songe style. The head contains the magic power as well as the small mirrored box built into the body of the figure. The effect is intensified by several attributes: a horn, or spearhead, feathers on the head and bundles of snake or animal skins or pelts, and to complete the decoration little wooden dolls, glass beads and decorative studs.

Besides the fetish figures, which are direct incarnations of magic power, some objects, which were really made for other purposes, are sometimes provided with the magic substances and thus take their place in the magic ritual. Usually they are rattles and percussion instruments, which have to be drummed incessantly throughout the rites to invoke the supernatural powers. In Gabon there are iron bells with seated mirror fetish figures. And all over the lower Congo region and in Loango, small wooden bells and slit-drums are used for this purpose. The Mayombe make fine boat-like instruments with handles in human form. The magic substance is placed in the head of the figure on the handle and covered with a round clay cap.

The problem of divination has been solved in several ways in Africa. The human mind has invented countless techniques to interpret supernatural signs, and to foretell the future. The instruments that have been used not only show the manifold possibilities of divination but are often pure works of art in themselves. It is only possible to discuss a few groups and therefore I have selected those which, apart from their primary function, fulfill the requirements of a work of art.

The *ifa* oracle of the Yoruba has already been mentioned. A similar oracle bowl is also found among the Venda in Rhodesia. Cryptogrammatic oracle signs are scratched on the border and in the interior. In Tanzania the Makonde use wooden plaques with animal figures or circle ornament and the Jokwe magicians of Angola use a flat, steep-sided basket, called *ngombo*, the contents of which are consulted. The basket—it is made in spiral fashion—is shaken and the magician reads the answer to the question from the pattern of objects resulting from the movement of the basket. A well-versed magician employs several dozen of these small objects, which can be divided into two categories: first the stylized small human figures with bent knees and little arms cut into the body, with slit eyes and sketchy hair; secondly animal material such as cut out oval or rectangular pieces of animal skin, cocks' feet, tortoise

Cat. 26

Cat. 25

Cat. 22, 24

Pl. 108; Cat. 23

Pl. 109

Cat. 112

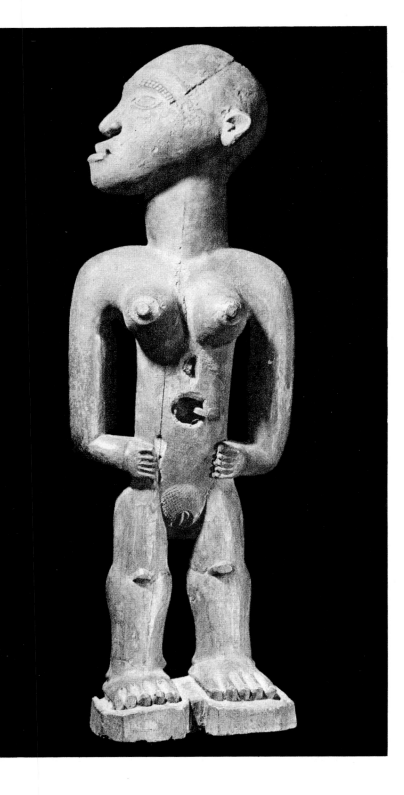

Pl. 107 Lower Congo. Female fetish figure with averted face, probably a tomb figure. Dark brown wood with traces of red painting, h. 64 cm. Ethnographisch Museum, Antwerp.

Pl. 108 Songe (Congo-Kinshasa). Male fetish figure. Detail. Wood, cowrie shells, animal hide, snakeskin, brass, fibres, overal height: 51.5 cm. Museum voor Land- en Volkenkunde, Rotterdam. (Cat. 23)

Pl. 109 Mayombe (lower Congo). Wooden bell with human face. H. 20 cm. Koninklijk Museum voor Midden-Afrika, Tervuren.

shells, small horns, teeth, shells and so on. There is also a rattle and a stick with a zebra tail.

The friction oracle appears in many variations all over the Congo. It consists principally of a fixed lower part with a flat surface and a smaller piece fitted over it. These oracle appliances are known by several names and are usually described as *katatora* in the literature on the subject. The finest examples take the shape of animals. For instance, the so-called *itombwa* oracle of the Kuba is carved as a crocodile with a small skittle-like knob on its flat back. In many Congo tribes the body of the animal is stylized into a boat-shaped rump on four small pillars. In place of the animal's head there is *Pl. 112, 113 sometimes a human face. A special variety called *iwa* has been developed by the Zande; the disc-shaped underside rests on two pillars and has a long, horizontally fixed handle that bends under. The lid is also round, *Pl. 110 but has a vertical handle. The Luba have a friction oracle in the form of two seated figures looking at one another whose arms merge.

Consultation with the oracle is relatively easy: the smaller, upper part, already covered with a particular substance, is carefully rubbed backwards and forwards on the flat surface of the fixed portion. The question is posed and the answer is negative or positive according to whether the disc sticks or slides gently on.

Finally another sophisticated oracle should be mentioned, used by the soothsayers of the Baule, but also *Pl. 111 known to the Guro. This is the so-called mouse oracle. It consists of a cylindrical, often beautifully carved wooden vessel with a fretwork base and cover. Some examples have a human figure on the edge carved in

the fine style typical of the Baule. The interior of the vessel is divided into two by a piece of wood with an opening connecting the upper with the lower part. A mouse is shut inside. Now the oracle bones are laid out on a small metal plate and a handful of rice thrown over them as a lure for the mouse. As the creature runs up and down across the metal plate gathering the rice, it disturbs the bones. After a while the mouse is taken away and the answer to the problem is read from its arrangement of the bones.

One last category of pieces must be mentioned, although in themselves they have little to do with oracles but do belong to the world of magic. These are the *kabila* figures of the Luba in the Congo. From the functional viewpoint the bowl is the most important part, but the interest of the composition is entirely centred on the carved figure carrying the bowl. We have already seen the extraordinary sensitive carving of female figures in Luba art, and the seated or kneeling female figures of the *kabila* are no exception. Some *kabila* figures are even known—like the stools and female figures—that were carved by the hand of the Master of Buli himself. The female figures carrying bowls are sometimes called beggar-women, and are used for various purposes. The magicians are supposed to have used them as containers for magic ingredients used against sickness. They were also set up before the hut of a pregnant woman, so that passers-by could put a gift in the bowl.

Pl. 111   Baule (Ivory Coast). Mouse oracle, supported by a seated male figure. Wood, h. 25 cm. Musée de l'Homme, Paris.

Pl. 110   Luba (Congo-Kinshasa). Katatora friction oracle in the form of two people embracing. Light-brown wood, h. 11.5 cm. Ethnographisch Museum, Antwerp.

Pl. 112   Luba (Congo-Kinshasa). Kabila, kneeling female figure with a vessel in the form of a gourd, used for divination. Brown wood, h. 29 cm. Ethnographisch Museum, Antwerp.

Pl. 113   Luba (Congo-Kinshasa). Kabila, seated woman with vessel, used for divination. Black wood, h. 46.5 cm. Museum voor Land- en Volkenkunde, Rotterdam.

INTELLECTUAL COMMUNICATION AND TECHNOLOGY

We have already learned a good deal about the life of the African from the discussion of aspects and objects in their functional capacity. Three different aspects still remain, which play their part in analyses in cultural anthropology. Two may be taken together: intellectual communication and technology. Both represent essential elements for the understanding of every culture, yet they scarcely enter into a discussion on art.

Literary language—poems, epics and litanies such as were also created in Africa—must certainly be regarded as art, but the subject of this book is the tangible, plastic arts. Language therefore is irrelevant to our discussion.

Technology is also difficult to reconcile with art, even though the results of certain technical methods may be works of art. For instance the suitability to its purpose of the hook on the head of a spear is a technical matter, as too the description of a trap made of rattan and its efficiency for catching certain animals. But here there is no question of art. Where technical procedures are helpful and necessary to explain the whole artistic picture, I have described them briefly. But an intensive exploration of this aspect would go beyond the bounds of our theme.

So we come to the last aspect of all and one of the most important for our subject.

PLAY

The element of play has a not unimportant share in the development of new forms of culture. It influences every aspect and is responsible for the dynamism that keeps a culture alive. By play I mean the game in the narrow sense. Huizinga in his book "Homo Ludens" (1938) first pointed out the function of play within a culture. Play is an inborn urge, man plays by nature without learning. It is actually a flight from reality into fantasy, in which one tries to occupy oneself in a way that has nothing to do with the everyday world. Two pairs of opposing concepts are at work here: freedom and constraint; the alien and the familiar. Inextricably bound up with play are the elements of fighting and the theatre; a game, for example, presupposes a fight over something. It is a competition to find the best player. These characteristics, however, are not necessarily limited to pure play. Play can be an expression of an abnormal and neurotic way of life, for instance when something is played continually from fear of reality. On the other hand it can be sublimated in various ways and act as an unconscious mainspring for the most widely differing activities. Ludik —or the play-element—is divided into three: true play, art, and knowledge. Clearly then almost every aspect of a culture is affected by the element of play. In other words the aspect of play extends so far into other cultural fields that a clear-cut definition is impossible. But it must be recognized that an urge to play is behind every expression of art. Of course it is also possible to take art as a starting-point and to consider it in the light of play, as we have done in this book. Art being our central theme we must now consider the influence of the play element on it. It must, however, be repeated that the outlines are hazy. Although different important elements of other aspects that have been discussed before will reappear, the essential impulse must be ascribed to the element of play.

First then, music and the dance. Both are exceptionally strongly developed in Africa and could be described without exaggeration as the pulse and rhythm of African life. It is not possible to give an exhaustive treatment of African music here—there are monographs on the subject—but one or two main themes can be indicated. It is important to remember that African music knows no written notation. A musical idea is spontaneously sounded, remembered and added to the earlier repertoire. This type of musical phrase is generally short and for one voice only, it is not extended or developed, but repeated several times. The repetitive element is very strong in African music.

The measure is stated aloud and the accents, though often surprising to the ear of a European, give the music its tension, its rhythm. The ceaseless beat, in which several rhythms may be played together, producing a complicated polyrhythm, is one of the most important characteristics of African music.

The percussive character of the music is also remarkable, for percussion instruments supply the major part of the music. Even where stringed instruments are played they are struck vigorously in a rhythmical beat.

Instruments are of all kinds, but here, too, a brief summary of the categories must suffice. Certain instruments will therefore be selected as examples and examined in the light of their artistic quality.

Idiophones: the sound waves are produced in the body of the instrument itself when it is struck or if the keys cause it to vibrate. Slit-drums, xylophones, rattles,

bells, *sanzas* and so forth belong to this group. The small slit-drums we have already encountered as magic instruments. There are, however, large ones, played to accompany the dance. In many districts they are richly carved, often like a stylized animal. The giant drums of the Zande, for example, have the form of a cow. Cat. 109

Typically African are the *sanzas*. They comprise a resonator on which narrow keys of iron or other material are fastened at one end, so that, held above the resonator by a bridge, they can vibrate freely when they are touched with the thumb. Gourds are sometimes used as resonators. Nearly every tribe has invented its own variation of the *sanza*. Many are prettily decorated with fine carving, poker-work and beads, as for instance in Angola and the Congo. The Zande even have anthropomorphic *sanzas*. Cat. 120 / Pl. 114

Aerophones: The sound is produced by vibrating a column of air. To this category belong buzzers, flutes, trumpets, horns, oboes, fifes and so on. The elephant's tusk inspired several tribes to produce a richly decorated transverse trumpet. In the Congo, decoration is usually limited to simple squares or circle ornament, but the old trumpets of Ife and Benin, carved with luxurious decoration of human and animal figures in high relief, are the products of a highly developed art of carving. Cat. 116, 117

Membranophones: The sound waves are produced by a membrane—an animal skin, stretched taut over an opening. The drums belong to this class; drums which are so inherent a part of African music that they are repeatedly described as the voice of Black Africa. There are drums with one skin and drums with two. Shapes Cat. 110, 111 / * Cat. 119

Pl. 114 *Zande (Congo-Kinshasa). Sanza, musical instrument with bamboo keys, in human form. Light-brown wood, h. 61 cm. Koninklijk Museum voor Midden-Afrika, Tervuren.*

Pl. 115 *Mangbetu (Congo-Kinshasa). Kundi bow-harp, the neck in the form of a hermaphrodite figure with two heads. Wood, leather, glass beads, h. 55 cm. Museum Rietberg, Zurich.*

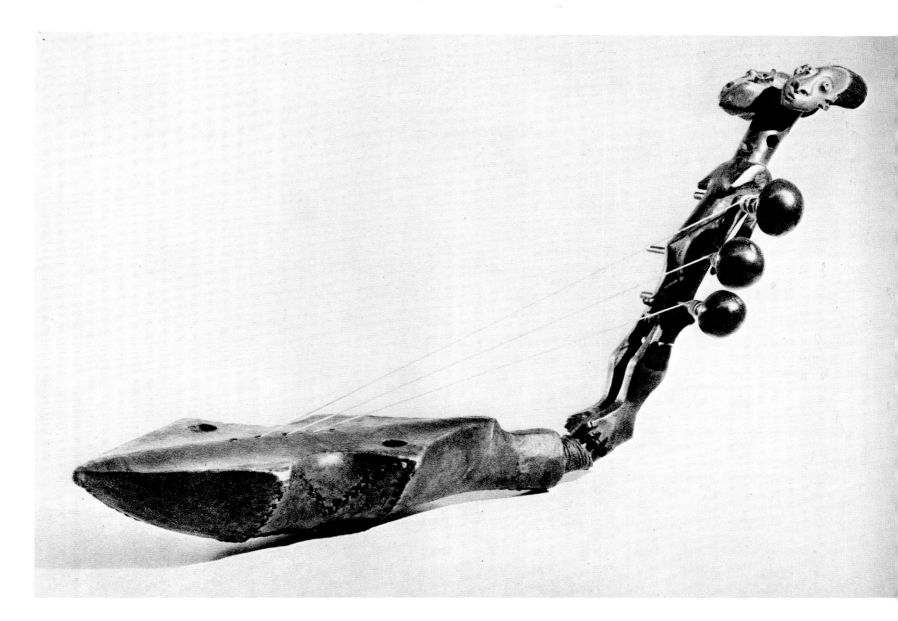

Pl. XXIII divide the drums into types—cylindrical, conical, gourd, hour-glass and beaker drums. A complete survey of the artistic qualities of African drums is impossible for there are far too many kinds and it would go beyond the confines of our theme. We must, therefore be content with the statement that the drum, as an essential part of the life of the African, is not only a musical instrument, but may also be an original work of art to which the artist has turned all his talent.

Chordophones: This technique depends on the vibration of one or more taut strings. There are many possibilities: *Zithers:* the strings are stretched over a resonator and fixed at both ends. *Harps:* the taut strings form a surface, standing perpendicular to the upper surface of the resonator. The strings are stretched between the resonator and one or more supporting arms, fastened to the resonator. A variation of this, the bow-harp, is widespread in Africa. A curved arm rises from the resonator and the strings are stretched between the two. The bow-harps of the Zande are famous, they are anthropomorphic and the curved arm has developed into a neck carrying one or two small human heads. Their neighbours, the Mangbetu, decorate the necks of their bow-harps with elongated small heads. The bow-harps of the Pangwe in Gabon are very different: here the finely-carved human heads are placed on both sides of the base of the neck. Often only a single, and therefore larger, head emerges from the resonator at the base of the neck. The Baule carve three-dimensional animal figures in this position. *Lutes:* the strings are drawn taut between the resonator and the neck, which is an extension of the box. They run almost parallel to its upper surface. Variations are the bow-lutes, on which every string is stretched taut onto a single bent neck, and the harp-lutes, the strings of which are pulled over a high comb and lie in a perpendicular plane to the resonator. The bow-lute is principally found in the Congo. An example of the harp-lute is the *kora*, which has a resonator made from a gourd. The *kora* is the instrument preferred by professional wandering singers in West Africa, especially in Senegal and Guinea. They use the instrument as an accompaniment to their songs of praise.

Musical instruments serve—although some may be part of a band—primarily as an accompaniment to the dance. African dancing has a tradition, yet the choreography is flexible enough for the cheerful invention of forms. The true nature of the African is revealed in the dance and he uses every opportunity to express his feelings in rhythmic movement. The African dance is on the whole enormously dynamic and virile. Without any seeking after stylization the whole body becomes a direct and expressive instrument, spontaneously building lively rhythmic movements into the form of a dance. The style and choreography of a particular dance determines the ornament and outfit of the dancer as regards costume and attributes. Nothing is left to chance, although the abundant and bizarre make-up may give exactly the opposite impression to an uninitiated observer.

These traditional effects of the element of play apart, another aspect stands out, namely the idea of entertainment, which plays an important part, when all kinds of tensions have to be released. The sacred and exclusive are profaned, every one can take part in exercises of this kind, which have a completely public character. It is noticeable that the same musical instruments and often the same masks are produced, although normally they appear only before a small exclusive group. For example the *gelede* masks of the Yoruba and the fine death masks of the Ibo. There are, too, profane masks and clown masks such as are found among the

* Pl. 115
* Pl. 116
Pl. 117
* Cat. 118

Pl. 116 *Zande (Congo-Kinshasa). Bow-harp in human form. Wood, leather, h. 48 cm. Deutsches Ledermuseum, Offenbach (Main).*

Pl. 117 *Masai (Kenya). Necklace. Twisted copper spirals with glass and stone beads sewn on leather bands. Shells pendant surrounded by pearls and an iron chain decoration. Diam. 21 cm. Deutsches Ledermuseum, Offenbach (Main).*

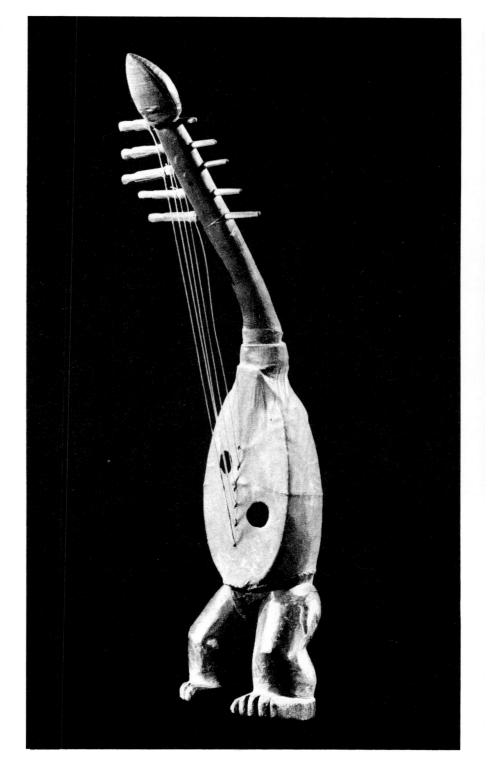

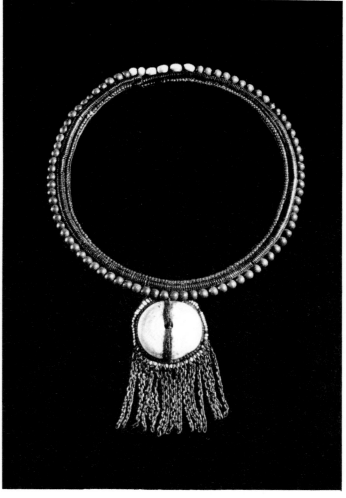

Pende in the Congo and the Makonde in Tanzania. The acrobatic dances and stilt-dances of the Ivory Coast, and the dance dramas of the miners in Johannesburg all belong to this group, not to mention modern developments, which have led to the formation of whole African ballets. These ballets have also made modern African dancing popular abroad.

The element of play is also found in other regions of

Pl. 118   Kongo (Sundi sub-style, lower Congo). Travelling European, borne by two men in a hammock. Wood, white, black and reddish-brown painting, l. 111 cm., h. 43,5 cm. Museum voor Land- en Volkenkunde, Rotterdam.

Pl. 119   Bambara (Mali). Marionette with a cloak of twisted fibres. Wood, h. 66 cm. Museum voor Land- en Volkenkunde, Rotterdam.

African art and in particular the sculpture inspired by non-African sources and subjected to a completely new interpretation by African art. The plastic figurative art from the region of the lower Congo is well-known and is remarkable for its playful interpretation of Europeans. But however pretty—and also amusing Pl. 118

Pl. 120   Gio (Liberia). Mankala or wari, *board game in the form of a goat,
with a hollowed-out bowl. Dark-coloured wood, l. 77 cm. Museum für
Völkerkunde, Basle.*

Pl. XXIV   Marka (Mali). *Head of a marionette, decorated with sheet
metal. Detail. Overall height: 63 cm. C. P. Meulendijk Collection, Rotterdam.*

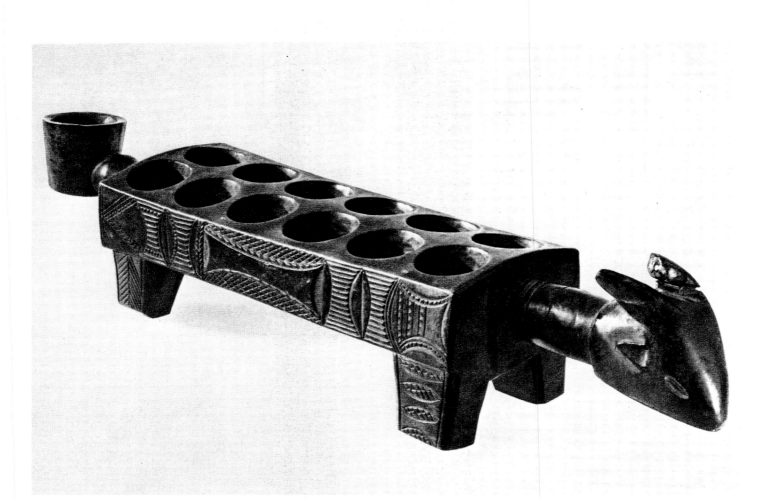

—these carvings may appear, it must not be forgotten
that the playfulness conceals more serious ideas. We
have already mentioned the representations of bicycles
in passing. Their form testifies to the power of observation of the African artist. In the ivory-carvings,
priests, huntsmen, officials as well as European women
are well observed and reproduced. Otherwise it is rare,
or at least very unusual to find deviations from a particular style in traditional African art and it seems prob-
able that these exceptions should therefore be attributed to a playful mood. For instance, some figures
have faces, seen, not as usual, frontally, but turned sideways. And in the lower Congo there are models which
depart absolutely from tradition, for example the man
climbing a palm-tree in search of palm-wine.

The marionettes, made by the Bambara in Mali and   Pl. XXIV
the Ibo and Ibibio in Nigeria could technically be also
described as toys, even though they have a different

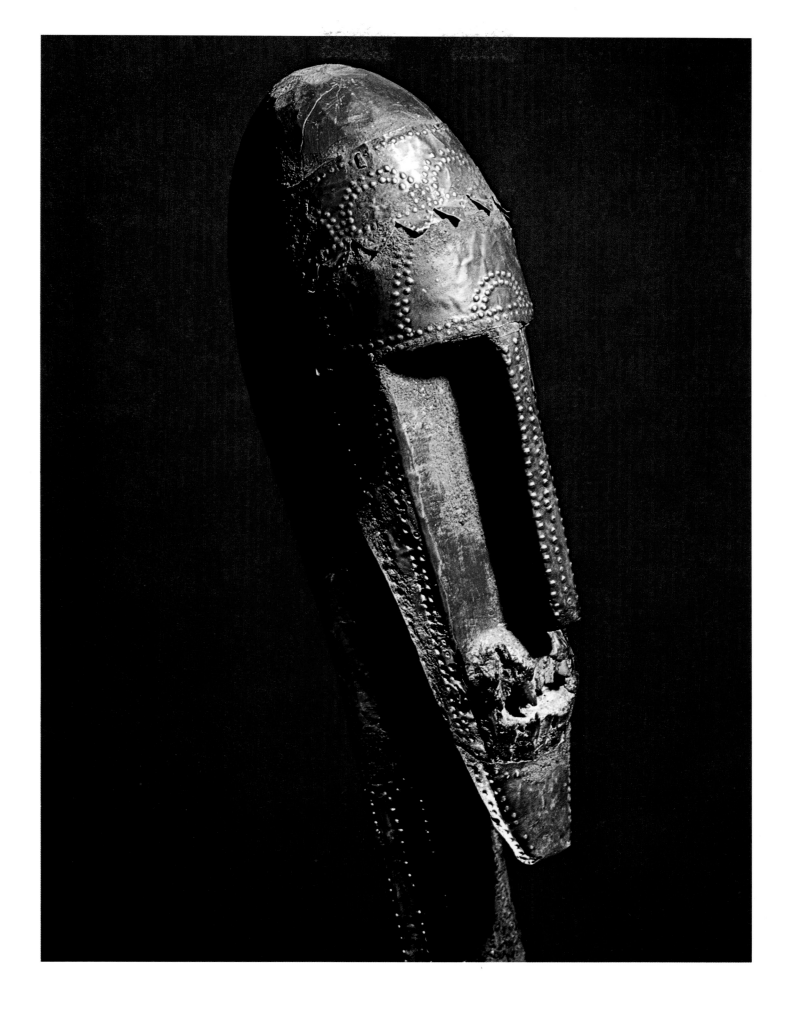

function. Those of the Bambara look very archaic with their sharply defined nose. Arms and legs are movable and can be lifted sideways on strings. The clothes consist mostly of rags or cloaks made of twisted fibre. Despite the really crude and rough carving these marionettes are extraordinarily expressive. Ibo marionettes are more finely polished and worked than those of the Bambara. Their arms can be moved forwards.

★ Pl. 119

★ Cat. 97

Finally one more plaything, solely a play object, should be mentioned. It is a game played with dice known all over Africa and even in many parts of Asia. Apart from many local names in literature it is usually given the description *mankala* or *wari*-game. The simplest form is a thick, rectangular board furnished with two rows of bowl-shaped hollows. Kola or some other kind of nuts belong to it and are preserved in a single bowl. Many ethnographical collections have *wari* games, which are fine works of art. The board is often shaped like a stylized animal. Here again we see how the African enjoys beautifying even the things necessary to everyday life.

★ Pl. 120

These few examples must suffice. I should only like to add that the plastic art of Africa consists of other things beside figures and masks, despite the contrary impression often gained by looking at collections outside Africa. The aesthetic sense of the African is seen in every aspect of life. And every style is a strong homogeneous unit, exemplified in the large as well as the small things—an ancestor figure, or a musical instrument, the pillar of a house or a snuff-box. African art is realized in all those objects and I have tried to bring the reader closer to it.

MODERN DEVELOPMENTS

Although this book has been devoted to the traditional art of Black Africa—and primarily to plastic sculpture —it is essential in conclusion to consider briefly the modern developments of African art.

The foregoing narrative has been presented partly in the present, partly in the past, because many of the circumstances described no longer exist, and the things which belonged to them are only to be seen in collections. On the other hand where cultures still pay attention to traditional laws much is still alive. Many are the factors, foreign, historical, political and religious, which have gradually changed our former stereotyped picture of Africa and fitted it into modern life. But this reality is so difficult to survey, and has so many facets, that one should hesitate to interpret things too clearly and unequivocally.

Long before the Second World War intensive processes of acculturation had begun which radically disturbed the trusted, traditional surroundings of many Africans, substituting for them the doubtful blessings of Western civilisation. The introduction of the clumsily unified Western systems of education and of Christianity was the chief driving force. Africans were suddenly able to see beyond the confines of their tribe. They learned that there was another, larger world full of undreamed possibilities and they wanted to belong to it. The immediate result, however, was that much of the old and valuable was destroyed and disappeared for ever. Thus a situation of conflict arose, which quickly reached a state of tension after the Second World War and finally developed into the immense urge for freedom that has led to the independence of African peo-

ples and the foundation of modern African states on the Western pattern.

It is not yet possible to see clearly what effect this revolution will have on the new art of Africa. The situation is still far too confused, contradictory, differing according to locality and sometimes full of latent factors. Yet there are signs everywhere that point to an African renaissance; a new, still uncertain adventure, displayed in its extreme form by the intense search for an African identity, a *présence africaine*, for a neo-African culture or *négritude*. Relevant are the writings of poet-statesmen such as the Senegalese Birago Diop, Léopold Sedar Senghor and also Aimé Césaire from Martinique. They take as their starting-point the old, traditional values of African cultures and try to give them new meaning more suited to the modern world.

When we come to consider the plastic arts, which have begun to take the first uncertain steps towards development in the Western sense, the impression is difficult to avoid that a real African identity has still to be discovered.

The young African artists now work in studios, founded by Europeans and which have developed well in several new states, for instance at Accra in Ghana; in Poto-Poto, Congo-Brazzaville; in Kinshasa and Lubumbashi (Elizabethville); Kampala, Uganda and so on. Experiments and innovations are continual. Models are taken not only from their own familiar culture, but also from other African cultures. The young artists are also inspired by non-African examples and at the same time have learned to master foreign techniques. It is of course understandable that many great difficulties have to be overcome; while the attempt to build all the fascinating new things into a particular formula is challenging, we must not be surprised that such themes as slavery, freedom and independence are often the only result, or that the African is caught in imitation of Western styles. Wherever the artists do turn back to the traditional, indigenous and immense variety of styles of their forefathers then really fine pieces of small sculpture are produced. The Kuba figures are attractive examples of this type of art. They have a cheerful frivolity caused by the asymmetric position of arms and legs or an unusual position of the head—such as is rarely seen in traditional art.

It is remarkable that painting, a typically Western art form, has found great favour, although it was scarcely practised at all in traditional Africa. Of course in the Congo, Tanzania and in the Central African Republic, on the Ivory Coast and in several other territories they used to paint the outside walls of the houses, but this kind of painting was generally not very much developed. Apart from magic and religious motifs such wall-paintings have scenes from daily life, or, more recently, scenes taken from Western magazines. The artistic quality is generally however rather poor.

Modern fresco painting, on the other hand, as practised in the studios, has developed quickly. In Kinshasa, especially, a style has developed which is already being applied to modern architecture. These wall-paintings display an extraordinary freshness and originality. The techniques are new and non-African, but the content is pure African. There are animal figures of every kind

in a rhythmical grouping and the intervening spaces are filled with decorative elements such as plants, flowers and dots.

Painting has also become popular in Poto-Poto. But here scenes with human figures are preferred. They are strongly abstract with elongated bodies and long arms and legs, and they are grouped together with a well-defined sense of rhythm. The whole composition is always lively and strongly reminiscent of the dance.

Besides these expressions of pure indigenous art there are also some works of art inspired by Christianity. The African artist was very skilful in forming these non-African ideas into purely African forms. The Christian sculpted figures of the Yoruba are an especially good example. A new Yoruba style has traditional symbols —riders, robes and ornaments of the *oni*—while their luminous colours are to be found in figures of the Madonna, the Magi and figures of Saints. Christianity has affected modern sculpture in South Africa too and in Rwanda, Congo and Burundi, where African elements are discovered in the decoration of the cathedrals, in church music and song.

We must now look for a moment at a completely different category of African sculpture, which is probably not even recognized by many as art and is therefore neglected. That is the non-traditional art made everywhere in African villages uninfluenced by studios and offered for sale to tourists in the large cities. One must not however be deceived: many pieces for sale in the markets and shops of Lagos, Accra, Abidjan, Brazzaville, Kinshasa, Mombasa, Dar-es-Salaam, Johannesburg and Cape Town by the hundred, are not to be reckoned as art. They are mass-produced in small workshops out of all kinds of materials and all look exactly the same.

Old, traditional motifs are often copied, yet the personal character is lacking and the expression that makes a work of art. But every now and then a good piece can be found among the rubbish, when its original form and convincing power of expression draw our attention. These few exceptions prove that despite commercialism and modern Western influence the African characteristic is not to be suppressed. It is certainly capable of expressing itself through new art forms.

I am of the opinion that these currents, although they are at present only sporadic, have the power to take shape and spread. Herein lies the best chance for a neo-African art. It is difficult to foresee if or how this process will develop, or which peoples are the most likely to bring such a renaissance to success. The Makonde of Tanzania are certainly capable of infusing new life into wood-carving and the Yoruba have also shown in their applied arts that a successful combination of the old and modern is possible. I have already mentioned examples from the Congo, but neither the Baule, Senufo and Fon should be passed over, for their efforts to reinstate metal-casting. Undoubtedly the people of the Cameroun grasslands are equally capable of developing new styles from the rich mine of their past.

It is then true that everywhere, where traditional art has blossomed, it has left a fruitful field for the modern African artist seeking to establish his identity in the surroundings of the new Africa.

CATALOGUE

THE MASKS: The survival of the legendary past in drama

Masks are used in the *rites de passage* of individuals or of the community. They are also protectors of the community and guardians of tradition.

Cat. 1   Dan-Kulime (Dahua village, Ivory Coast). Mask representing an 'avenger'. Wood, h. 20 cm. Ethnographisch Museum, Antwerp.

Cat. 2   Gere (Ivory Coast). Mask with stylized horns. Wood, woven fibres, textile, h. 35 cm. Stella Mertens Collection, Paris.

Cat. 3   Ibibio (south-east Nigeria). Mask of the *ekpo* society. Wood, h. 46 cm. C. P. Meulendijk Collection, Rotterdam.

Cat. 4 Landana Island (mouth of the Shiloango, lower Congo). Mask with fur beard. Wood, 25 cm. Musée d'Ethnographie, Neuchâtel. (Pl. 38).

Cat. 5 Mau (Touba region, Ivory Coast). Mask representing the protective spirit of the *komo* society. Wood, antelope horns, clay, leather, iron, fibres, h. 69 cm. R. Jacobsen Collection, France.

Cat. 6 Bobo-Fing (Orodara village, Upper Volta). Helmet mask with a helmet-like superstructure. Black wood painted red and white, the cloak made of dyed red vegetable fibre, h. 43 cm. Museum für Völkerkunde, Basle.

Cat. 7   Mende (Sierra Leone). Helmet mask of the *poro* society. Black wood, the eyes and teeth in laid with tin, h. 52 cm. C. P. Meulendijk Collection, Rotterdam.

Cat. 8   Yoruba (Nigeria). Helmet mask of the *gelede* society. Dark brown wood heightened with white, h. 27.5 cm. Museum voor Land-en Volkenkunde, Rotterdam.

Cat. 9   Bamessing or Bekom (Cameroun grasslands). Helmet mask used for fertility rites. Dark wood heightened with white, h. 43.5 cm. Ethnographisch Museum, Antwerp.

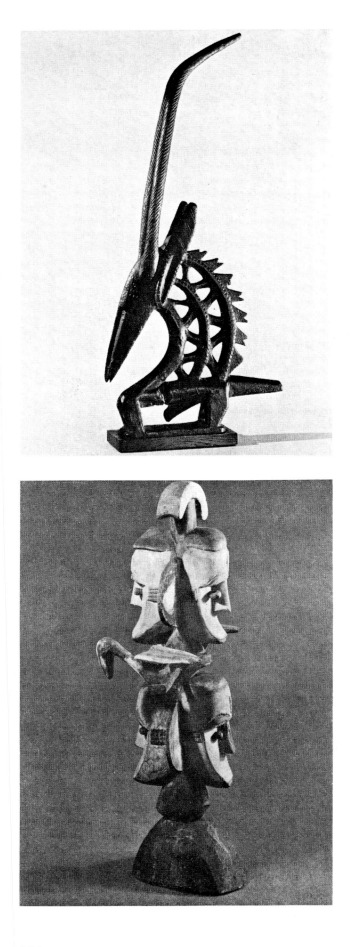

Cat. 10   Bambara (Mali). Mask superstructure in the form of a male antelope: *chi wara*, vertical style. Wood, h. 81 cm. Dr. M. Kofler Collection, Riehen/Basle.

Cat. 11   Ijo (south-east Nigeria). Mask superstructure with two pairs of Janus-heads. Wood, white touched up with black, h. 58.2 cm. Rijksmuseum voor Volkenkunde, Leiden.

Cat. 12   Baga (Guinea). *Nimba* large mask with superstructure, of the *simo* society. Wood, fibre cloak, h. 110 cm. Museum voor Land- en Volkenkunde, Rotterdam.

Cat. 13-15 Lega (Congo-Kinshasa). Three amulet masks of the *bwame* society.

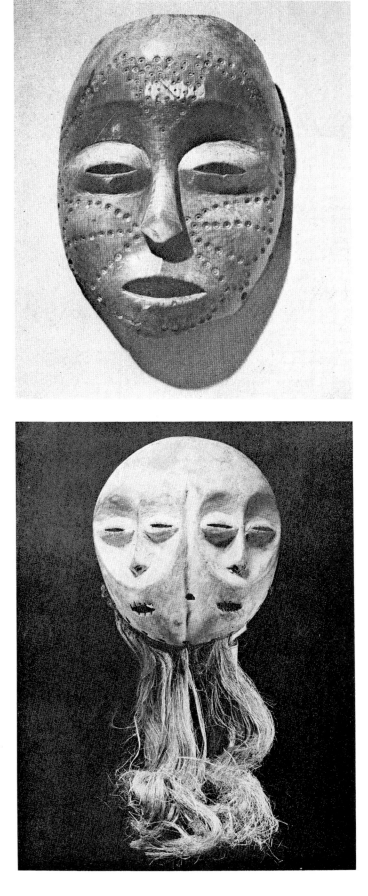

Cat. 13 Wood, h. 23 cm. Dr. M. Kofler Collection, Riehen/Basle.

Cat. 14 Brownish-red ivory, h. 19.5 cm. Pablo Picasso Collection, France.

Cat. 15 Kindu region. Janus-faced mask. Wood, painted white with kaolin, and a fibre beard, h. 25 cm. Musée d'Ethnographie, Neuchâtel.

Cat. 16 Songe (Congo-Kinshasa). *Kifwebe* initiation mask. Dark wood with white grooves, h. 37 cm. Rijksmuseum voor Volkenkunde, Leiden.

Cat. 17 Teke (Congo-Brazzaville). Stylized mask. Wood painted red, white and black, h. 35 cm. Musée de l'Homme, Paris.

Cat. 18 Kwele (Congo-Brazzaville). Stylized mask with three pairs of eyes. Wood, black and white, h. 38 cm. Ch. Lapicque Collection, Paris.

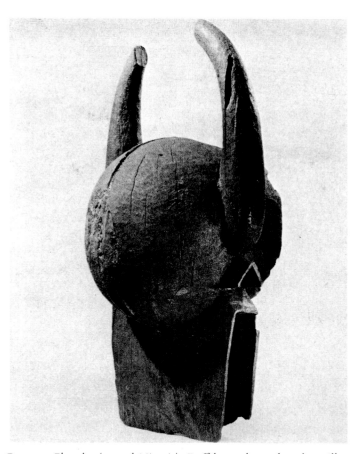

Cat. 19 Senufo (Ivory Coast). *Kponiugo* buffalo mask, of the *lo* society. Wood with fibre cloak, l. 83 cm. L. Nevelson Collection.

Cat. 20 Chamba (central Nigeria). Buffalo mask, used at the millet sowing. Wood, l. 70 cm. Museum für Völkerkunde, Basle.

Cat. 21 Bamileke (Cameroun grasslands). Buffalo mask. Dark-brown wood, l. 73 cm. Dr. M. Kofler Collection, Riehen/Basle.

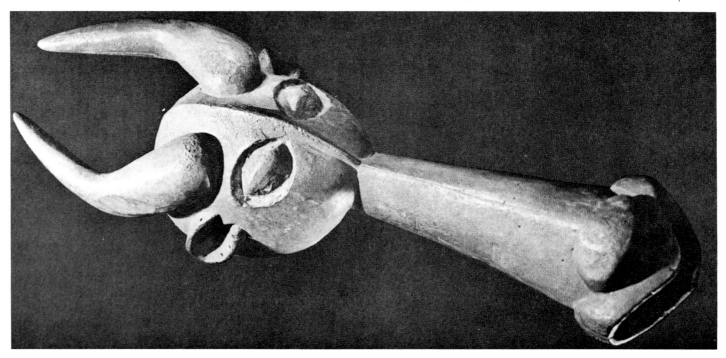

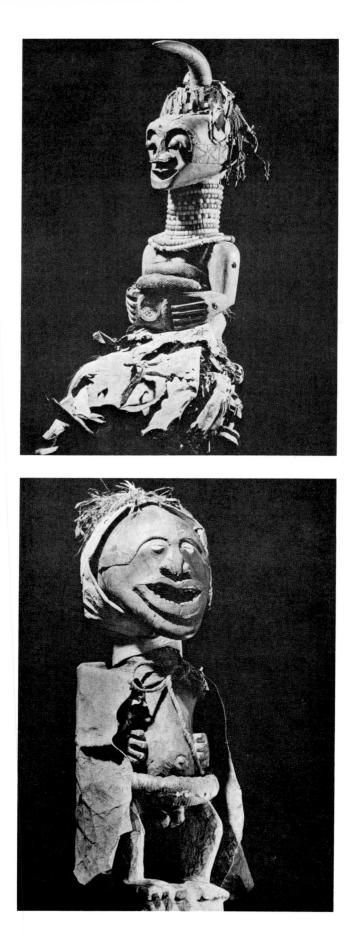

The object receives power from the magic substances — blood, broth, paste, nails, mirrors, and so on — fastened to it to fulfil a definite aim, be it good or evil.

Cat. 22   Songe (Congo-Kinshasa). Fetish figure surrounded with small wooden figures. Light-brown wood, blackened face, horn, glass beads, metal, animal hide and snakeskin, h. 40.5 cm. Ethnographisch Museum, Antwerp.

Cat. 23   Songe (Congo-Kinshasa). Male fetish figure. Wood, h. 51.5 cm. Museum voor Land- en Volkenkunde, Rotterdam. (Pl. 108).

Cat. 24   Songe (Congo-Kinshasa). Male fetish figure. Wood, metal, necklace of large glass beads, h. 30 cm. Koninklijk Museum voor Midden-Afrika, Tervuren.

Cat. 25   Lower Congo. Fetish figure in the shape of a seated dog. Wood, metal, glass, h. 13.5 cm. Museum voor Land- en Volkenkunde, Rotterdam.

Cat. 26   Kongo (lower Congo). Nail fetish with a mirror. Wood, glass, iron nails, textile, feathers, h. 46 cm. Museum voor Land- en Volkenkunde, Rotterdam.

Cat. 27   Songe (Bekalebue sub-style, Congo-Kinshasa). Fetish figure with Janus-face in the style of the *kifwebe* masks. Wood, woven raffia, the fringes made of lengths of twisted raffia, h. 73 cm. Museum für Völkerkunde, Basle.

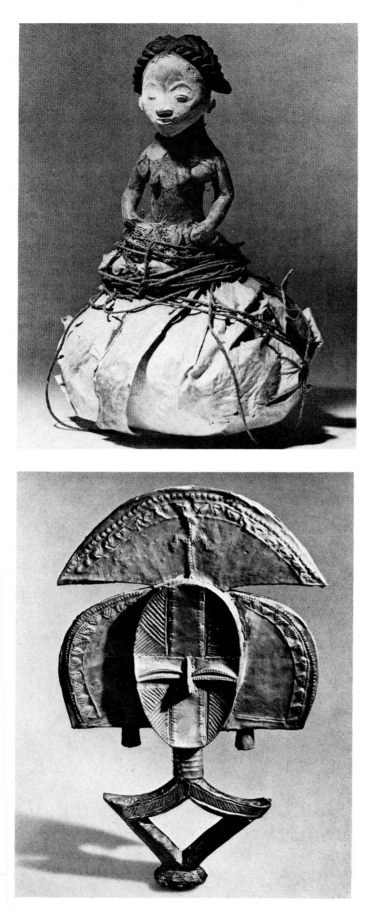

Cat. 28 Lumbo (Gabon). Female guardian figure with a bag of bones. Wood, white face, goatskin, twisted lengths of raffia, h. 30 cm. Musée de l'Homme, Paris.

Cat. 29 Kota (Gabon). *Mbulu-ngulu*, guardian figure for a basket for a skull and bones. Wood, covered with sheet brass, h. 62 cm. Dr. M. Kofler Collection, Riehen/Basle.

Cat. 30 Kota (Udumbo village, Gabon). *Mbulu-ngulu*, guardian figure with the basket for a skull and bones. Wood, covered with copper and brass bands, feathers, basket work, fibres of twisted animal skin, h. 58 cm. Musée de l'Homme, Paris.

FETISH

Cat. 31-33   Baule (Ivory Coast). Three images of the ape god *Gbekre* or *Mbotumbo*.

Cat. 31   With a sacrificial bowl. Wood, textile, h. 53.5 cm. Musée de l'Homme, Paris.

Cat. 32   Wood, h. 70.7 cm. Ethnographisch Museum, Antwerp.

Cat. 33   With a sacrificial bowl. Wood, textile, h. 73 cm. R. D'Haese Collection, Belgium.

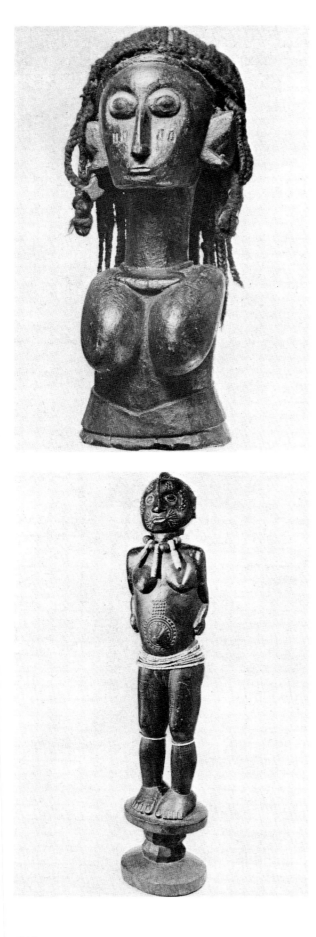

Important ancestors who are remembered by their heirs are commemorated by stylized portraits.

Cat. 34 Baga (Guinea). Torso of a female ancestor figure. Black wood heightened with white, wool hair, h. 47 cm. C. P. Meulendijk Collection, Rotterdam.

Cat. 35 Tiv (Central Nigeria). Female ancestor figure. Black wood, necklace with bone amulets and large glass beads and strings of beads, h. 89 cm. 19th century. C. P. Meulendijk Collection, Rotterdam.

Cat. 36 Bambara (Mali). Seated female ancestor figure. Blackened wood, h. 61 cm. Formerly Jean Matisse Collection.

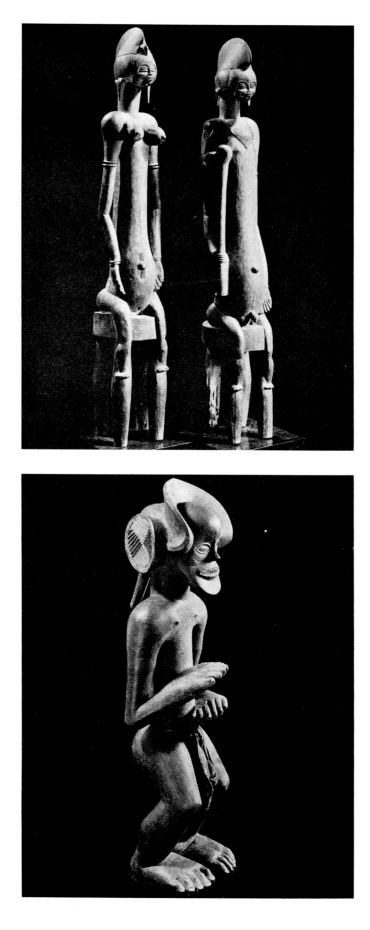

Cat. 37 Baule (Ivory Coast). Seated male ancestor figure. Wood, h. 57 cm. Dr. M. Kofler Collection, Riehen/Basle.

Cat. 38 Senufo-Kiembara (Ivory Coast). *Tugubo*, seated ancestor couple. Used for initiation into the *lo* society. Wood, h. 103. 2 cm. and 100.8 cm. Ethnographisch Museum, Antwerp. (Pl. 37)

Cat. 39 Jokwe (Angola). Male ancestor figure. Wood, textile, h. 47 cm. Rijksmuseum voor Volkenkunde, Leiden. (Pl. 28)

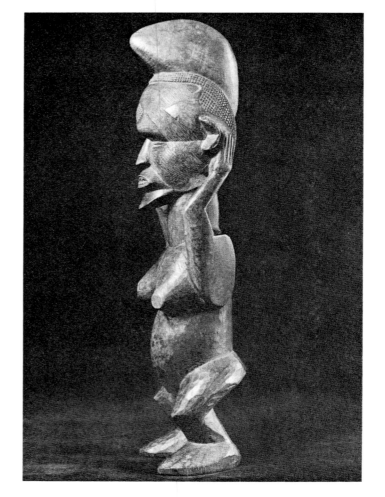

Cat. 40 Yoruba (Nigeria). The *orisha* Eshu or Elegba, the divine trickster figure, with pointed cap and flute. Wood, h. 34 cm. C. P. Meulendijk Collection, Rotterdam.

Cat. 41 Dogon (Mali). *Andumbulu*, male ancestor figure with a staff, presented as an old man. Used for the rain ceremony. Wood, h. 54 cm. Dr. M. Kofler Collection, Riehen/Basle.

Cat. 42 Teke (Congo-Brazzaville). Female ancestor figure, used as a fetish. Brown wood, h. 34 cm. C. P. Meulendijk Collection, Rotterdam.

THE HUMAN FIGURE: Symbol of earthly life

Man, bearer of life and yet mortal, is unmerciful in the observation of his own sufferings and joys, and portrays them with humour and irony.

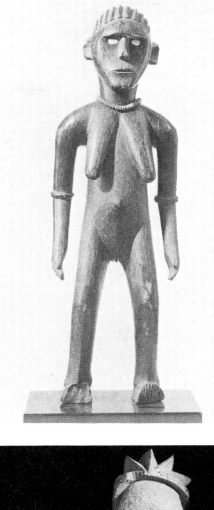

Cat. 43   Dogon (Mali). Ancestor couple. Wood, h. 57 cm. Dr. M. Kofler Collection, Riehen/Basle.

Cat. 44   Mossi (Upper Volta). Female figure. Wood, the eyes inlaid with bone, glass beads, leather armbands, h. 64 cm. C. P. Meulendijk Collection, Rotterdam.

Cat. 45   Suku (Congo-Kinshasa). Male figure. Wood, necklace made of horns, h. 93.6 cm. Koninklijk Museum voor Midden-Afrika, Tervuren.

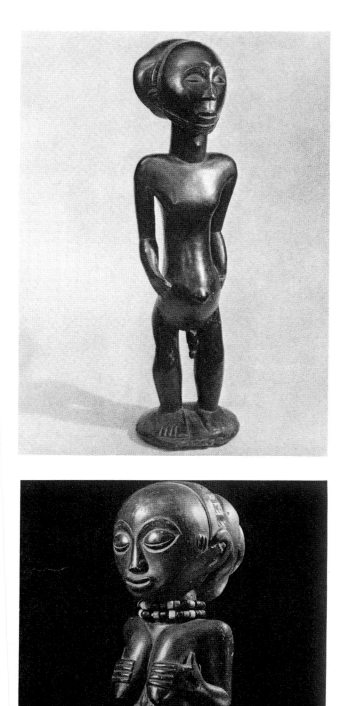

Cat. 46   Luba-Hemba (Congo-Kinshasa). Male ancestor figure with a cruciform hair-style. Black wood, h. 88 cm. Ethnographisch Museum, Antwerp.

Cat. 47   Luba-Hemba (Uruha region, Congo-Kinshasa). Female ancestor figure with cruciform hair-style. Black wood, glass beads, h. 41 cm. C. P. Meulendijk Collection, Rotterdam.

Cat. 48   Luba-Hemba (Uruha region, Congo-Kinshasa). Seated pipe-smoking male figure with cruciform hair-style. Black wood, h. 51 cm. C. P. Meulendijk Collection, Rotterdam.

Cat. 49 Ngbaka (north Congo-Kinshasa). Female ancestor figure with an amulet of glass beads hanging round her neck. Wood, glass, h. 29.5 cm. Koninklijk Museum voor Midden-Afrika, Tervuren.

Cat. 50 Mbole (Congo-Kinshasa). Female figure. Used for initiation into the *lilwa* society. Wood, black and yellow, white face, h. 69.5 cm. Ethnographisch Museum, Antwerp.

Cat. 51 Mbala (Congo-Kinshasa). Mother-and-child figure. Brown wood with traces of red painting, h. 52.cm. Ethnographisch Museum, Antwerp.

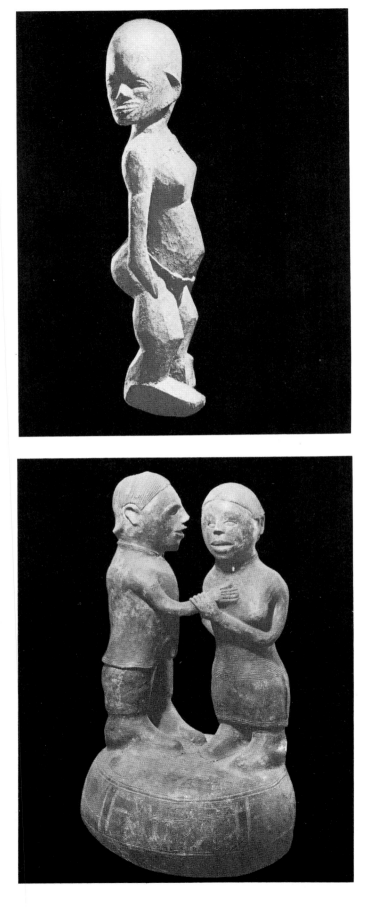

Cat. 52 Lobi (Upper Volta). Female figure with head turned aside. Wood, string of cowrie shells, h. 49 cm. Museum Rietberg, Zurich.

Cat. 53 Kakongo (Muba village, lower Congo). Clay vessel with figures of a man and wife. Individualized representation of Voanica Muba. Last quarter of the 19th century to early 20th century. Clay, h. 47.5 cm. Museum Rietberg, Zurich.

Cat. 54 Zulu (Union of South Africa). Male figure. Light-brown wood, animal hide, h. 59.5 cm. Musée de l'Homme, Paris.

Cat. 55   Dan (Ivory Coast). Smith at work. Brass cast, h. 9.5 cm.
Koninklijk Instituut voor de Tropen, Amsterdam.

Cat. 56   Agni (former kingdom of Krinjabo, Ivory Coast). Seated
tomb figure. Clay, h. 44 cm. Koninklijk Instituut voor de Tropen,
Amsterdam.

Cat. 57   Sierra Leone. *Nomoli*, crouching figure. Steatite, h. 14 cm.
L. van Bussel Collection, The Hague.

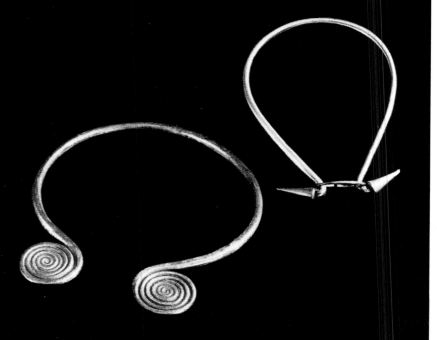

THE ARTIST: Material comes to life

Nearly all natural raw materials have inspired the artist to fashion them into form through his creative talent.

Cat. 58 Baule (Adioukrou village, Ivory Coast). Gold mask. H. 9.5 cm. Musée de l'Homme, Paris.

Cat. 59 Wolof (Senegal). Artificial plait with two gold buttons. Diam. 5.5 cm. Koninklijk Museum voor Midden-Afrika, Tervuren.

Cat. 60 Logo and Fajelu (north-east Congo/Buganda). Two neckbands. Silver, diam. 22.3 cm. and 19.2 cm. Koninklijk Museum voor Midden-Afrika, Tervuren.

Cat. 61   Bambara (Mali). Female figure as a staff finial. Detail. Wrought iron, overall height: 82 cm. Dr. M. Kofler Collection, Riehen/Basle.

Cat. 62   From Kete Krachi (Togo). Male mask. Made under the influence of the Yoruba bronze founder Ali Amonikoyi. Brass cast, h. 28 cm. Early 20th century. Museum Rietberg, Zurich.

Cat. 63   Ashanti (Ghana). *Kuduo* covered vessel, with musicians on the lid. Used in the death ritual. Bronze, h. 21 cm. Koninklijk Instituut voor de Tropen, Amsterdam.

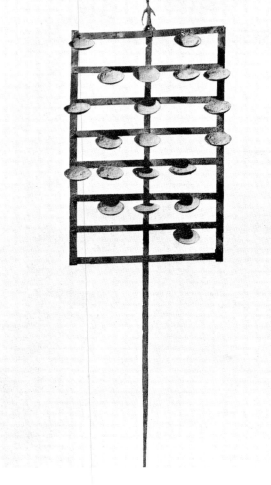

Cat. 64   Yoruba (Nigeria). Staff with birds. Used in the cult of healing of the *orisha* Osanyin. Wrought iron, h. 60 cm. Dr. M. Kofler Collection, Riehen/Basle.

Cat. 65   Senufo (Ivory Coast). Ring of silence in the form of a buffalo head with human features. Brass cast, h. 9.5 cm. Dr. M. Kofler Collection, Riehen/Basle.

Cat. 66   Senufo (Ivory Coast). Oil lamp. Wrought iron, h. 157.5 cm. E. Hajdu Collection, France.

Cat. 67-69   Pende (Congo-Kinshasa). *Minyaki* amulet masks.
Ivory.

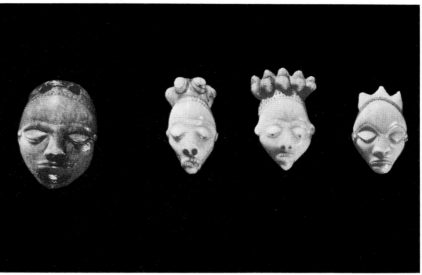

Cat. 67   H. 6 cm. Dr. M. Kofler Collection, Riehen/Basle.

Cat. 68   H. (from left to right): 6.3 cm., 5.7 cm., 6 cm., 5.2 cm.
Ethnographisch Museum, Antwerp.

Cat. 69   Amulet pipe with a mask. H. 8.5 cm. Ethnographisch
Museum, Antwerp.

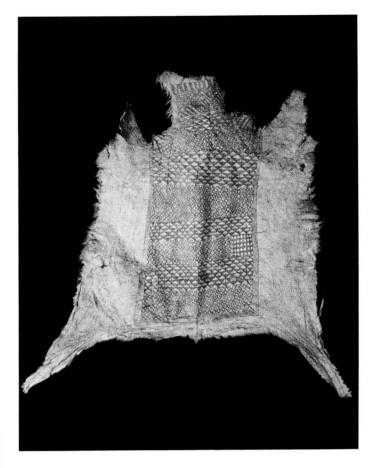

Cat. 70 Lake Bangweolo (south-east Congo-Kinshasa). Cloak made from the skin of the marsh antelope. The pattern scratched in and coloured with black mud dye, 106 × 95 cm. Deutsches Ledermuseum, Offenbach (Main).

Cat. 71 Hausa (north Nigeria). Man's robe, embroidered. Cotton, dark blue and white. Koninklijk Instituut voor de Tropen, Amsterdam. (Pl. 11)

Cat. 72 Ashanti (Ghana). *Adinkra* cloth, made of eight bands sewn together, with coloured embroidery at the seams and printed with different patterns. Used at funeral and other festivities. Cotton, 307 × 183 cm. Museum voor Land- en Volkenkunde, Rotterdam.

By their basic function, form and decoration useful things can tell something of the society to which they belong. The tiniest detail reveals the joy in decoration.

Cat. 73 Dan (Ivory Coast). *Po*, ceremonial spoon in the form of a man. Wood, h. 56 cm. A. Magnelli Collection, Meudon, France.

Cat. 74 Kran (Duékoué village, Ivory Coast). *Gasua* fetish head. Black clay, the eyes and teeth of aluminium, boar's teeth, pieces of mirror glass, tufts of raffia fibre, feathers, h. 32 cm. Museum für Völkerkunde, Basle.

Cat. 75 Yoruba (Nigeria). *Ifa* oracle board. Brown wood, diam. 42 cm. Museum für Völkerkunde, Basle.

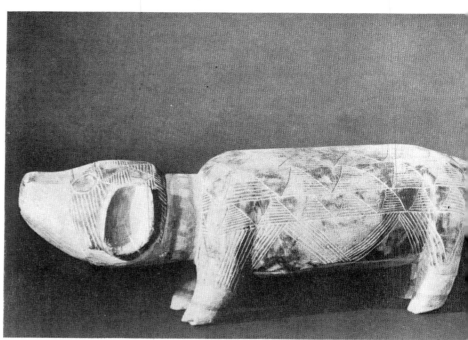

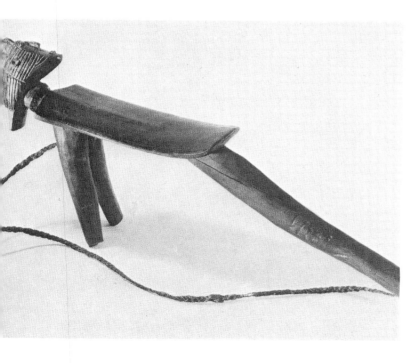

Cat. 76 Zambia. Comb with superstructure in the form of a European. Wood, h. 19 cm. Museum für Völkerkunde, Basle.

Cat. 77 Bobo-Gbe (Upper Volta). Stool in the form of a club, with a human head. Wood, l. 52 cm. Museum voor Land- en Volkenkunde, Rotterdam.

Cat. 78 Ovambo (South West Africa). Neck-support in the shape of a quadruped. Wood with red triangles, l. 47. 5 cm. Musée de l'Homme, Paris.

Cat. 79 Yoruba (Nigeria). *Ile ori* or *ibo ori,* fetish basket for the preservation of a man's head to which protective powers were attributed. Leather, textile and cowrie shells, h. 31.2 cm. Ethnographisch Museum, Antwerp.

Cat. 80 Baule (Ivory Coast). Bobbin-holder with a portrait head. Dark brown wood, h. 20.5 cm. J. Fribourg Collection, Paris.

Cat. 81 Yoruba (Dahomey). Oil lamp. Clay, h. 51 cm. Musée de l'Homme, Paris.

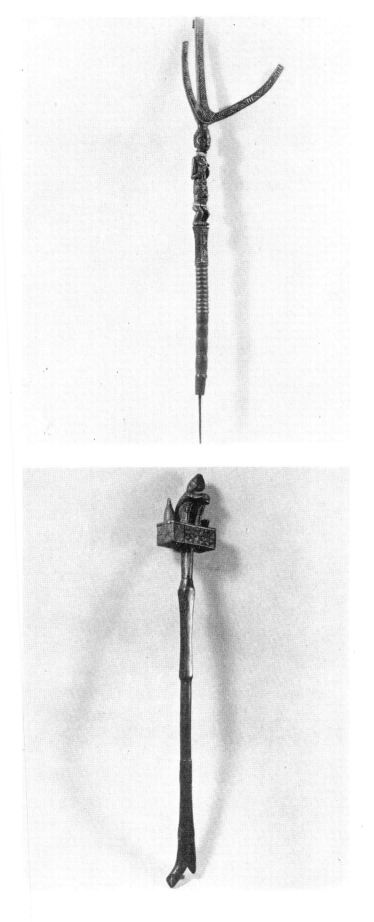

Cat. 82 Luba (Congo-Kinshasa). Arrow-rest, supported by a female figure. Wood, glass beads, iron, h. 86 cm. Museum voor Land- en Volkenkunde, Rotterdam. (Pl. 81)

Cat. 83 Mayombe (lower Congo). Dignitary's staff with a finial in the form of a crouching figure carrying a bottle and beaker for palm-wine. Wood, h. 52 cm. Koninklijk Museum voor Midden-Afrika, Tervuren.

Cat. 84 Mfinu/Teke (Congo-Kinshasa). Fly-swat with two small heads. Wood, wire, monkey's hair, textile, h. 45.5 cm. Koninklijk Museum voor Midden-Afrika, Tervuren.

Cat. 85 Zande (Congo-Kinshasa). Box and cover in the form of a neck-support with two heads. Light brown wood with dark brown accents, l. 38.2 cm. Koninklijk Museum voor Midden-Afrika, Tervuren.

Cat. 86-87 Rotse (Zambia). Two covered bowls for preserving food.

Cat. 86 Handle in the form of two buffaloes. Dark wood, l. 45.5 cm. Ethnographisch Museum, Antwerp.

Cat. 87 Handle in the form of an elephant. Dark wood, l. 47.5 cm. Musée d'Ethnographie, Neuchâtel.

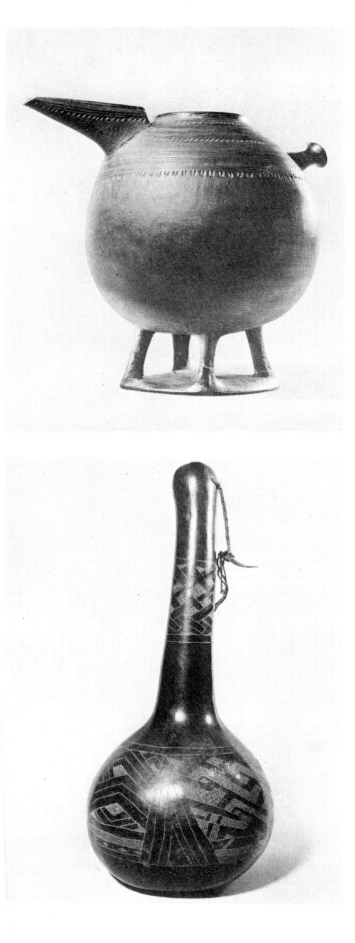

Cat. 88   Shi (Lake Bukavu, south-east Congo-Kinshasa). Milk can. Wood, h. 26.4 cm. Koninklijk Museum voor Midden-Afrika, Tervuren.

Cat. 89   Kuba (Congo-Kinshasa). Gourd bottle with a pattern of interwoven bands, h. 44.1 cm. Koninklijk Museum voor Midden-Afrika, Tervuren.

Cat. 90   Western Songe (Congo-Kinshasa). Gourd with a cover and glass beads, h. 25 cm. Koninklijk Museum voor Midden-Afrika, Tervuren.

Cat. 91 Bena Lulua (Congo-Kinshasa). Snuff-box in the shape of a man. Dark brown wood, h. 8.5 cm. Ethnographisch Museum, Antwerp.

Cat. 92 Jokwe (Congo-Kinshasa). Drinking vessel for palm-wine supported by two figures. Brown wood, h. 6.7 cm. Koninklijk Museum voor Midden-Afrika, Tervuren.

Cat. 93 Bambara (Mali). Ointment jar. The lid with a female figure. Wood, h. 46 cm. Dr. M. Kofler Collection, Riehen/Basle.

Cat. 94   Bamum (Cameroun grasslands). Head of a chief's pipe in human form. Black clay, h. 31.5 cm. Museum voor Land- en Volkenkunde, Rotterdam.

Cat. 95   Bamum (Cameroun grasslands). Chief's pipe, its head in the form of a human face. The superstructure shows the spider pattern. Clay, handle covered with coloured glass beads, h. 110 cm. Ethnographisch Museum, Antwerp. (Pl. 24).

Cat. 96   Dogon (Mali). Head of a pipe. The cover bearing the figure of a rider with a gun. Brass cast, h. 15 cm. Museum voor Land- en Volkenkunde, Rotterdam.

Cat. 97   Bambara (Mali). Female marionette, representing Fatimata. Wood, hair, textile, h. 100 cm. Musée de l'Homme, Paris.

Cat. 98   Herero (South West Africa). Doll. Wood with leather and strings of glass beads wound around it, h. 25 cm. Museum für Völkerkunde, Basle

Cat. 99   Mambwe (Tanzania/Zambia). Doll. Wood with strings of glass beads wound around it, h. 18.5 cm. Musée de l'Homme, Paris.

Cat. 100 Tonga (Zambia). Stool. Blackened wood, the mask light brown, h. 25 cm. Musée d'Ethnographie, Neuchâtel.

Cat. 101 Bamileke (Cameroun grasslands). Stool with fretwork carving representing animal heads. Wood, h. 46 cm. Musée d'Ethnographie, Neuchâtel.

Cat. 102 Cameroun grasslands. Chief's stool supported by three human figures and three leopards. Light brown wood with dark brown accents, h. 67 cm. Museum voor Land- en Volkenkunde, Rotterdam.

Cat. 103 Bamileke (Cameroun grasslands). Door post from a chief's house. Mother-and-child figure and two warriors. Wood, h. 197 cm. R. Jacobsen Collection, France.

Cat. 104 Bamileke (Foumban, Cameroun grasslands). Lintel over a door of a chief's house. Wood, l. 113 cm. Musée de l'Homme, Paris.

Cat. 105 Senufo (region of Sinématiali, Ivory Coast). Door taken from a mask house with a relief carving of mythological subjects and a lock in the form of a lizard. Wood, 106 × 69 cm. Museum Rietberg, Zurich.

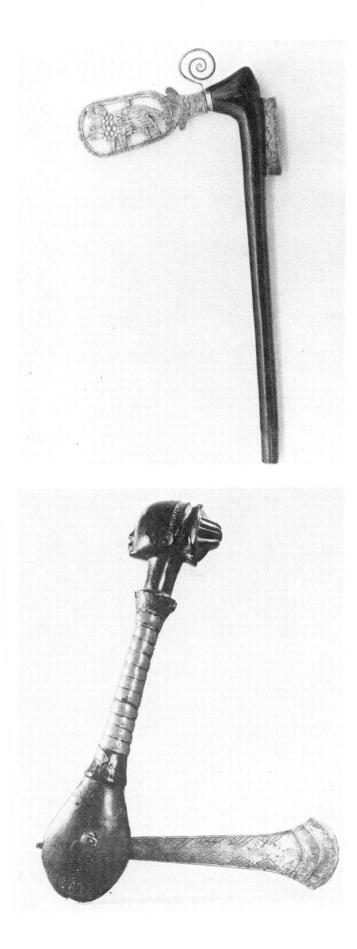

Invented to preserve and defend human life against the world, weapons have become symbols of rank and prestige.

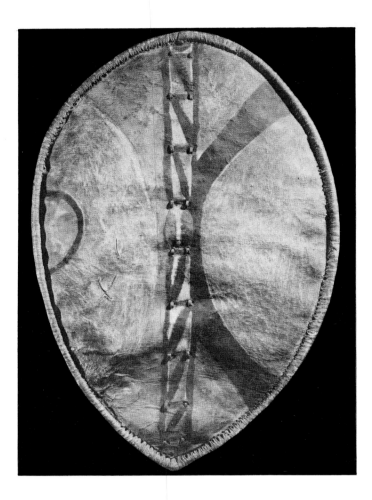

Cat. 106 Fon (Dahomey). Ceremonial axe. Power symbol of the dignitary. Wood and iron, l. 42 cm. Koninklijk Instituut voor de Tropen, Amsterdam.

Cat. 107 Luba-Hemba (Congo-Kinshasa). Ceremonial axe with head of a woman. Wood, iron, copper bands, l. 36.5 cm. Museum Rietberg, Zurich. (Pl. 8)

Cat. 108 Masai (Kenya). Warrior's shield. Animal skin, painted red, white and black, l. 94 cm. Deutsches Ledermuseum, Offenbach (Main).

MUSIC: Rhythm and pulse of life

Music and dance are not only forms of expression in which man can give vent to his feelings, but are also essential companions of all the stages of a man's life.

Cat. 109   Central African Republic. Slit drum in the form of a stylized buffalo. Wood, h. 80 cm., l. 229 cm. Musée de l'Homme, Paris.

Cat. 110   Probably Huana (Congo-Kinshasa). Skin drum. The lower part carved in the form of human hands. Wood, animal skin, h. 40 cm. Deutsches Ledermuseum, Offenbach (Main).

Cat. 111   Baule (Ivory Coast). Ceremonial skin drum, richly carved with mythological symbols. Wood with traces of painting, animal hide and knotted strings, h. 134 cm. Musée de l'Homme, Paris.

Cat. 112   Fang (Gabon). Iron bell, crowned with a fetish figure carrying a small mirror glass box. Wood, rubbed with *tukula* powder, glass, textile, h. 53 cm. Museum voor Land- en Volkenkunde, Rotterdam.

Cat. 113 a, b   Pangwe (Gabon). Bell, surmounted by a female fetish figure, carrying a child in a sling on the back. Wood, h. 20.5 cm. L. van Bussel Collection, The Hague.

Cat. 114   Zande (Congo-Kinshasa). Bell in the form of a stylized human figure. Wood, h. 44 cm. Ethnographisch Museum, Antwerp.

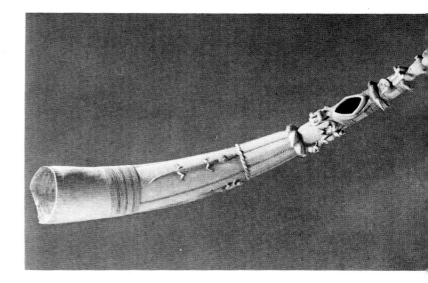

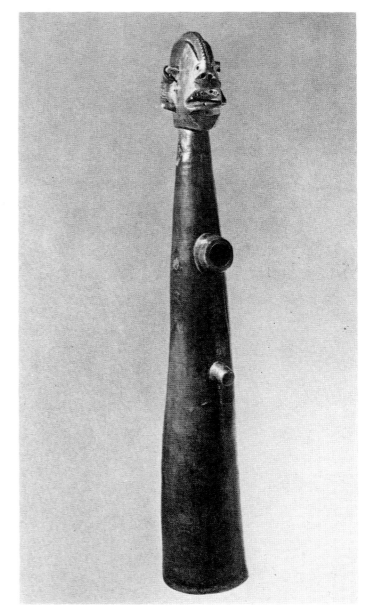

Cat. 115 Cameroun. Iron bell, the handle in the form of a double-figure in wood. H. 44 cm. Musée d'Ethnographie, Neuchâtel.

Cat. 116 Yoruba (Nigeria). Trumpet with human and crocodile figures carved in relief. Ivory, 1.65 cm. Musée de l'Homme, Paris.

Cat. 117 Tanzania. Trumpet used for ritual purposes, crowned with a head. Wood, iron, l. 85 cm. A. Magnelli Collection, Meudon, France.

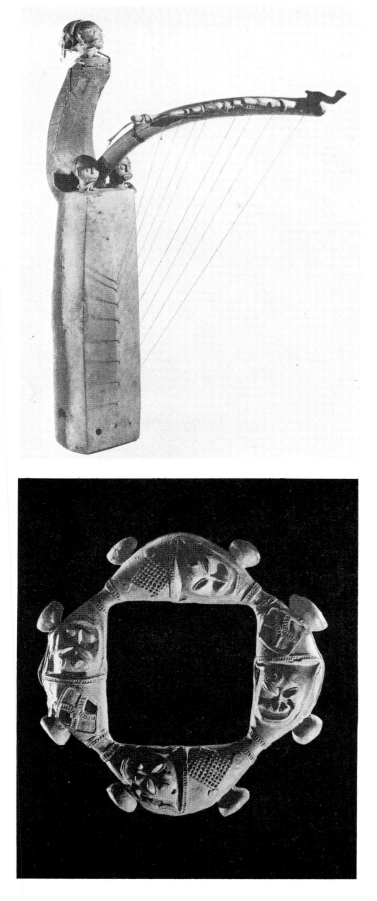

Cat. 118 Pangwe (Gabon). Bow harp with three ancestor heads. Wood, animal skin, glass beads, l. 72 cm. Museum voor Land- en Volkenkunde, Rotterdam.

Cat. 119 Yoruba (Nigeria). Dance rattle. Bronze, l. 20 cm. Dr. M. Kofler Collection, Riehen/Basle.

Cat. 120 Angola. *Sanza*. Small wooden board with twelve iron keys and glass beads for vibration. L. 23.5 cm. Musée d'Ethnographie, Neuchâtel.

APPENDIX

ACKNOWLEDGEMENTS

The help and cooperation of various ethnographical museums has enabled me to select photographs over a wide field of African art which complement the character of the work. It was my aim to introduce some of the lesser known pieces especially those that have so far not been published. The inclusion of pieces already familiar to the reader should serve as a further confirmation of their accepted status as the finest examples of African art, which are therefore not to be passed over.

My grateful thanks are due to the directors, keepers and assistants of the following museums for their help:

Belgium: Koninklijk Museum voor Midden-Afrika, Tervuren; Ethnographisch Museum, Antwerp.

England: The British Museum, London.

France: Musée de l'Homme, Paris.

Germany: Deutsches Ledermuseum, Offenbach (Main).

Netherlands: Rijksmuseum voor Volkenkunde, Leiden; Koninklijk Instituut voor de Tropen, Amsterdam; Museum voor Land- en Volkenkunde, Rotterdam.

Switzerland: Museum für Völkerkunde, Basle; Museum Rietberg, Zurich; Musée d'Ethnographie, Neuchâtel.

I am also deeply indebted to all the private collectors who have so willingly given me access to their collections. I am grateful to them, not only for a large part of the illustrations in this book, but for many hours of friendly discussion. My especial thanks are due to: Messrs. L. van Bussel, Den Haag; J. Fribourg, Paris; Dr. M. Kofler, Riehen/Basle; C. P. Meulendijk, Rotterdam.

I am also especially indebted to Mme Marie-Jean Béraud-Villars, Administrator of the "Société des Amis du Musée de l'Homme", Paris, who gave me permission to use photographs of African works of art, which were being shown in the exhibition entitled: "Arts primitifs dans les ateliers d'artistes", and which belong to the following artists and collectors: Jacques Boussard; Georges Braque (C. Laurens); Roel D'Haese; Theo Dobbelmann; Eugène Dodeigne; Etienne Hajdu; Robert Jacobsen; Charles Lapicque; Alberto Magnelli; René Matisse (Jean Matisse); Stella Mertens; Louise Nevelson; Pablo Picasso.

Finally I would like to thank Hans Hinz for his technical skill and artistic sensitivity; his photographs do the African works of art full justice.

The photographs other than those of Hans Hinz were placed at our disposal by:

The British Museum, London: Pl. 13, 14, 21, 85, 86, 89, 91

Prof. Dr. Hans Carrol, Toronto: Pl. XVI

Deutsches Ledermuseum, Offenbach (Main): Pl. XX

Frau Prof. Dr. Elsy Leuzinger, Zurich: Pl. VI, XXIII; Pl. 23

Musée de l'Homme, Paris: Pl. 1, 2, 16, 17, 41, 42, 44, 101; Cat. 2, 5, 14, 17, 18, 19, 28, 30, 31, 33, 36, 55, 58, 73, 78, 81, 97, 99, 103, 104, 109, 111, 116, 117

René S. Wassing, The Hague: Pl. XIV, XIX

BIBLIOGRAPHY

L'Art nègre, sources, évolution, expansion (Catalogue, festival mondial des arts nègres). Dakar – Paris 1966.

Atlas van Belgisch Congo en Ruanda-Urundi. Brussels – Amsterdam 1955.

BALANDIER, G.: *Afrique ambiguë.* Paris 1957.

BAUMANN, H., R. THURNWALD and D. WESTERMANN: *Völkerkunde von Afrika.* Essen 1940.

BEIER, U.: *The Story of Sacred Wood Carvings from one Yoruba Town.* Lagos 1957.

BEIER, U.: *Contemporary Art in Africa.* London 1967.

BITTREMIEUX, L.: *Mayombsche Namen.* Leuven 1934.

BURSSENS, H.: *Yanda beelden en Maui sekte bij de Azande.* Tervuren 1962.

CARROL, K.: *Yoruba Religious Carving.* London 1967.

DARK, PH.: *Benin Art.* London 1960.

DARYLL FORDE, C. (ed.): *African Worlds. Studies in the cosmological diras and social values of African peoples.* London 1959.

DAVIDSON, B.: *Africa, History of a Continent.* London 1966.

DELACHAUX, TH.: "Méthodes et instruments de divination en Angola", in: *Acta Tropica,* vol. 3, 1946, pp. 41-72 and pp. 138-149.

DELANGE, J.: "Le Bansonyi du pays Baga", in: *Objets et Mondes,* II, part I, Spring 1962, pp. 3-12.

DIETERLEN, G.: *Essai sur la religion Bambara.* Paris 1951.

DITTMER, K.: "Die sakralen Häuptlinge der Gurunsi im Obervolta-Gebiet und die feudalen Fürstentümer im Sudan", in: *Tribus,* 9, Sept. 1960, pp. 68-80.

DITTMER, K.: *Kunst und Handwerk in West-Afrika* (Catalogue of an exhibition at the Hamburgisches Museum für Völkerkunde und Vorgeschichte). Hamburg 1966.

ELISOFON, E. and W. FAGG: *The Sculpture of Africa.* New York 1958.

FAGG, W.: *Nigerian Images.* London 1963.

FAGG, W. and PLASS, M.: *African Sculpture, an anthology.* London 1964.

FISCHER, E.: "Die Gelbgußmaske des Ali Amonikoyi (aus Togo) im Museum für Völkerkunde in Basel", in: *Tribus,* 15, Aug. 1966, pp. 89-95.

FRASER, D. (ed.): *The Many Faces of Primitive Art.* New York 1966.

FROBENIUS, L.: *Das unbekannte Afrika.* München 1923.

GASKIN, L. J. P.: *A Bibliography of African Art.* London 1965.

GERBRANDS, A. A.: *Art as an Element of Culture, especially in Negro Africa.* Leiden 1957.

GERBRANDS, A. A.: *Afrika. Kunst uit het Zwarte Werelddeel.* Recklinghausen 1967.

GLÜCK, J. F.: "Die Gelbgüsse des Ali Amonikoyi (Ilorin)", in: *Jahrbuch des Linden-Museums,* 1951, pp. 27-71.

GOLDWATER, R.: *Bambara Sculpture from the Western Sudan.* New York 1960.

GOLDWATER, R.: *Senufo Sculpture from West Africa.* New York 1964.

GRIAULE, M.: *Masques Dogons.* Paris 1938.

GUTKIND, P. C. W.: *The Royal Capital of Buganda.* The Hague 1963.

HABERLAND, E.: *Galla Süd-Äthiopiens.* Stuttgart 1963.

HERSKOVITS, M. J.: *Dahomey, an ancient West-African Kingdom.* New York 1938.

HERSKOVITS, M. J.: *Man and his Works. The Science of Cultural Anthropology.* New York 1949.

HIMMELHEBER, H.: *Die Dan, ein Bauernvolk im westafrikanischen Urwald.* Stuttgart 1958.

HIMMELHEBER, H.: *Negerkunst und Negerkünstler.* Brunswick 1960.

HIMMELHEBER, H.: "Gelbgußringe der Guéré (Elfenbeinküste)", in: *Tribus,* 13, Dec. 1964, pp. 13-23.

HIMMELHEBER, H.: "Deutung bestimmter Eigenarten der Senufo-Masken. Nördliche Elfenbeinküste", in: *Baessler-Archiv,* XIII, Heft 1, 30. Sept. 1965, pp. 73-82.

HIMMELHEBER, H.: "Figuren und Schnitztechnik bei den Lobi. Elfenbeinküste", in: *Tribus,* 15, Aug. 1966, pp. 63-87.

HIRSCHBERG, W.: "Die Künstlerstraße in Foumban (Kamerun)", in: *Tribus,* 9, Sept. 1960, pp. 90-106.

HOGBIN, S. and A. H. M. KIRK-GREENE: *The Emirates of Northern-Nigeria.* London 1966.

HOLAS, B.: *Les Senoufo.* Paris 1957.

HOLAS, B.: *Cultures matérielles de la Côte d'Ivoire.* Paris 1960.

HOLY, L.: *The Art of Africa. Masks and Figures from Eastern and Southern Africa.* London 1967.

HUET, M. and KEITA FODEBA: *Les hommes de la danse.* Lausanne 1954.

IHLE, A.: *Das alte Königreich Kongo.* (Studien zur Völkerkunde, I.) Leipzig 1929.

JACOBS, M. and B. J. STERN: *General Anthropology.* New York 1955.

JAHN, J. H.: *Muntu, Umrisse der neoafrikanischen Kultur.* Cologne 1958.

"Kinderpüppchen der Mossi in Obervolta" (L. Meurer: "Die Puppentypen und ihre Bedeutung"; E. Kafando: "Zur Geschichte der Puppen".), in: *Tribus,* 13, Dec. 1964, pp. 25-30.

KJERSMEIER, C.: *Centres de style de la sculpture nègre africaine.* 4 vols. Paris 1935-8.

KORABIEWICZ, W.: *African Art in Polish Collections.* Warsaw 1966.

LAUDE, J.: *Les arts de l'Afrique noire.* Paris 1966.

LECOQ, R.: *Les Bamiléké.* Paris 1953.

LEIRIS, M. and J. DELANGE: *African Art.* London and New York 1968.

LEUZINGER, E.: *Africa.* London 1960.

LEUZINGER, E.: *Afrikanische Skulpturen* (Catalogue of an exhibition at the Museum Rietberg in Zurich). Zurich 1963.

MAQUET, J. J.: *Afrique, les civilisations noires.* Geneva 1962.

MARQUART, J.: *Die Benin-Sammlung des Reichsmuseums für Völkerkunde in Leiden.* Leiden 1913.

MARSHALL THOMAS, E.: *The Harmless People.* London 1959.

MARSHALL THOMAS, E: *Warrior Herdsmen.* London 1965.

MEEK, C. K.: *Tribal Studies in Northern Nigeria.* London 1931.

MEYEROWITZ, E. L. R.: *The Akan Traditions of Origin.* London 1952.

MEYEROWITZ, E. L. R.: *The Akan of Ghana.* London 1958.

MEYEROWITZ, E. L. R.: *The Divine Kingship in Ghana and Ancient Egypt.* London 1960.

MEYEROWITZ, E. L. R.: *At the Court of an African King.* London 1962.

MURDOCK, G. P.: *Africa, its Peoples and their Culture History.* New York 1959.

Musée de l'Homme: *Arts primitifs dans les ateliers d'artistes* (Catalogue of an exhibition at the Musée de l'Homme, Paris). Paris 1967.

NADEL, S. F.: *A Black Byzantium*. London 1942.

OLBRECHTS, F. M.: *Plastiek van Kongo*. Antwerp 1946.

PAULME, D.: *Les gens du riz ; Kissi de Haute-Guinée française*. Paris 1954.

RATTRAY, R. S.: *Ashanti*. Oxford 1913.

SASSERATH, J. S.: *Le Ruanda-Urundi*. Brussels 1948.

SCHWEEGER-EXELI, A.: "Probleme mediterraner Kultureinflüsse in Westafrika", in: *Tribus*, 9, Sept. 1960, pp. 81-89.

SCHWEEGER-HEFEL, A.: "Die Kunst der Kurumba", in: *Archiv für Völkerkunde*, vols. XVII/XVIII, 1962/1963, pp. 194-260.

SEGY, L.: "The Ashanti Akua'ba Statues as Archetype and the Egyptian Ankh", in: *Anthropos*, 1963, vol. 58, part 5-6, pp. 839-76.

SELIGMAN, G. G.: *Races of Africa*. 3rd ed. London 1957.

SKINNER, E. P.: *The Mossi of Upper Volta*. Stanford 1964.

SOUSBERGHE, L. de: *L'art Pende*. Gembloux 1958.

TARDITS, C.: "Panneaux sculptés Bamoun", in: *Objets et Mondes*, II, part 4, winter 1962, pp. 249-60.

TEMPELS, P. (ed.): *Bantu Philosophie. Onthologie und Ethik*. Heidelberg 1956.

TESSMAN, G.: *Die Pangwe*. 2 vols. Berlin 1913.

TORDAY, E. and T. A. JOYCE: "Les Bushongo", in: *Annales du Musée du Congo Belge*, Brussels 1910.

VANDENHOUTE, P.: *Classification stylistique du masque Dan et Guéré de la Côte-d'Ivoire occidentale*. (Publication of the Rijksmuseum voor Volkenkunde, Leiden). Leiden 1948.

VERGER, P.: *Dieux d'Afrique*. Paris 1954.

WILLET, F.: *Ife in the History of West African Sculpture*. London 1967.

WINGERT, P. S.: *The Sculpture of Negro Africa*. New York 1950.

ZWERNEMANN, J.: "Spiegel- und Nagelplastiken vom unteren Kongo im Linden-Museum", in: *Tribus*, 10, Sept. 1961, pp. 14-32.

MAP I: AFRICAN TRIBES

1. Wolof
2. Tukuleur
3. Serer
4. Diola
5. Mandingo
6. Baga
7. Malinke
8. Sarakole
9. Kasonke
10. Peul
11. Susu
12. Bulom
13. Bambara
14. Dogon
15. Songhai
16. Kurumba
17. Gurma
18. Mossi
19. Gurunsi
20. Lobi
21. Bobo
22. Senufo
23. Diula
24. Kono
25. Toma
26. Kissi
27. Temne
28. Mende
29. Kpelle
30. Kru
31. Bakwe
32. Kran
33. Gere
34. Dan
35. Guro
36. Baule
37. Agni
38. Tamberma
39. Mamprusi
40. Konkomba
41. Dagomba
42. Abron
43. Akan
44. Ashanti
45. Fanti
46. Kabre
47. Ewe
48. Fon
49. Yoruba
50. Bini

51. Ibo
52. Ijo
53. Ibibio
54. Ekoi
55. Anyang
56. Tiv
57. Jukun
58. Nupe
59. Afo
60. Hausa
61. Fulani
62. Kanembu
63. Kanuri
64. Matakam
65. Kirdi
66. Sara
67. Mbum
68. Bekom
69. Bali
70. Tikar
71. Bamum
72. Bamileke
73. Baya
74. Banda
75. Nsakara
76. Zande
77. Mangbetu
78. Ababua
79. Ngbandi
80. Bwansa
81. Ngombe
82. Bwaka
83. Yangere
84. Kwele
85. Yanzi
86. Pangwe
87. Fang
88. Kota
89. Lumbo
90. Kuyu
91. Teke
92. Bembe
93. Vili
94. Mayombe
95. Kongo
96. Yaka
97. Mbala
98. Suku
99. Lele
100. Huana

101. Dengese
102. Akela
103. Ekonda
104. Kundu
105. Mbole
106. Mongo
107. Wangata
108. Ngelima
109. Genia
110. Mbuti
111. Rega
112. Bembe
113. Buye
114. Tetela
115. Songe
116. Luba
117. Tabwa
118. Hemba
119. Bena Kanioka
120. Salampasu
121. Kuba
122. Kete
123. Bena Lulua
124. Pende
125. Holo
126. Jokwe
127. Ngola
128. Lunda
129. Yeke
130. Bemba
131. Mbangala
132. Ngangela
133. Luena
134. Mbunda
135. Ovimbundu
136. Ovambo
137. Rotse
138. Totela
139. Bauchi
140. Bushmen
141. Herero
142. Ngawaketse
143. Hottentots
144. Xhosa
145. Mpondo
146. Sotho
147. Zulu
148. Ndebele
149. Swazi
150. Chopi

151. Tonga
152. Venda
153. Shona
154. Matabele
155. Ngoni
156. Makua
157. Makonde
158. Swahili
159. Zaramo
160. Nyamwesi
161. Twa
162. Hutu
163. Tutsi
164. Sukuma
165. Masai
166. Chagga
167. Kamba
168. Kikuyu
169. Kavirondo
170. Nandi
171. Ganda
172. Ankole
173. Acholi
174. Lugbara
175. Bunyoro
176. Karamojong
177. Suk
178. Turkana
179. Latuko
180. Dinka
181. Nuer
182. Shilluk
183. Nuba
184. Galla
185. Danakil

A Ife
B Benin
C Nok

276

MAP II: AFRICAN STATES

1. Morocco — Rabat
2. Ifni — Ifni
3. Algeria — Algiers
4. Rio de Oro
5. Mauritania — Nouakchott
6. Mali — Bamako
7. Senegal — Dakar
8. Gambia — Bathurst
9. Portuguese Guinea — Bissao
10. Guinea — Conakry
11. Sierra Leone — Freetown
12. Liberia — Monrovia
13. Ivory Coast — Abidjan
14. Upper Volta — Ouagadougou
15. Ghana — Accra
16. Togo — Lome
17. Dahomey — Porto Novo
18. Nigeria — Lagos
19. Niger — Niamey
20. Chad — Fort Lamy
21. Central African Republic — Bangui
22. Cameroun — Yaoundé
23. Spanish Guinea
24. Gabon — Libreville
25. Congo — Brazzaville
26. Cabinda
27. Congolese Democratic Republic — Kinshasa
28. Angola — Luanda
29. Zambia — Lusaka
30. Rhodesia — Salisbury
31. Botswana — Gaberones
32. South-West Africa — Windhoek
33. Union of South Africa — Pretoria
34. Lesotho — Maseru
35. Swaziland
36. Mozambique — Lourenço Marques
37. Malawi — Zomba
38. United Republic of Tanzania — Dar es Salaam
39. Burundi — Bujumbura
40. Rwanda — Kigali
41. Buganda — Kampala
42. Kenya — Nairobi
43. Somali — Mogadishu
44. Ethiopia — Addis Ababa
45. French Somaliland — Djibouti
46. Sudan — Khartoum
47. United Arab Republic — Cairo
48. Libya — Tripoli
49. Tunisia — Tunis

INDEX

Translator's notes

Plangi: "Tie and dye work is one of the resist-dyeing textile processes the resistance being accomplished by binding or knotting the cloth tightly to prevent the penetration of the dye. A Malay term 'plangi' is increasingly being used in place of 'tie and dye' to designate this process." (Verla Birrel, Textile Arts, Harper & Bros, New York, 1959).

Gelbguss: Bronze-or brass-casting. The alloy differs from one region to another, hence the word is interchangeable between the alloys.

Printed and bound in Hong Kong.